Towa
NEW SO(

W. Paul Cockshott
and
Allin Cottrell

SPOKESMAN

First published in Great Britain in 1993 by
Spokesman
Bertrand Russell House
Gamble Street
Nottingham, England
Tel. 0602 708318

British Library Cataloguing in Publication Data available on request from the British Library.

ISBN 0-85124-544-7
ISBN 0-85124-545 5 pbk

Printed by the Russell Press Ltd, Nottingham
(Tel. 0602 784505)

CONTENTS

Acknowledgements

We wish to thank Maria Black, Ron Buchanan and Greg Michaelson for useful discussions of the ideas in this book. Allin Cottrell also wishes to acknowledge assistance in the form of research grants from Elon College, North Carolina, and the Kerr Bequest at the University of Edinburgh.

Introduction

'Socialism has been tried. Seventy years after the Bolshevik revolution, history's verdict is that it has failed.' All those still inclined to call themselves socialists in the 1990s are obliged to offer some response to this widely held view. This book is our response. It may be useful first, however, to distinguish our view from some responses to be found among the Left in the West.

Presumably, most socialists will wish to say that the sort of social system they seek is substantially different from the Soviet model. But the grounds for this claim may be various. The first distinction to make is between social democrats and those we might call 'idealist marxists'. The former might argue that the failure of Soviet socialism has little to say about the future of, say, Scandinavian-style social democracy. This may be true. It so happens that the period of crisis of Soviet socialism has coincided with an onslaught on social democratic ideas and institutions, particularly although not exclusively in Britain and the USA, but one might argue that this connection is, if not fortuitous then at any rate less than logically necessary: even if the crisis of the Soviet system is terminal, that is, one can imagine the political 'pendulum' swinging back towards social democracy in the West. As we shall see, however, there are some grounds for doubt on this score. Idealist marxists, on the other hand, tend to claim that failure in the Eastern bloc should not count against marxism, since the Soviet system represented the betrayal rather than the realisation of marxian ideals. While the social democrats say that Soviet socialism was not the kind of socialism they wanted, these marxists say that the USSR (post-Lenin, perhaps) was not really socialist at all. Social democrats may accept that the Soviet system was indeed marxist, and they reject marxism; idealist marxists cling to their theory while claiming that it has not yet been put into practice.

Our position is distinct from both of these views. First of all, we argue that social democracy sells short the historic aspirations of socialism; it represents an insufficiently radical solution to the ills of modern capitalist societies. In contrast to the social democrats, we believe that there is much of value in the classical marxian project of radical social transformation. On the other hand, we reject the idealist view which seeks to preserve the purity of socialist ideals at the cost of disconnecting them from historical reality. We recognise, that is, that the Soviet-type societies were in a significant sense socialist. Of course, they did not represent the materialisation of the ideals of Marx and Engels, or even of Lenin, but then what concrete historical society was ever the incarnation of an Idea? When we use the term 'socialism' as a social-scientific concept, to differentiate a specific form of social organisation by virtue of its specific mode of production, we must recognise that socialism is not a Utopia. It is quite unscientific to claim that because the Soviet system was not democratic, therefore it cannot have been socialist, or more generally to build whatever features of society one considers most desirable into the very definition of socialism. Our view can be summed up as follows:

1. Soviet society was indeed socialist.
2. This society had many undesirable and problematic features.
3. The problems of Soviet society were in part related to the extremely difficult historical circumstances in which the Bolsheviks set about trying to build socialism, but that is not all: important policy mistakes were made (just as possible in a socialist society as in capitalism), and furthermore the problems of Soviet socialism in part reflect serious weaknesses in classical marxism itself.
4. The failure of the Soviet system is therefore by no means irrelevant to marxian socialism. We must reflect carefully on the lessons to be learned from this failure.
5. Nonetheless, unlike those who delight in proclaiming the complete historic rout of marxism, we believe that a different type of socialism—still recognizably marxian, yet substantially reformulated—is possible. The Soviet Union was socialist, but other forms of marxian socialism are possible.
6. This claim can be sustained only by spelling out in much more detail than hitherto both the sorts of economic mechanisms and the forms of political constitution which socialists consider both desirable and feasible. This we try to do in the book.

In this introduction, we begin to offer some answers to certain questions arising from these statements: Why is social democracy inadequate? In what sense was the USSR socialist? Insofar as the shortcomings of Soviet society arose from policy mistakes and lacunae in marxist theory, what were those mistakes and lacunae? What is the basis for the claim that a revival of socialism is both possible and desirable? We cannot answer these large questions in any detail here; our intention is to sketch the outlines of answers, and to point forwards to the chapters which will flesh out the sketches.

Why is social democracy inadequate?

Social democracy has traditionally stood for a 'mixed economy', for the mitigation of the inequalities of capitalism by means of a system of progressive taxation and social benefits, for parliamentary democracy and civil liberties. At their most successful, social democratic parties have certainly succeeded in improving the conditions of the working class, compared to a situation of unregulated capitalism; in Britain the National Health Service remains the most enduring monument to this sort of amelioration. Nonetheless very substantial problems remain.

First, capitalist economic mechanisms tend to generate gross inequalities of income, wealth and 'life-chances' (as discussed in chapter 1), and social democracy has had little real impact on these inequalities, which have indeed worsened over the last decade or so. Only a radical change in the mode of distribution of personal incomes, such as that advocated in chapter 2, offers a real prospect of eliminating gross inequality. Secondly, the 'mixed economy' is problematic in two important ways. In the mixed economies that have existed to date, the socialist elements have remained subordinated to the capitalist elements. That is, the commodity and wage forms have remained the primary forms of organisation of production and payment of labour respectively. 'Socialist' activities have had to be financed out of tax revenue extracted from the capitalist sector, which has meant that the opportunities for expansion of 'welfare' measures and the 'free' distribution of basic services have been dependent on the health of the capitalist sector and the strength of the tax base. Only when the capitalist sector has been growing strongly have social democratic governments been able to 'deliver the goods'. In this way, the capacity of social democratic governments to reshape the class structure of society has been inherently self-limiting: attempts at radical redistribution always threaten to destroy the engine of capitalist wealth-creation on which those governments ultimately depend.

Linked to the foregoing, if the mixed economy is a mixture of capitalist and socialist elements, there has been little serious attempt to define the principles of operation of the socialist sector. This leaves the whole idea of a mixed economy vulnerable, in a world context where the planned economies are disintegrating. Advocates of the unfettered market can argue, in effect, that if planning is being rejected in its heartlands, why should it be tolerated in the West, even as a subordinate element of the system? Insofar as Western social democrats have no coherent idea of what planned and non-commodity forms of production are ultimately about, and how their efficiency can be assessed, they are ill-placed to defend their favoured 'mixture', except in a rather vague and moralising manner.

From this point of view, our attempt to define the principles of a socialist economic mechanism might be seen as providing the socialist backbone which is conspicuously lacking in contemporary social democracy: even those who disagree with our advocacy of a fully planned economy might find some value in our arguments, insofar as they illuminate the undeveloped component in the mixed economy's 'mix'.

In what sense was the USSR socialist?
Here we base ourselves on the classical marxist analysis of society. In Marx's view, the most basic distinguishing feature of different modes of social organisation is the manner in which they ensure the 'extraction of a surplus product' from the direct producers. This requires a little explanation. The 'necessary product', on this theory, is the product required to maintain and reproduce the workforce itself. This will take the form of consumer goods and services for the workers and their families, and the investment in plant, equipment and so on that is needed simply to maintain the society's means of production in working order. The 'surplus product', on the other hand, is that portion of social output used to maintain the non-producing members of society (a heterogeneous lot, ranging from the idle rich, to politicians, to the armed forces, to retired working people and children), plus that portion devoted to net expansion of the stock of means of production. Any society capable of supporting non-producing members, and of generating an economically progressive programme of net investment, must have some mechanism for compelling or inducing the direct producers to produce more than is needed simply to maintain themselves. The precise nature of this mechanism is, according to marxist theory, the key to understanding the society as a whole—not just the 'economy', but also the general form of the state and of politics. Our claim is that the Soviet system put into effect a mode of extraction of the surplus product quite different from that of capitalism. To put this point in context, some more general historical background may be useful.

Consider, first, the distinction between feudal and capitalist society. Under feudalism, the extraction of a surplus product was plainly 'visible' to all. The specific forms were various, but one typical method involved the peasants working their own fields for so many days in the week, and the lord's land for the rest. Alternatively, the peasants might have to surrender a portion of the produce of their own fields to the lord. If such a society is to reproduce itself, the direct producers must be held in some form of direct subordination or servitude; political and legal equality is out of the question. A religious ideology that speaks of the distinct 'places' allotted to individuals on this earth and of the virtues of knowing one's proper place, and that promises a heavenly reward for those who fulfil their role in God's earthly scheme, will also be very useful.

Under capitalism, on the other hand, the extraction of the surplus product becomes 'invisible' in the form of the wage contract. The parties to the contract are legal equals, each bringing their property to the market and conducting a voluntary transaction. No bell rings in the factory to announce the end of the portion of the working day spent producing the equivalent of the workers' wages, and the beginning of the production of profits for the employer. Nonetheless, the workers' wages *are* substantially less than the total value of the product they generate: this is the basis of Marx's theory of exploitation. The degree of exploitation that is realised depends on the struggle between workers and capitalists, in its various forms: over the level of wages, over the pace of production and the length of the working day, and over the changes in technology that determine how much labour time is required to produce a given quantum of wage-goods.

Soviet socialism, particularly following the introduction of the first five-year plan under Stalin in the late 1920s, introduced a new and non-capitalist mode of extraction of a surplus. This is somewhat obscured by the fact that workers were still paid rouble wages, and that money continued in use as a unit of account in the planned industries, but the social content of these 'monetary forms' changed drastically. Under Soviet planning, the division between the necessary and surplus portions of the social product was the result of *political decisions.* For the most part, goods and labour were physically allocated to enterprises by the planning authorities, who would always ensure that the enterprises had enough money to 'pay for' the real goods allocated to them. If an enterprise made monetary 'losses', and therefore had to have its money balances topped up with 'subsidies', that was no matter. On the other hand, possession of money as such was no guarantee of being able to get hold of real goods. By the same token, the resources going into production of consumer goods were centrally allocated. Suppose the workers won higher rouble wages: by itself this would achieve nothing, since the flow of production of consumer goods was not responsive to the monetary amount of consumer spending. Higher wages would simply mean higher prices or shortages in the shops. The rate of production of a surplus was fixed when the planners allocated resources to investment in heavy industry and to the production of consumer goods respectively.

In very general terms this switch to a planned system, where the the division of necessary and surplus product is the result of deliberate social decision, is entirely in line with what Marx had hoped for. Only Marx had imagined this 'social decision' as being radically democratic, so that the production of the surplus would have an intrinsic legitimacy. The people, having made the decision to devote so much of their combined labour to net investment and the support of non-producers, would then willingly implement their own decision. For reasons both external and internal, Soviet society at the time of the introduction of economic planning was far from democratic. How, then, could the workers be induced or compelled to implement the plan (which, although it was supposedly formulated in their interests, was certainly not of their making)?

We know that the plans were, by and large, implemented. The 1930s saw the development of a heavy industrial base at unprecedented speed, a base that would be severely tested in the successful resistance to the Nazi invasion. We are also well aware of the characteristic features of the Stalin era, with its peculiar mixture of terror and forced labour on the one hand, and genuine pioneering fervour on the other. Starting from the question of how the extraction of a surplus product was possible in a planned but undemocratic system, the cult of Stalin's personality appears not as a mere 'aberration', but as an integral feature of the system. Stalin: at once the inspirational leader, making up in determination and grit for what he lacked in eloquence and capable of promoting a sense of participation in a great historic endeavour, and the stern and utterly ruthless liquidator of any who failed so to participate (and many others besides). The Stalin cult, with both its populist and its terrible aspects, was central to the Soviet mode of extraction of a surplus product.

What can be learnt from the failure of Soviet socialism?

The crisis of Soviet socialism appears to stem from two sources. On the one hand there is popular revulsion against the undemocratic and authoritarian practices of old-style Soviet politics, and on the other hand there is a widespread sense that the basic economic mechanisms in operation since the 1930s have outlived their usefulness, and that to retain these mechanisms would condemn the peoples of the (erstwhile) USSR to stagnant standards of living and chronic shortages of consumer goods. Compared with the evident continuing vitality of the advanced capitalist economies, such conditions became increasingly intolerable to the people.

To some extent these two issues are linked. As the USSR moved from the era of Stalin to that of Brezhnev, the earlier system of terror and compulsion was mitigated. At the same time, however, the pioneering spirit that had animated broad layers of the Soviet population during the early years of socialist construction, and also during the resistance to fascism, eroded. In other words, both pillars of the Soviet mode of extraction of a surplus product (in a planned yet undemocratic system) were undermined. It should also be noted that Stalin was not averse to using substantial wage differentials as a means of stimulating work effort, while Brezhnev moved towards a more egalitarian policy. Socialists can applaud egalitarianism, of course, but if individualistic monetary incentives are undermined there is nonetheless a need to promote other kinds of incentives—for instance those stemming from a sense of democratic participation in a common endeavour. And if good work is not to be rewarded by much higher pay, it still must be rewarded (and be seen to be rewarded) by opportunities for promotion and advancement. Such alternative incentives were almost completely absent in the corrupt and cynical political culture of the Brezhnev period. Apathy became widespread. While an earlier generation had known socialism as a noble ideal—imperfectly realised or perhaps even gravely distorted in the Soviet Union, but still worth upholding—an entire generation grew up under Brezhnev for whom the Soviet Union and socialism were simply *equated*, as in the system's own propaganda. If they hated the Soviet system, then they hated socialism.

The diagnosis so far leads to somewhat ambiguous conclusions. Our emphasis on the problems facing the USSR as an *undemocratic* planned system might seem to suggest that deep-going democratic reforms might have been enough to revitalise Soviet society and the Soviet economy. That is, if undemocratic planning were replaced by democratic planning, then the enthusiasm of the population might be enlisted for the task of economic modernisation, still within the broad framework of a planned and non-capitalist system. Of course, this view is now very widely seen as falsified by the brute facts of recent Russian history: reform did not stop at *glasnost*, nor even at *perestroika*, conceived as a re-structuring of the *socialist* economy, but moved on, apparently inexorably, to the destruction of the old planning system in its entirety and the project of transition to a market economy.

Various interpretations of this history are possible. One view is the simple anti-socialist one, that centralised planning and state ownership are inherently inferior to the market system, and that given a free choice in the absence of political/ideological coercion people will automatically choose the market. Democracy inevitably leads to the rejection of the socialist economic mechanism. This book contains a set of arguments designed to show that this conclusion is unwarranted, *i.e.* that an efficient and productive socialist economic mechanism is both possible and preferable to capitalism (from the standpoint of the interests of the working majority at any rate). But if that is true, how do we explain the rejection of the socialist economy in the USSR and elsewhere? Two points are particularly relevant. First, as we have already noted, by the 1980s there were many Soviet citizens for whom socialism was *nothing other* than the Brezhnev system. This is what they were told *ad nauseam*, and they had little reason to doubt it. The notion that a very different kind of socialism is possible and desirable depends upon the classic arguments, proposals and ideals of the founders of socialism; and those whose only acquaintance with these ideas was in the form of turgid official apologetics are unlikely to entertain such a notion. Secondly, there can be little doubt that the economic stagnation that beset the Soviet Union in the latter days of the old economic mechanism was not solely and simply the result of a lack of democratic participation. There *were* serious technical/economic problems with that mechanism; but we shall argue that such problems are not inherent in socialist planning as such.

Our view is, then, that a thorough democratisation *plus* substantial reforms in the planning mechanism might, in principle, have created the opportunity for a revitalised Soviet socialism. Unfortunately, though, the historical experience of the bleak decades of inefficient and dictatorial rule, buttressed ideologically by an ossified official marxism, seems to have ruled this out as a practical political option for the present.

What is the theoretical basis for a new socialism?

The principal bases for a post-Soviet socialism must be radical democracy and efficient planning. The democratic element, it is now clear, is not a luxury, or something that can be postponed until conditions are especially favourable. Without democracy, as we have argued above, the leaders of a socialist society will be driven to coercion in order to ensure the production of a surplus product, and if coercion slackens the system will tend to stagnate. At the same time, the development of an efficient planning system will most likely be impossible in the absence of an open competition of ideas. The failure of Soviet Communists to come up with viable *socialist* reform proposals over recent years is testimony to the malign effects of a system in which conformity and obedience were at a premium. Capitalist societies can achieve economic progress under conditions of political dictatorship, for even under such dictatorship the realm of private economic activity is relatively unregulated and the normal processes of competition remain operative, while the suppression of working-class organisation may permit a higher rate of exploitation. Under socialism, there can be no such separation of oppressive state from 'free' economy; and if criteria of ideological 'correctness' dominate in the promotion of managers and even in economic-theoretical debate, the long-run prospects for growth and efficiency are dim indeed.

On the counts of both democratic institutions and efficient planning mechanisms, we have to say that the problems which emerged in the Soviet case reflect certain weaknesses in classical marxism. Marx, Engels and Lenin were much stronger in their critiques of capitalism than in their positive theorising concerning socialist society. As regards democratic institutions, the Bolsheviks initially latched onto the soviets of workers' and soldiers' deputies as the favoured form. While this may have been tactically astute, we argue that the soviet form is inherently inadequate and indeed dangerous and that we must look elsewhere for the principles of a socialist democratic constitution. As regards planning mechanisms, Marx and Engels had some interesting suggestions, but these were never developed beyond the level of rather vague generalities. The Soviet planners improvised their own system, which worked for certain purposes in its time, but the development of their thinking about socialist economic mechanisms was limited by what they saw as the need to conform to the canons of marxism—to avoid and indeed denounce any theoretical methods, such as marginal analysis, that appeared tainted by 'bourgeois' connotations. Western marxists have argued that this tendency was based on a misinterpretation of Marx. Quite likely so, but the fact that Marx did not attempt to spell out the principles of operation of a planned economy at any length made such a misreading possible. At any rate, socialism will never again have any credibility as an economic system unless we can spell out such principles in reasonable detail.

Synopsis of the book
In the remainder of this introduction we offer a synopsis of the main arguments to come, in the light of the problems and issues identified above. Chapters 1 and 2 tackle issues connected with inequality and inequity. The first gives an overview of the bases of

inequality in capitalist society—bases which, as we have suggested above, social democratic amelioration is unable to eradicate. The second shows how a consistent socialist system of payment could substantially eliminate inequality. The payment system outlined in chapter 2 depends on the idea that the total labour content of each product or service can be calculated. Chapter 3 justifies this claim, while developing the argument that economic calculation in terms of labour time is rational and technically progressive.

Chapters 4 to 9 then develop various aspects of an efficient system of economic planning, a system capable of ensuring that economic development is governed by the democratically constructed needs of the people. Chapter 4 establishes some basic concepts and priorities, and distinguishes a number of different 'levels' of planning, namely strategic planning, detailed planning, and macroeconomic planning, which are then examined in detail in chapters 5, 6 and 7 respectively. Chapter 8 outlines a specific mechanism for ensuring that the detailed pattern of production remains in line with consumers' preferences, while avoiding excessive queues and shortages. Chapter 9 examines the information requirements for the type of planning system we envisage, and makes a link between the issue of accurate information and the incentives and sanctions faced by individuals. In the course of these chapters we draw a number of contrasts between the sort of system we are proposing, and the system commonly regarded as having failed in the Soviet Union.[1]

While chapters 4 to 9 deal with the planning of a single economy in isolation, chapters 10 and 11 extend the argument to consider issues arising from trade with other economies, an important practical concern in a world of increasing interdependence.

Chapters 12 to 14 move beyond the economic to further social and political questions. Chapter 12 makes a connection between socialist objectives and the concerns brought to light by feminists. It investigates the possibilities for domestic communes as an alternative to the nuclear family 'household', and shows how such communes could function within the broad structure of a planned economy. Chapter 13 considers the political sphere, and proposes a radical form of democratic constitution capable of giving ordinary people real control over their lives. As mentioned earlier, we are critical of the soviet model of democracy. We are equally critical of parliamentary systems, and our own proposals stem from a re-examination of the mechanisms of classical (Athenian) democracy in the modern context. Chapter 14 examines the question of property relations, and elaborates the specific forms of property required as a basis for the preceding economic and social forms.

In a final chapter we tackle some contrary arguments put forward by sceptical socialists in recent years. In this context we reply to arguments in favour of 'market socialism' as an alternative to the sort of planning we advocate.

The overall theme which animates the book, through all its various detailed arguments, will, we hope, be clear. That is, we take as our ultimate aim the greatest possible fulfilment of the potential of each human being, as individual and as a member of society. This fulfilment requires dignity, security and substantive equality (though not, of course, uniformity), as well as productive efficiency. It also requires that humans find sustainable ways of living in balance with the overall environment of the planet. We argue that these aims can best be met through a cooperative, planned form of social economy under a radically democratic political constitution—a post-Soviet socialism.

Note to Introduction
1. In this book, we develop our own proposals for socialist planning from first principles, without making a great deal of reference to the existing literature. For a detailed discussion and critique of the historic 'socialist calculation debate' see Cottrell and Cockshott (1993a); and for a more detailed examination of the theory and practices of Soviet-type economic planning see Cottrell and Cockshott (1993b).

CHAPTER 1

Inequality

One of the main aims of socialism is to overcome the gross inequalities of income, rights and opportunities that are associated with capitalism. Socialism makes its primary appeal to those who suffer most from the inequalities of capitalism. Conversely, those who benefit, or believe that they benefit from inequality and privilege, have in the main opposed socialism.

The wealthy are easily convinced that attempts to achieve social equality are futile where they are not misguided, but their poorer fellow citizens may need some persuasion. To this end, it is argued that inequality is both functional and inevitable. Unequal incomes are necessary in order to provide the incentives to make people work hard and efficiently; whatever their initial intentions, even socialist countries will find that they have to introduce inequality to make the economy work. It is interesting how the advocates of social inequality think that the wealthy respond to quite different incentives from the poor. If the rich are to be persuaded to work, they require the stimulus of still greater wealth: hence the paramount importance of reducing taxes on high incomes. When dealing with the poor, in contrast, it is held that there is nothing like the propect of still greater poverty as a work incentive: hence the paramount importance of strictly limiting the benefits to which they are entitled.

We strongly disagree with both these contentions. We want to show that although a modicum of economic inequality may be inevitable, this amount is tiny compared to what exists today. We think that it is possible to run a society that is efficient, humane and basically equal. In this chapter we outline the first principles of a sustainable economic mechanism that would produce such a society.

Sources of inequality

Those who suffer under the present dispensation do not need to be told how bad things are; they know this already. The important questions are: what are the causes of the present contrast between poverty and wealth, and what can be done about it? Of these, logically the most important question is the first. What really causes inequality in the present society? The most important causes are:

1. Exploitation of those who work
2. Inheritance of wealth by a minority
3. Unemployment
4. Infirmity and old age
5. The economic subordination of women
6. Differences in skills and ability

Exploitation

In everyday speech, we talk of exploitation wherever the strong take advantage of the weak. Economic exploitation involves people not being adequately paid for the work they do. It might be a wife forced to skivvy without pay for her husband or an employee working to enrich his employer. In an exploitative relationship the person who is being exploited does not get back out of it what he or she puts in. The idea tends to be rather vague and imprecise in personal relationships, but in the cash relationship between worker and employer it takes on a precise meaning. A worker is exploited if the wages she gets are worth less than the product of the work that she does.

The idea is very simple. We can best show it by first imagining a situation where exploitation does not exist. Suppose a worker is employed for 40 hours a week. If he is not to be exploited, then the wages he gets for that work should allow him to buy goods and services that took 40 hours of work to produce. Although goods do not come with their labour content stamped on them, like the calorific content on cereal packets, it is in principle possible to calculate labour content. It is clear that in this case there would be no exploitation. A week's work as a cook or a bus driver would just be exchanged for the same amount of work (in terms of time) by those who supply the employee with her wants and necessities: farmers, clothworkers, bakers, actors, etc.

In practice this does not happen in a capitalist society. Although the labour contract between employer and employee is formally a voluntary agreement, its terms are effectively dictated by the employer. Someone who has been unemployed for a while, or who fears unemployment, will be glad of any job and won't be too particular about the conditions. The employer does not face the same constraints. There are usually many applicants for each job, so that if one person tries to negotiate his rate of wages there will be someone else who will undercut him.

In those rare circumstances in which there is a severe shortage of labour, and wages rise to non-exploitative levels, then the employers have the option of leaving their capital in the bank to earn interest. They would rather do this than hire labour at wage levels which would threaten their profits. Finally they can think of moving their business abroad to a third world country with much lower wage levels.

All of these factors conspire to force employees to sell themselves at exploitatively low wage rates. Just how low can be seen by looking at the breakdown of the British National Income shown in Table 1.1. For each sector of the economy we examine how the value added through labour is distributed between wages and profits. By value added we mean the difference between the total sales of a company and the costs of its non-labour inputs to the production process: fuel, raw-materials, depreciation on machinery etc.

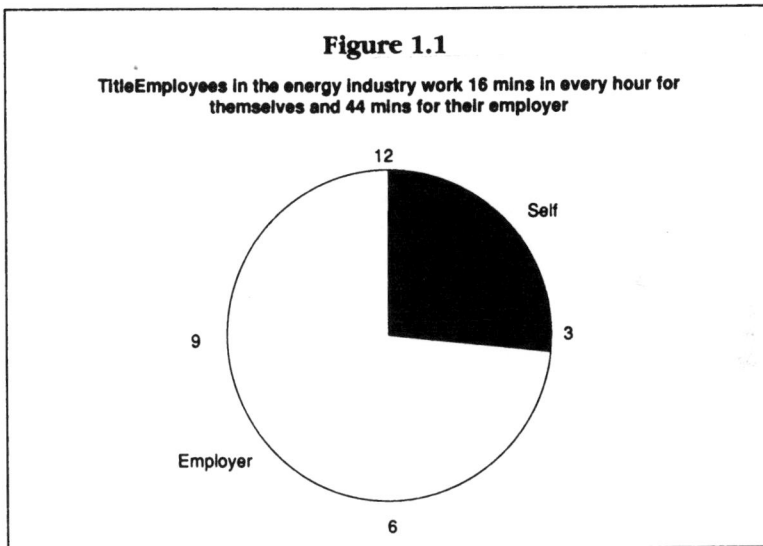

Figure 1.1

TitleEmployees in the energy industry work 16 mins in every hour for themselves and 44 mins for their employer

These figures are derived from the 1983 *National Income and Expenditure Blue Book* published by the Central Statistical Office. The two columns show total wages and profits for various sectors of the economy. The total value added is the sum of wages and profits. We can see that the share of value added that goes towards wages varies substantially from one sector to another. In 1982, the share of value added going to workers in the energy industry was only 27 per cent. That is equivalent to energy workers working 16 minutes in every hour for themselves, and 44 minutes per hour for their employers' profit.

In other industries the rate of exploitation is lower. In manufacturing, for example, about 75 per cent of value added goes

Table 1.1:
Calculating the rate of exploitation, 1982

Industry or sector	Wages	Profits and other property income less stock appreciation
Energy	7241	18796
Manufacturing	44337	14105
Construction	7774	5706
Distrib & Catering	21526	8445
Transport	7443	2868
Communications	4359	2494
Banking etc	15205	13835
Rent	0	14690
Other Services	11176	3367
Agriculture, Forestry, Fish	2044	3708
Totals	*121105*	*88014*
	(= 57%)	(= 43%)

Raw rate of exploitation	for self	for others
(minutes per hour worked)	34.4 (57%)	25.6 (43%)

Further breakdown of banking and financial services

Wages and Salaries	15205	
Service Charges	10589	(= wages + trading profits)
Trading Profits	–4616	

Assume labour of bank employees paid for at 60% of value created. Income from service charges breaks up as:

Wages and salaries	6353.4
Surplus value	4235.6
Total	10589

Adjusted contribution of banking sector

to total wages	6353.4
to total surplus value	22686.6

Adjusted Totals

Wages and Salaries	112253.4
Property Income	96865.6

Adjusted rate of exploitation	for self	for others
(minutes per hour worked)	32.2 (53%)	27.8 (47%)

All figures in £ million.
Source National Income and Expenditure, 1983 edition, Central Statistical Office.

towards wages. To arrive at an estimate of the average level of exploitation of employees for the economy as a whole, we start by adding up wages and profits for various capitalist sectors of the economy. If we look at the totals of wages and of property income we find that only about 60 per cent of all value added went to the workers who created it.

On closer examination, it turns out that this is an overestimate of the amount that workers are paid. The point is that the banks and financial institutions cannot be treated as producers of wealth in the same sense as manufacturing or catering. The financial sector derives its income from two sources: service charges levied on the holders of current accounts, and interest receipts from loans. The former is termed trading income, the latter non-trading income. The financial sector provides services like clearing cheques and providing accounts. The value of these services is measured by their service charges. The service charges less the related wage bill appears as gross trading profit in the official statistics. These trading profits must be distinguished from the total profits earned by the banks, which will be boosted by non trading income in the form of interest.

The gross trading profits of the financial sector are consistently negative, indicating that the running costs of the banks are only

Figure 1.2

The average employee worked 32 minutes in the hour for herself in 1987

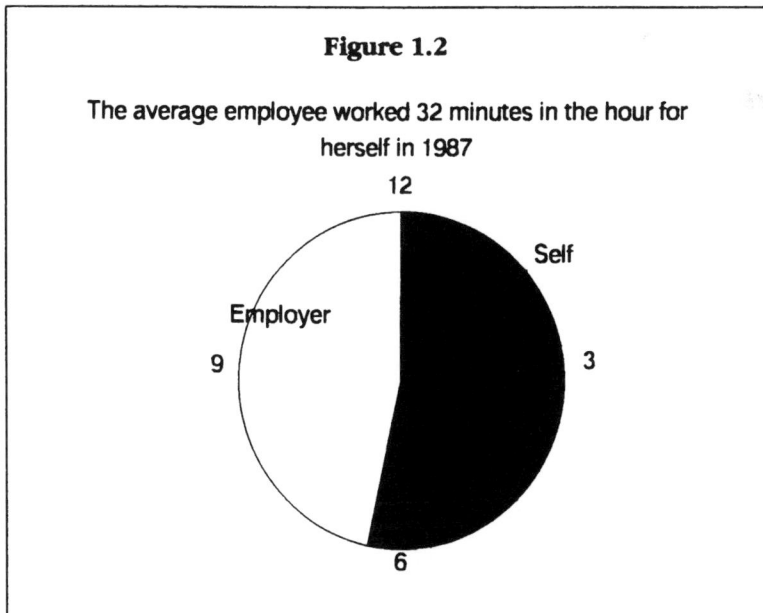

partly met by their trading income. This means that only some of the labour employed by the banks goes towards the provision of marketed services; the remaining labour is an additional cost that the banks incur in managing loans and collecting interest. This cost has to be met by the wealth producing sector of the population, via payments of interest.

When we calculate the total national wage bill for the capitalist sector, we should only include the wages of those bank employees who produce marketed services; other bank wages should be treated as part of surplus value. These adjustments are made in the bottom half of Table 1.1. The adjusted result gives a somewhat higher estimate for the rate of exploitation.

From this result, we can work out how much of income actually does go back to wealth-producing employees. This is shown in the adjusted figures for wages and property income. Using these we find that workers in the capitalist sectors of the economy only get back 53 per cent of the value added by their labour. In effect they work 32 minutes in every hour for themselves and 28 minutes to support various exploiting or unproductive groups in society.

The exploitation of employees is associated with gross inequalities in income and wealth.[1] The proceeds of exploitation are devoted to two main purposes. They are either distributed as dividends or interest payments, or they are used to finance capital accumulation on the part of the company. In either case the beneficiaries of this are the owners of shares, bonds and other financial assets. If profits are devoted to dividends they benefit directly. If they are directed into capital accumulation, shareholders benefit indirectly through the appreciation of share values.

Shares are very unevenly distributed among the population. The 1975 Royal Commission on the Distribution of Income and Wealth reported that the bottom 80 per cent of the population owned less than 4 per cent of shares. Even now, in a country with a highly developed stock market like Britain, the majority of working class people own no shares at all. Those workers who do own them will often only have a few hundred pounds' worth, so that income from shares makes up an insignificant part of their total earnings; the amount that they earn from shares will be less than they have to pay as interest on personal debts and mortgages. Quite aside from their exploitation by their employers, they will suffer from a net exploitation by the financial institutions.

The uneven distribution of income is self-perpetuating. A very small proportion of the population own the majority of shares. The Royal Commission reported that some 330,000 people owned 55 per cent of all shares and 58 per cent of all land. This section of the population is able to live off property income. Such people may also choose to work and obtain additional income from directors' fees, etc. In either case they have enough income to reinvest a large part of it in additional shares or other financial assets. Because they can afford to save a much larger fraction of their income than the average employee, this class will continue, from one generation to the next, to hold the greater part of the nation's financial capital.[2]

This small minority is the final beneficiary of the systematic underpayment of the working population. So long as the present market system continues, this is bound to be the major source of economic inequality.

Unemployment

A secondary, but still important source of economic inequality is unemployment. People with a job can easily forget, or fail to realise, just how low one's income falls if one is unemployed. Dozens of ordinary minor expenditures that the employed think nothing of—buying a cup of coffee, using public transport, visiting the cinema—all suddenly seem outrageously expensive. Those unemployed for a long period who exhaust their limited savings, or who have never had the opportunity of paid employment, are dependent upon state benefits nicely calculated to suffice for bare survival. In some capitalist countries, and to an increasing extent in Britain, even this is unavailable to whole sections of unemployed people. These groups are driven into an underworld of crime, prostitution or dependence upon charity.

The difference between the conditions of the employed and the unemployed attracts a great deal of political attention. Politicians talk of the emergence of a new underclass of long term unemployed. Princes worry in coded terms about the 'inner cities'. Nonetheless, unemployment is a secondary source of inequality. For one thing, it only affects a minority of the labour force; unemployment fluctuates, but it is usually less than one in seven of the fit adult population. More importantly, unemployment works to maintain the exploitation of those in employment. Unemployment acts to create a buyer's market for labour; for every job there will be several applicants. Exploitative wage rates will not be questioned by those who have no alternative. Unions will hesitate to strike for higher pay if they know that the employer can readily hire strike-breakers from among the unemployed. Whole workforces can be dismissed and alternative labour hired at lower rates.

Unemployment is the regulator of exploitation and is maintained as such by government policy. The economic policies that will bring about full employment are well known. In Britain, they were followed for some two decades after the second world war, and kept unemployment down to about one in 30 or one in 40 of the labour force. They could be applied now. The economic levers for creating full employment remain the same. The reason why they are not applied is because of what happened during those 20 years.

Those were the days when a Conservative Prime Minister (Harold Macmillan) could honestly say to the working classes that they 'had never had it so good'. Full employment meant an unprecedented period of continuously rising real wages. Following a half century of stagnation, real take home pay almost doubled.[3] But over the same period the share of company output that went towards profits halved from 23.4 per cent in 1950 to 12.1 per cent in 1970 (Bacon and Eltis, 1978). In other words, employees used the labour shortage to reduce their exploitation. Attempts by companies to maintain their profit share by increasing prices led to inflation.

Since the mid 1970s it has been accepted by politicians of both leading political parties that full employment policies are impractical, and if resumed would once again trigger off inflation. An economy based upon the systematic exploitation of employees required the creation of a surplus in the labour market, and that required unemployment.

There is no logical reason why unemployment should entail poverty and deprivation. If there was no work available, then a civilised society might pay those temporarily idle, but willing to work, a decent income. If somebody is idle through no fault of his own, why should he suffer a drop in income? If, as many people mistakenly believe, the source of unemployment is technological change, the advance of the robot and the computer, there would be no bar to such a rational and humane policy. But unemployment is due to a change in public policy. Once governments accepted unemployment as a permanent necessity for regulating the labour market, they then set about degrading the unemployed.

From year to year the real level of benefit paid to the unemployed is eroded, while the conditions that must be met to obtain it become more and more stringent. Vulnerable groups like teenagers have their rights to benefits withdrawn; grants for clothing and furniture are replaced by loans; the unemployed are made liable for the Poll Tax, etc.

By reducing the unemployed to absolute indigence, the government depresses the lower end of the wage scale. When youngsters are compelled to work for what are generously called training schemes at £25 per week, is it any wonder that starting rates for adults are as low as £1.70 per hour? These rates, moreover, are paid for what is often part-time work of one of two dozen hours per week. The poverty of the unemployed is a gateway to poverty for the employed.

Infirmity and old age

A person need not be poor just because he is old, disabled or otherwise unable to work. Upper class retired people with substantial property live a prosperous life. It is only those who lack property, and are dependent upon selling their labour, who are thrown into hardship by injury or old age. Because this is the condition of most of the population, the majority of the old and the disabled live in relatively straitened circumstances, dependent upon a niggardly state pension.

The low level of these pensions is the result of political decisions. It is official policy to encourage people to rely upon private pension and insurance schemes, and people will be less willing to take these out if they feel they can rely upon an adequate statutory pension. This creates pressure to hold down the level of the state pension. The politicians who take these decisions know that they personally will have more substantial reserves to fall back upon when they retire. This fact cannot fail to have an influence upon them, but they not just acting from pure self-interest. When they encourage the use of private pensions they are going along with the logic of capitalist private property. Private pension schemes prolong the income differentials established during working life into retirement; they thus add security and stability to the basic class structure. Over and above this they give the middle classes an incentive to save. Through saving they take a stake in the capitalist financial system, and with that a political interest in its perpetuation.

It would be different if there were no private pensions and if decisions on state pension levels were taken by people who expected to have to rely upon these pensions themselves. Then it would be reasonable to expect the basic state pension to be higher in relation to average earnings than it is now.

Women's economic subordination

The nations of western Europe have a social system that is made up of several different forms of economy. Socialists have traditionally been most aware of the capitalist and state capitalist sectors. When people talk of the mixed economy it is the mixture between these two components that they mean: the mixture between private industry and nationalised industry. In addition to this and sometimes confused with it, is the distinction between the genuinely socialist elements of the economy (like the National

Health Service and parts of the education system) and both the private and state capitalist sectors. These are seen as the the most important component of the mixed economy. What is overlooked in this view of things is the very large part still played in our social system by domestic economy.

We believe that just as the capitalist economy is responsible for one set of economic inequalities—those between rich and poor—so the domestic economy is ultimately responsible for another set of inequalities—those between women and men.

The domestic economy is marked by the unpaid performance of labour services in the family. The majority of those who directly produce these services are married women; the non-producers who get the benefits of these labour services are children and husbands. It is another feature of the domestic economy that neither the results of work nor the work itself is paid for. If a wife cooks a meal for her family she is not paid for the time she spends working, nor is the meal itself sold. If the family members go out to a restaurant they may have a meal that is identical in nutritional terms, but its social character will be quite different. The meal is bought as a commodity and it is produced by waged employees of the restaurant.

Because the domestic economy is essentially non-monetary its contribution to the national product is not included in official statistics. If we measured its contribution in terms of the effort that is put in, however, the sheer numbers of housewives and others involved, and the length of hours that they work, could make it the biggest sector of the economy.

The domestic economy has undergone a long decline in relative importance during the capitalist epoch. When classical writers spoke of the economy or *oikonomia* they were speaking of household management, of the organisation of domestic production (see Tribe, 1978). Such a large proportion of economic activity took place within the household that money-making was viewed by Aristotle as an unnatural activity. It seemed by nature to be opposed to the normal productive activities that occur within the household. When bourgeois economic thought was formalised by Adam Smith, a complete inversion took place. Now, production for the market was seen as the characteristic form of economic activity. This view of economic activity as being primarily market-oriented reflects the fact that the capitalist system really is superior to the domestic economy.

During periods of rapid growth the capitalist economy expands at the expense of the domestic sector. Historically the most important stage of this process is the replacement of domestic food production by capitalist agriculture. In Britain this process was complete by the early years of the 19th century, but in other parts of Europe the process continued well into the last quarter of the 20th. Ironically socialist revolutions have generally occurred in countries like China where the domestic economy was still dominant in the production of food. In an advanced capitalist country the scope of the domestic economy has become much more restricted. It is confined to the fields of: (1) the final steps in food preparation; (2) the care of preschool infants; (3) part of the care of school age children; (4) part of the cleaning and maintenance of domestic premises; and (5) part of the care of the elderly and infirm.

Over the period of capitalist development one can see that several areas of production have been almost completely lost by the domestic economy: (1) the cultivation of crops; (2) care of domestic animals; (3) milling; (4) slaughtering; (5) food preservation; (6) spinning and weaving; and (7) house construction. These activities have all been transferred to the capitalist sector. The process continues. Examples are the increase in restaurants and the sale of prepared or quick-to-prepare meals. These reduce the amount of food production carried out by the domestic sector. The purchase of boarding school services by bourgeois and upper middle class families is another example.

These transfers between sectors have happened mainly because the market sector is more efficient. In some cases, it is true, coercion was used to annex land and eliminate domestic farming (enclosures in England, the clearances in Scotland); but even in those countries where coercion has not been used domestic agriculture has declined. Capitalism brings about technical advances in all the activities it organises. Competition between producers encourages the adoption of the most efficient techniques, and the productivity of labour goes up. The areas that were once part of domestic production now have much less work expended on them. The labour freed from them is now available to run the whole gamut of new industries and branches of production that have grown up in the modern era.

Although much labour is still expended in domestic production it produces relatively little in physical terms. In contrast to this the physical productivity of the market economy is continually growing. More and more goods become available from the capitalist sector whilst the productivity of the domestic sector remains relatively stagnant. It is not entirely stagnant; improvement in domestic means of production has been considerable. The replacement of wood or dung fires by gas or electric stoves, the replacement of wells by plumbed water, and of washing tubs by washing machines, means that significantly less labour now needs to be expended to carry out the same tasks. But these improvements have been external to the domestic economy; they result from the importation of capitalist technology. On its own, the domestic economy has never shown much ability to innovate.

The domestic economy has lost out to socialism as well. In industrialised countries it is standard for the state to provide free, compulsory education for children. This affects the domestic economy in two ways. To an extent it reduces the work of the mother who is no longer responsible for the children all day. On the other hand it removes a potential labour force from the domestic sector, since children are held in school well beyond the age at which they would have been expected to start productive work in earlier economic systems. One of the tragic effects of the reversion to domestic agriculture in China has been the tendency of peasant families to withdraw their children from schools; they are more use as farm hands. A domesticated workforce is all too often an illiterate one.

More recently the state has undertaken part of the task of looking after the elderly. Unlike encroachments by the capitalist sector, which occur spontaneously, the replacement of domestic labour by free public services requires direct political decisions. Areas of current conflict between the socialist and domestic modes of production include the feeding of children (free school meals) and the care of infants (nursery provision). There is considerable further scope for the extension of the semi-socialist sector at the expense of the domestic sector in the areas of food production, cleaning and child care.

As stated above, in the domestic system married women typically perform unpaid work for their husbands and children. This particular form of exploitation is highly mystified. Cloaked as it is in the ideologies of sexual and maternal love, people tend to overlook it. Because of its very private nature, the class contradictions between exploiter and exploited tend to appear in the form of personal antagonisms. The economic class struggle is manifest in arguments, moral pressures, wife beating, desertions and divorces.

Economic class struggles, even those between employers and employees, appear to the participants as basically private disputes. What makes a collection of private disputes a class conflict is that it involves a class of individuals who share common attributes and are opposed by another class of individuals. It is because conflicts of interests between husband and wife or between employer and employee do not just occur one or twice in isolated instances, but occur in parallel millions of times over, that they must be recognised as conflicts between classes of people.

It becomes clear to the participants in these disputes that these are class issues when the disputes are politicised. That is to say one side or the other demands that state action be taken to redress grievances. This is especially true of domestic class contradictions, since it is only in the political arena that women can cooperate with each other in large numbers to fight against their exploitation. In this case as in others it is in the interests of the exploiters to keep the contradiction privatised and personalised.

All political class struggle requires both a class-conscious leadership and a programme of demands around which the class can be united. So far, perhaps the most important issue in women's political struggle has been the struggle over abortion rights. So long as the domestic mode of production persists, control over fertility is essential to women who wish to control their own labour time.

The struggle of women as a class against domestic exploitation can take on a revolutionary character only if its objective becomes the replacement of the domestic economy by more advanced forms of production relations. Unless there is persistent propaganda for alternative ways for people to live together, prepare food, care for children and provide each other with emotional support, it will not be possible to raise the contradiction between men and women out of personal politics up to the level of political class struggle. In this sense we can view the contradiction between men and women as still being a suppressed or latent contradiction in British politics.

We believe that women's struggles can best be given a revolutionary content by putting forward a concrete image of a communal way of life that can supplant the present day patriarchal family. That task will be taken up in chapter 12.

Summary

In this chapter we have drawn attention both to the degree of inequality generated by a market economy and to some of its causes. We have examined the economic roots of inequality in the exploitation of labour. Opposition to this, the attempt to eliminate it, lies at the moral heart of any socialist political economy. In the chapters that follow, we shall show that by consistently upholding the principle that human work is alone the source of value, it is possible to construct an economic system that is both just and efficient.

Notes to Chapter 1

1. It would not be quite correct to say that inequality is 'caused by' exploitation. The two conditions are mutually reinforcing. Underlying inequality in the ownership of productive assets forces the majority of non-owners to submit to exploitation by selling their labour to the owners, which in turn gives rise to the wide disparity of incomes.
2. This is quite apart from the fact that direct ownership of real industrial capital is now chiefly exercised by impersonal enterprises rather than individual capitalists. On this point see Cottrell (1984).
3. *Historical Abstract of Labour Statistics 1886-1968*, Department of Employment and Productivity, 1971.

CHAPTER 2

Eliminating Inequalities

Our object in this book is to describe a set of principles and economic mechanisms which will, among other benefits, prevent the types of inequalities described in the last chapter. We believe that the inequalities caused by the capitalistic exploitation of employees and by unemployment can be effectively eliminated. We believe that the elimination of these inequalities among the economically active population would create political conditions favourable to ending much of the economic privations experienced by older people. We think that the progressive development of new forms of communal family can go a long way towards eliminating sexual inequalities. Finally we think that although there may be some residual economic inequalities associated with differences in skill or training, these can be reduced to a fraction of what they now are.

The relevant economic principles are not new. They date back to the first part of the 19th century, to the early days of socialism. In a certain sense their ancestry can be traced back further, to the classical economists of early capitalism: Adam Smith and David Ricardo. The basic idea is that a just society can only be established on the principle that *those who work are entitled to the full proceeds of their labour.* This was for a long time the most distinctive and popular of socialist principles. It sought a remedy for the exploitation of the workers by according them the right to get back out of each day's work, in terms of wages, as much as they had put in during the day, in terms of time and effort. Along with this went a second principle: *only work is a legitimate source of income.*

This excluded all sources of income such as rent, dividends or interest which derive from the ownership of property rather than the personal efforts of their recipients. The exclusion of unearned incomes is obviously a necessary consequence of the first principle, since in a society where the producers were entitled to the full proceeds of their labour there would be nothing left over to supply unearned incomes.

These are rather old, some would say obsolete, socialist principles. Mere age does not invalidate an economic doctrine. A 'new' right that revels in the rediscovery of the 18th century economics of Adam Smith is ill placed to throw the charge of archaism at the revival of a socialist doctrine that grew up as the 19th century riposte to the consequences of *laissez faire* capitalism.

The great merit of these original principles is that they provide a coherent foundation for an entire system, not just of economic organisation, but also a whole new legal, moral and social order. They imply a monetary system based upon time rather than upon arbitrary and meaningless currency units like Pounds, Dollars or Ecu. People would be credited with hours worked rather than money at the end of the week. Payments for goods and services would also be in terms of time. You would pay for a garment that took two hours to produce with two hours of your own time. An economy based upon time-prices would have built into it the democratic presumption of human equality.[1]

Marx outlined the sort of system we have in mind as follows:

> Accordingly, the individual producer gets back from society—after the deductions—exactly what he has given it. What he has given it is his individual quantum of labour. For instance, the social working day consists of the sum of the individual hours of work. The individual labour time of the individual producer thus constitutes his contribution to the social working day, his share of it. Society gives him a certificate stating that he has done such and such an amount of work (after the labour done for the communal fund has been deducted), and with this certificate he can withdraw from the social supply of means of consumption as much as costs an equivalent amount of labour. The same amount of labour he has given to society in one form, he receives back in another. (Marx, 1974, p. 346)

Note that these *certificates* of labour performed are quite distinct from money. They can only be obtained by labour and can only be exchanged against consumer goods. In another passage Marx argues that Robert Owen's so-called 'labour money' was not money at all:

> On this point I will only say that Owen's 'labour money', for instance, is no more 'money' than a theatre ticket is. Owen presupposes directly socialized labour, a form of production diametrically opposed to the production of commodities. The certificate of labour is merely evidence of the part taken by the individual in the common labour, and of his claim to a certain portion of the common product which has been set aside for consumption. But Owen never made the mistake of presupposing the production of commodities, while, at the same time, by juggling with

money, trying to circumvent the necessary conditions of that form of production. (Marx, 1976, pp.188–9)

When Marx says that labour certificates are no more money than a theatre ticket we can draw certain implications:

1. The certificates do not circulate; they can only be directly exchanged against consumer goods.
2. Like many tickets they would be non-transferable. Only the person who had performed the labour could use them.
3. They would be cancelled after a single use, just as a theatre ticket is destroyed on entry to the theatre. When individuals withdrew goods from a shop their vouchers would be cancelled. The shop, as a communal organisation, has no need to buy in goods, it is just allocated them, so its only interest in the labour vouchers is for record-keeping purposes.
4. They would not serve as a store of value. They could have a 'use by' date on them. Unless individuals redeemed their share of this year's output by the end of the year, it would be assumed that they did not want it. If labour tokens are not spent then the goods that embodied the labour would not be used. Many goods are perishable and they would have to be disposed of somehow.

Nowadays one need not think in terms of paper certificates of work done. Instead we can envisage the use of some form of *labour credit card* which keeps track of how much work you have done. Deductions from your social labour credit account could be made by filling in a slip, or using a direct debit terminal.

We are presented by Marx with a model—a skeletal one but a clear one—of a socialist society in which there are no commodities (*i.e.* goods produced specifically for exchange on a market). People are paid in labour credits for work done. Deductions are made for communal needs. Goods are distributed on the basis of their labour content, with corresponding deductions from people's credit accounts. Production is organised on a directly social basis with intermediate products never assuming the form of commodities.

Since the socialist principle of payment in terms of labour time was first advanced various objections to it have been raised. The first is that human beings are not equal so that it is neither just nor economically efficient to pay them equally. We will examine this argument in detail below.

It has also been argued that although calculation in terms of labour time may be fine on Robinson Crusoe's island it would never be practical in a real economy because of the sheer complexity of the problem. We will argue that modern computer technology

Table 2.1:
Value created by an hour's labour in 1987

UK Gross National Product at market prices	£420 billion
less Capital Consumption	£48 billion
equals Net National Product	£372 billion
Employed Workforce	25.7 million
So: National Product Per Employee	**£14,474**
Hours worked per week	40
Weeks per year	48
So: Total hours worked per year	**1920**
So: Value created per hour = £14,474/1920 =	**£7.53**

Note that this underestimates the amount of value created by an hour's labour since a part of the workforce is employed part time and works less than 40 hours per week.

would have little difficulty in keeping track of how much work goes into making things. This issue is examined in chapter 3.

Another objection to the use of labour prices, one advanced by Karl Marx in his critique of Proudhon (Marx, 1936, pp.55–56), was that labour money was incompatible with the operation of a market. This argument says that attempts to fix the prices of goods in terms of their labour costs of production would fail when confronted with fluctuations in supply and demand. We examine this argument in chapter 8.

First of all, however, we examine what the benefits of a socialist system of payment would be in practical terms.

Benefits of income redistribution
How much better off would the average person be under the socialist system of payment?

How much would one hour's labour produce?
We estimate that in Britain in 1987 an hour's labour produced goods worth about £7.50. This means that payment in terms of labour money would be equivalent to an hourly rate of £7.50 per hour in 1987 money.

Table 2.1 shows how this is worked out. The data come from the 1988 edition of the *United Kingdom National Accounts*. We start off with the Gross National Product of the country. We subtract from this the figure for capital consumption. Capital consumption is the rate at which the nation's capital stock is wearing down or decaying; prudence requires that a corresponding part of the Gross National Product be set aside to replace the decaying capital stock. In recent years this has not always been done and elements of the country's infrastructure—such as the transport system, sewage and housing stock—have been allowed to deteriorate. A policy of skimping on capital replacement is cheap in the short run but costs dear in the end. The needs of the future should be treated more seriously; so in our calculation capital consumption is deducted to arrive at the Net National Product. This is what was available in 1987 to meet the needs of society during the year.

We then divide this by the number of employees to obtain the National Product per Employee: about £14,500. This is the average amount of value that each employee produced in 1987.[2] If we divide this by the average yearly number of hours worked we come up with the result that an hour's labour creates a value of about £7.50.

For a 40 hour week this would give an income of £300 before tax. We are not claiming that everybody would be free to spend all of this each week. In a socialist economy the level of personal taxation to support education, health services, public investment, scientific research, and so on might be higher than at present. As against this, less tax would have to be needed to fund social security in a fully employed socialist economy. But an allocation of national income through the taxation system is fundamentally different from exploitation because the tax system can be subject to democratic control. In a democracy the citizens can influence the level of taxation, so that taxes would represent resources which people have consented to allocate to public purposes. In contrast to this the distribution of income brought about by the market economy is not, and can never be, the result of democratic decisions.

Whether an egalitarian pre-tax income of £300 per week seems a large or a modest sum is a matter of perspective. If you think it modest then you are either misled by the scale of inflation since 1987 or you have no idea how poorly paid most people are.

The *New Earnings Survey*[3] shows that the median weekly income for women workers in 1987 was £145. The median income is the mid-point in the income distribution: half of the women workers earned less than £145 per week and half earned more.

Figure 2.1 shows a more detailed breakdown of women's earnings. It can be seen that more than 75 per cent of women manual workers earned less than £145 per week. Even among non-manual workers, only 25 per cent earned more than £213 per week. Contrasting this chart with the egalitarian pay scale of £300 a week, it appears that half of the female workforce would see their incomes more than doubled by payment on socialist lines. A further quarter would see their incomes rise by about 50 per cent. Even among the top quarter of female employees, the majority would probably see substantial increases in pay. It is clear that women

Figure 2.1
Comparison of actual earnings with egalitarian pay in 1987

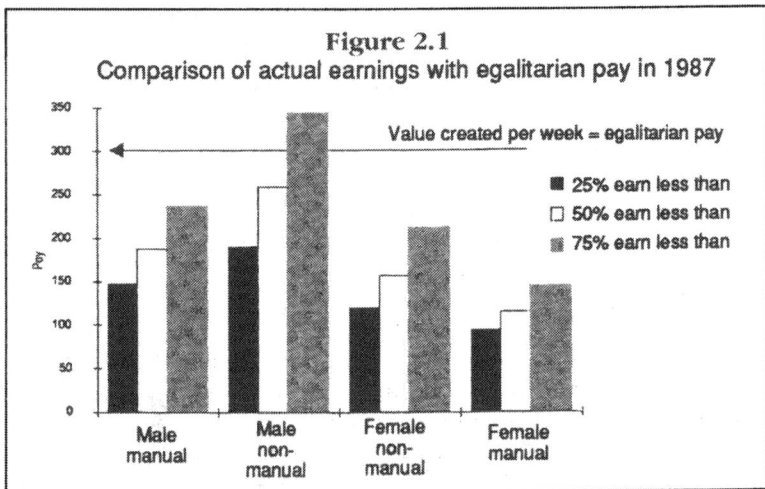

Value created per week = egalitarian pay

■ 25% earn less than
□ 50% earn less than
▨ 75% earn less than

would benefit immensely from the socialist principle of payment according to labour time. Does the same hold true for men?

As Figure 2.1 shows, although men are generally paid about a third more than women, the great majority of men would also benefit from the socialist principle of payment according to labour. The only category earning above the £300 level was the top quartile of male white collar workers. What this shows is that the great majority of employees are exploited. The gains that they would make if they were no longer exploited would more than offset any erosion of differentials that they might suffer under an egalitarian pay scheme. The very substantial increase that almost all employees would experience is possible because property income is abolished under a socialist system of payment. Socialism involves employees as a group benefiting at the expense of shareholders and other property owners.

Equality more effective than growth
This is an important point to grasp, since it is often alleged that there is very little to be gained from a socialist redistribution of income. Proponents of capitalism argue that the real living standards of those on low pay are better raised by allowing the whole economy to grow. As it grows, those at the bottom of the social heap will benefit from wealth that 'trickles down' from the top. The falsity of this argument can be seen by looking at the figures.

The long term rate of growth of the UK economy is 2.5 per cent per annum. How many years would it take a woman earning the median wage to get up to £300 per week at this growth rate? The answer is 30 years: check it on your calculator. Socialist redistribution could achieve directly what would otherwise take the better part of a working lifetime. With socialism the employee can have her cake and eat it too. She gets a once and for all rise in income through redistribution, but economic growth does not stop, so she will continue to enjoy rising earnings year by year.

Advocates of capitalism counter that inequality is essential to economic growth since it provides incentives. They point to the mid-1980s as evidence. As a result of policies designed to increase inequality the British government claims to have fostered a sustained economic growth rate of 3 per cent. This was not sustained for any great period, but was slightly above what the British economy had achieved in the recent past. Let us allow that this extra half a percent per year represents the fruits of inequality (rather than of North Sea oil). How long would it take for this half a percent per annum to give the same benefit as redistribution of income?

It would take 150 years. That is six generations of women. And this is disregarding the fact that increases in inequality mean that working women are likely to experience a lower growth in incomes than those on higher incomes. It is questionable whether working women on median incomes have got any of that extra half percent.

Inequalities of labour
Up to this point, we have been assuming that labour is essentially homogeneous. We have said that socialism was originally based upon the democratic presumption that human beings were equal, and that their labour should thus be treated alike. We implicitly assume that each hour of labour produces the same amount of value and all workers should on this account be paid at an equal rate of, let us say, one labour token per hour. While we might argue on philosophical grounds that all people are equal, we can not deny that there are real differences in people's ability to work. Let us explore the consequences of this inequality of labour. We want to see what the implications are for social inequality: Must inequality in skills or training lead to class differences?

We don't think so. Workers differ in at least two ways—with respect to the degree and form of their education or training, and with respect to 'personal qualities' such as their willingness to work hard, their ability to cooperate well with colleagues and so on. These two kinds of distinction give rise to two issues. The first issue is whether people with greater skills or ability need to be paid more than those with less. The second issue is whether, for all its philosophy of human equality, any socialist economy is going to be forced to recognise distinct types of labour for planning (allocation) purposes. We shall deal with these issues in turn.

Differential payment for education/skill?

We first examine the relationship between skill or education level and individual payment for work. In capitalist economies relatively skilled or educated workers are generally better paid. What are the reasons for this? To what extent do these reasons also apply in a socialist economy?

One generally accepted explanation for at least part of this salary premium is that it functions as compensation for the expense of education or training, and for earnings foregone. The extent to which workers in capitalist economies are responsible for the financing of their own education or training is variable, but in all cases there is an element of earnings foregone, in that people could earn more—at first—by going straight into employment after the completion of basic education than they receive during the years of additional education. In order to generate a sufficient supply of educated labour, therefore, the more highly educated workers must be paid a premium once they move into employment. So the argument goes.

How realistic is this? Is it really a 'sacrifice' to be a student compared, for instance, to leaving school and working on a building site? Compared to many working-class youngsters, students have an easy time. The work is clean. It is not too demanding. There are good social facilities and a rich cultural life. Is this an experience that demands financial compensation in later life?

Even if the compensation argument is an accurate reflection of reality in capitalist countries this does not mean that professional workers should obtain the same sort of differentials in a socialist system. The costs of education and training then would be borne fully by the state. Not only would the education itself be free, as it has been in Britain, but in addition students could receive a regular wage during their period of study. Study is a valid and socially necessary form of work. It produces skilled labour as its 'output', and should be rewarded accordingly. So there need be no individual expense or earnings-loss on the part of a student, for which compensation is required.

In present day society, the class system prevents a large part of the population from ever reaching their full potential. Children grow up in working-class neighbourhoods without ever realising the opportunities that education presents. Their career aspirations are stunted from infancy. Many assume, with some realism, that all that is open to them is menial work, and who needs an education for that?

Some of this is just a reflection of the jobs that children see open to their parents, and these jobs would not themselves change if a revolution in society instituted equal pay. Equal pay would not raise the educational and cultural level of people overnight; but the democratic presumption behind it would, over time, work in this direction. Equal pay is a moral statement. It says that one person is worth as much as any other. It says, 'Citizens, you are all equal in the eyes of society; you may do different things but you are no longer divided into upper and lower classes.' Talk of equality of educational opportunity is hollow so long as hard economic reality reminds you that society considers you inferior. Beyond what it buys, pay is a symbol of social status; and a levelling of pay will produce a revolution in self-esteem. Increased comfort and security for the mass of working class people would be accompanied by a rise in their expectations for themselves and their children.

If society values people equally in terms of money, it encourages them to aspire to equality in terms of education and culture. Education is an enrichment that goes beyond money, but 'to him that hath shall be given'. At present educational opportunity runs alongside money. Once working-class people win economic equality they will have the confidence to seek cultural and educational equality for themselves and their children. In the process a huge economic potential will be liberated. Human creativity and ingenuity is our ultimate resource—develop that through education and economic progress follows.

Specific labour shortages
Under capitalist conditions, aside from the general tendency for higher pay for greater education there may arise from time to time shortages of specific types of labour power (not necessarily the most highly educated), causing a temporary rise in the market price of such labour. The resulting premium payment is in the nature of a scarcity 'rent'.

We use the term 'rent' by analogy with rents that are charged for land. The term 'rent' is a metaphor in economics for a monopoly price that can be charged by the owner of some scarce resource. The essence of rent was captured in Mark Twain's advice: 'Invest in land. They have stopped making it.' Because land is in short supply, and because it is privately owned, the owners can extract payment from people who need it to farm or to live on. If some particular skill or specialism is in short supply relative to demand, then people with that skill are rather like landowners. The economy cannot function without their skill so they can demand extra payments for doing their work.

In some circumstances this premium may induce more recruits into the specific specialism in short supply. In other cases the premium may persist. There may be barriers to entry into the profession. The American Medical Association has a strong influence upon the medical schools that train new doctors and upon the rules governing immigration of doctors, and it uses this to control the number of new entrants to the profession. This enables doctors to charge higher fees.

In a socialist economy, too, there may well emerge shortages of specific skills relative to the demands of society, and there has to be a mechanism for enlarging supply. Within a socialised system of education and training and labour allocation it should be easier to project and advertise potential shortages, and to induce recruits into the needed specialisms with the promise of greater choice of work project if they pursue the targeted careers. If this did not ensure adequate numbers of people entering the trade or profession then either direction of labour or the payment of 'rents' over and above the regular labour tokens would be required.

Direction of labour sounds draconian, and the use of forced labour on Soviet construction projects in the '30s and '40s lived up to this image (although the widespread use of forced labour went hand in hand with increased differentials and incentive payments to persuade people to move voluntarily into new industrial specialisms). Both incentive payments and direction of labour sprang from the same need to re-allocate labour during rapid industrialisation. Both were unpopular, and the Khrushchev government essentially got rid of labour direction and greatly reduced the levels of wage differentials. The reductions in differentials continued under Brezhnev (see Lane, 1985).

It is likely that telling individuals that they must do this particular job, or paying them large differentials, will always be resented in a socialist country. The citizens of a socialist country tend to have strong egalitarian feelings. This is attested to by the popular resentment that is reportedly expressed against the higher incomes earned by members of the new co-operatives in Russia.

Direction of labour in a more subtle form occurs every day in capitalist countries. Workers from the North of England have to travel down to work in London, only getting to see their families at weekends. Unemployment benefit offices are instructed to remove benefits from people who turn down an offer of work. It is not called direction of labour but the effect is the same: a person finds that he has no choice but to take a particular job. This hidden coercion takes place whenever there is a shortage of jobs. Unemployment then forces you to take what is offered. The old Soviet techniques of special bonus payments and explicit direction of workers were needed because there was full employment. In the absence of these measures, in the Brezhnev years, workers tended to change jobs frequently so that enterprises had difficulty maintaining a stable workforce. A similar situation existed in Britain in the 1960s when unemployment was very low. If there are more jobs than workers, then some employers are willing to pay incentives to tempt workers away from their present jobs. Skills in especially short supply will be at a premium. When this happens in a capitalist country and some groups of manual workers start earning incomes in the professional range it creates a brief media sensation.

The economic plan in a socialist economy should be designed to use up the available labour resources, without either excess demand or excess supply. Nonetheless, overall balance in the supply and demand for labour does not deal with the problem of particular specialities experiencing shortfalls. Suppose there is a shortage of electrical technicians. If this is due to there being no training facilities for electrical technicians, then paying technicians more will not solve the problem. What is needed is an enhanced training program. Now suppose there is a shortage of deep sea divers. There are vacancies at the Aberdeen college of underwater technology, but not enough applicants. Some people with a spirit of adventure may be naturally drawn to the life of a diver, but others, fearing the dangers and hardships, hesitate to apply. What should be done?

In a market economy the answer is simple. Pay divers more than the average manual worker. Then you will find people willing to take risks for the extra money. Is this satisfactory? An alternative approach might be to accept that not many people want to risk their lives under the sea, and hold up offshore oil development until automatic machines can be built to do the job.

Divers are an extreme case. The fact remains that some jobs are less pleasant than others. Socialist society has to decide whether this problem is going to be dealt with by improving the conditions and quality of work, or by paying incentives to people who do the nasty jobs. If the whole economy is based upon labour money there are risks to paying incentives. There is a danger that the 'hour' would be devalued if people were paid two hours' tokens for every hour worked. These incentive payments would be at the cost of others who would suffer a fall in their income. To prevent inflation and give the public some control over differentials, these would have to be 'financed' out of general taxation.

Differential payment for 'personal qualities'?
Within any given stratum of workers defined by their level and form
of education or skill, there are clearly remaining differences in
aptitude, energy, cooperativeness, etc. Should such differences be
recognised in differential payment?

Before attempting an answer, consider the implications of the
question—we are touching here on the issue of the extraction of a
surplus product under socialist conditions. By the term 'surplus
product' we mean the extra that is produced over and above what
is needed to support the workers themselves. In a capitalist
economy the surplus appears in the form of the proceeds of
exploitation: profit, interest, rent.

The category of exploitation would not be applicable in a socialist
economy where the disposition of the surplus product is decided
democratically; there is, nonetheless, a need to ensure the
'extraction' of a surplus from the productive workers to provide for
the consumption needs of non-producers (soldiers, pensioners,
children, the sick, etc.) as well as accumulation of means of
production. In formal terms, this is achieved within the system we
are proposing by taxation of labour incomes and the collection of
ground rent (i.e. these 'revenues' of the state 'finance' transfers to
non-producers, social provision and accumulation, as discussed in
chapter 7). But the existence of this formal mechanism in no way
guarantees the real production of an adequate surplus; what really
matters is that workers should be sufficiently diligent and productive
(or if they choose to be less productive, that their personal
consumption is correspondingly limited). What methods could
ensure this?

For comparison, consider the situation in a capitalist economy.
Here the imperative to produce a surplus product takes the form
of the need for the firm to make a profit. We know the mechanisms
which enforce or induce a level of productivity conducive to the
making of profits. The worker enters into an employment contract
which contains, implicitly or explicitly, a conception of minimum
acceptable performance; this contract is then enforced by the
supervisory agents of the enterprise (managers, foremen, etc.),
backed up by the ultimate sanction of firing if the worker does not
meet the required performance standard or is otherwise
insufficiently obedient. The force of the firing sanction, of course,
depends in large measure on conditions outwith the control of the
individual firm, primarily the economy-wide state of unemployment
and the level of income maintenance available to unemployed
workers. Aside from this 'negative' control over labour power, the
enterprise has certain positive means of inducing productivity:

bonus payments and variable salaries; the prospect of promotion; the public advertisement of outstanding individual performance; and the creation of an environment in which workers feel that their suggestions for enhancing the productivity of the firm will be listened to and rewarded. The extent to which capitalist enterprises go in for the latter more 'enlightened' strategies is, of course, highly variable.

In a socialist economy the unemployment sanction is quite deliberately removed. Work is guaranteed for all. How else does the situation differ from capitalism?

We may well wish to argue that socialism should provide favourable general social conditions for the production of a surplus, if workers feel that they are working 'for the good of all' rather than for the profits of a 'boss'. But it would be naive to assume that this will solve all problems. Aside from making general use of the strategies of 'enlightened' capitalist enterprises (public recognition of worker achievement, construction of democratic working environment) there may still be some need to gear individual pay to productivity. Morale problems can develop if people believe that they are putting in more than the usual effort 'for nothing' or that a colleague is slacking, coasting along on the backs of his fellows.

One way of gearing reward to effort would be an economy-wide system for the grading of labour. For instance, there could be three grades of labour, A, B and C, with B labour representing average productivity, A above average and C below average. New workers might start out as 'B' workers and then have their performance reviewed (either at their own initiative or at the instigation of the project for which they work) with the possibility of being regraded as A or C. Note that these grades have nothing to do with education or skill level, but are solely concerned with the worker's productivity relative to the average for her trade or profession.

These grades of labour would be regarded for planning purposes as 'creating value' at different rates. Rates of pay would correspond to these differential productivities: grade B workers would receive one labour token per hour, A workers rather more, and C workers rather less. The rates of pay would have to be fixed in such proportions as to keep the total issue of labour tokens equal to the total hours worked. The exact rates of pay could be worked out automatically by computers once the number of people in each grade was known.

There need be no stigma attached to being a 'C' worker; such a worker basically chooses to work at an easier pace—and correspondingly accepts a somewhat lower rate of consumption. Not everyone has to be a *Stakhanovite*, and there is no call for resentment of the less productive workers if they make no pretence at being anything else. But in this way the highly productive worker's contribution is recognised and encouraged, while at the same time the planners get a more accurate fix on the distribution of social labour.

Skilled labour as a 'produced input'

We have indicated above that workers may be divided into groups of differing *individual productivities*, and recognised as such for planning purposes. The planners would know, for instance, that a given project requiring 1,000 person hours of average labour would only require, say, 800 person hours of grade A labour. Now the question arises whether the existence of different skills demands recognition by the planners, and if so how this should be organised.

In the short to medium run, the differentiation of labour by skill is both important and irreducible. The skills of a mining engineer, a surgeon and a computer programmer are not interchangeable. It follows that over this time horizon the planners cannot simply think in terms of the allocation of 'labour' as such, but must recognise the constraints imposed by the availability of specific skills. This implies that detailed records should be kept of the number of people qualified in each speciality. But then what becomes of the labour conception of value and the use of labour-time as a unit of account?

Well, in the long run workers can be retrained, and the democratic assumption of socialists is that, apart from certain extremely demanding tasks and certain impaired individuals, almost everyone can do almost anything. In the context of long-run planning, what matters is not the present availability of specific types of skilled labour, but rather the *cost of production* of those skills. And just as the value of machines can be calculated in terms of the amount of labour time required to make them, for the purposes of long term economic calculation, so can human skills.

We can envision the establishment of a baseline level of general education: workers educated to this level only will be regarded as 'simple labour', while the labour of workers who have received additional special education is treated as a 'produced input', much like other means of production. This notion of skilled labour as a produced input may be illustrated by example.

Suppose that becoming a competent engineer requires four years of study beyond the basic level of education. This four year production process for skilled engineering labour involves a variety of labour inputs. First, there is the work of the student—attending lectures, study in the library, lab work, etc. As stated earlier, this is regarded as valid productive work and is rewarded accordingly. It is counted as a 'simple labour' input. Second is the work of teaching, distributed over the number of students being taught. This is a skilled labour input. Third, there is the 'overhead' work connected with education (librarians, technicians, administrators). This may be a mixture of skilled and simple labour.[4]

This illustrates the general point that the production of skilled labour will typically require both simple and skilled labour as inputs. Measuring the current simple labour input is in principle quite simple; the more difficult question is how we treat the input of skilled labour. If skilled labour embodies a past labour input it will count as some multiple of simple labour, but how is the multiplier determined?

The very same question arises in relation to the evaluation of the skilled (*e.g.* teaching) input into the production of our skilled engineering labour, as in relation to the subsequent evaluation of the qualified engineer's labour. In the following discussion and the appendix to this chapter we deal with both aspects at once, employing the simplifying assumption that all 'skilled' labour requires the same quantity of labour input for its production.

Consider the analogy of inanimate means of production. The standard method for quantifying the labour 'passed on' from such means of production to the product is to 'distribute' the labour content of the means of production over the total volume of output to which those means contribute. For example, if a machine embodying 1,000 hours of labour gets used up in the course of producing one million units of product X, then the machine may be said to pass on $1,000 \div 1,000,000 = 0.001$ hours of labour to each unit of X. To take the calculation one step further, suppose that our machine is operated at a production rate of 100 units of X per hour. It follows that the machine 'transmits' $100 \times 0.001 = 0.1$ hours of embodied labour per hour of operation.

Now return to our skilled engineer and apply the same principle. Suppose that, once qualified, she works a 35 hour week for 45 weeks per year, *i.e.* 1,575 hours per year. And let the 'depreciation horizon' for her engineering skills be 10 years. (That is, at the end of this time she will need, or become eligible for, another period of full-time education to update her knowledge and skills or to change specialisms if she wishes.) She will work $1,575 \times 10$ hours in those 10 years, and to determine her rate of transmission of embodied labour during that working time we divide the total labour content of her education by 15,750.

The appendix to this chapter shows how it is possible to work out the total embodied labour content of skilled labour, using simple labour as unit of account. According to these calculations the

'transmission rate' might be of the order of
0.50 for depreciation over 10 years,
0.33 for depreciation over 15 years, or
0.24 for depreciation over 20 years.
The figure of 0.33, for instance, tells us that our engineer, whose skills are depreciated over a 15 year horizon, transmits 0.33 hours of embodied labour per hour worked. Unlike the machine, which *only* transmits labour embodied in the past, our engineer also *works* one hour per hour. The total direct plus indirect labour contribution of our engineer would therefore be 1.33 hours per hour, a multiple of the simple labour rate. In other words, if the planners are contemplating the employment of a million hours of skilled engineering labour in the context of a long-run plan, they should recognise that this is equivalent to a commitment of 1.33 million hours of simple labour.

We do not mean to imply that just because a skilled worker is rated as costing society a third more than a worker of average skill, then they should be paid a third more. This extra third represents the additional cost to society of using skilled labour. Society has already met the 'extra third' in paying for the worker's education, so there is no justification for paying the individual any extra. Although it has no implications for the distribution of personal income, the skilled labour multiplier is important in working out the true social cost of projects. A task that requires skilled labour is more costly to society even if the skilled workers are paid the same as unskilled ones.

Comparison with historically existing socialism
In closing this chapter, it may be useful to compare the Marxian model we are advocating with what was achieved in the socialist countries. To our knowledge the only instance of Marxian principles of distribution being applied in these countries was on the People's Communes in China during the 1960s and 1970s. There, goods were allocated according to a work-point system. The number of hours of work that members put in during the year was recorded and their share of the harvest was based on this. It may be that other socialist countries applied this principle too, but we do not know of it.

In general, the socialist economies retained money. They issued notes and coin which went into general circulation. This money was used in five distinct forms of circulation:
1. Exchanges between socialist state enterprises. The basis of this was the relative operational and managerial independence of state enterprises.

2. Exchanges between the collective farm sector and the state.
3. Exchanges between collective farms and urban workers at markets for agricultural produce.
4. Sale of products by family farms to urban workers, the basis for which was the continuation of family sideline production.
5. Exchanges between state retailing agencies and the employees of state enterprises.

It was often argued that in the first case money was not really functioning as money, since no transfers of ownership were involved. If enterprise A delivered goods to enterprise B, enterprise B might pay for them, but there was no real change of ownership since both were owned by the state.[5] There was some truth in this, since most of the deliveries were in accordance with a plan, but the rationalisation was only partially true. If there were no real change in ownership, why should there be even a nominal exchange of money?

If production was directly socialised, then there is no reason why enterprise B should pay A for the goods that A delivers. Instead unit B—a hospital, say—could be given a budget of x hours of labour. All work done by nurses, cleaners and doctors in the unit would be deducted from this budget. Any drugs, food, and medical supplies provided by the publicly owned pharmaceutical factories etc., would have their labour content deducted from the budget. But there would be no money payments from the hospital to its workers or suppliers. The workers would be credited by the state or commune for work done, and the pharmaceutical factories would not need to be 'paid' as they would have their own labour budgets.

We can see this system in embryo in the NHS where, prior to Tory re-organisation, hospitals did not pay for services such as laboratory tests and X-rays produced within the same Health Board.

In comparison the industrial sector of the socialist economies retained the commodity form to a far greater extent than seems necessary given socialist property relations. Stalin argued[6] that this continuation of the commodity form derived from the other types of exchange, primarily that between the collective farms and the state. This may have been true originally, but in some of the socialist countries—Bulgaria comes to mind particularly—the independent character of the collective farms *vis-à-vis* the state had all but vanished by the end of the 1960s. Yet the use of money remained in all cases.

If labour-value accounting had been prevalent in the economy as a whole one could have envisaged transitional forms of agricultural production in which the collective farm as an entity was credited for the mean labour content of products delivered, that is the average amount of labour required to grow a crop, which might be more or less than they actually used. This would have left collective farm labour still one stage removed from directly social labour, but would have been compatible with the elimination of money.

The final exchange system—the market for consumer goods—is the crucial one. It is here that fundamental class contradictions acted to prevent the completion of the Marxian socialist programme. For the Marxian view of socialism was radically egalitarian. There was to be no source of income other than labour, and *all labour was to be treated as equal.* Advancing to this point would have required the elimination of the perks and differentials enjoyed by the bureaucracy. The Marxian programme was incompatible with the perpetuation of any elite stratum. Marx applauded the principle employed by the Paris Commune, that public officials should get no more than average workers' wages.[7] In more recent years Mao and the left in China opposed differentials and pointed out that China still had far to go to achieve a socialist distribution system; they argued that the 8-grade wage system remained an obstacle to socialism.

China was exceptional in that the question of abolishing the bourgeois system of labour differentials became a burning political issue. It was one of the key issues in the Cultural Revolution. With the defeat of the left there and the hegemony of Deng's line, further advance towards realising the Marxist programme became impossible. In most of the other socialist countries the question of moving to payment on the basis of labour was never even on the agenda.

Socialist politicians, whether in the East or the West, are rarely keen on 'leveling'. Whilst being opposed to extremes of wealth, they feel that some level of differentials should be maintained. It is much easier to justify differentials ideologically if everything is still done in money terms. If accounting is done in terms of labour time, then the fraud of professional differentials becomes a little too transparent. Why should a secretary get paid only 30 minutes for each hour that she works, whilst professionals in the next office get paid 2 hours for each hour they put in?

The secretaries and cleaners would soon be saying: 'Now hold on there. What kind of socialism is it that makes one of you worth four of us?' That notorious proletarian levelling tendency (so primitive and unsophisticated), would come to the fore: 'We're a' Jock Tamson's bairns'; 'A man's a man for a' that'. This democratic sentiment has been at the heart of every proletarian revolutionary movement. By the late 19th century, the assertion that one man's labour was as good as another's had become the guiding doctrine of what was still called Social Democracy. Where bourgeois democracy proclaimed 'All men are equal', whilst qualifying this with, 'before the law', Social Democracy went on to demand real economic equality. What equal voting rights were to bourgeois democracy, equality of labour was to the proletariat.

Enemies of political democracy like South African whites deplore the way the doctrine of one man one vote ignores natural human inequality. Is a civilised white man really to be compared with a kaffir fresh out of the bush? Enemies of economic democracy deplore the Marxist doctrine of the labour theory of value for the way it falsely homogenises people. As a visiting Chinese student put it to to one of us: could he with his years of education count for no more than an ignorant drunken worker?

True, people are different. The work of a college professor is different from that of a labourer. The culture of a Boer is different from that of a Zulu. A man is different from a woman. To those at the top of the heap, difference justifies differentials. The view from the bottom is different.

Notes to Chapter 2

1. The implications of labour-time accounting for the democratic control of the economy are developed in chapter 13.
2. It should be borne in mind that during an inflationary period such figures rapidly get out of date. The reader should remember that by the time she reads this, the value each worker produces will be considerably higher.
3. Published annually by the UK government.
4. Note that the labour required for providing the subsistence of the student is not actually a cost of production of skilled labour. This labour would have to be performed by somebody, whether or not the studying takes place.
5. The points concerning property relations which are touched upon in the next few paragraphs are developed further in chapter 14.
6. In *Economic Problems of Socialism in the USSR* (Stalin, 1952).
7. In *The Civil War in France* (in Marx, 1974).

APPENDIX TO CHAPTER 2

Illustrative calculation of skilled labour multiplier

This appendix explains in more detail the calculation of the skilled labour multiplier discussed in the text. We first illustrate the calculation of the total embodied labour content of skilled labour.

1. On the part of the student. Assume 4 years of study at 40 hours per week for 45 weeks per year.

   Total: 7,200 hours.

2. Classroom teaching. Assume 15 hours per week, 35 weeks per year, for 4 years, distributed across an average class size of 30 (average of large lecture classes and smaller labs, seminars etc.).

   Total per student: 70 hours.

3. Tutorial work. Assume 2 hours per week, 30 weeks per year of one-on-one tutorials.

   Over 4 years, total = 240 hours.

4. Educational overheads. Let us suppose this amounts to a contribution equal to the classroom teaching labour.

   Total 70 hours.

Now examine the breakdown of this total labour content into simple and skilled. The student's own contribution is simple; the teachers' contribution is skilled; and let us assume for the sake of argument that the 'overhead' contribution breaks down 50/50 skilled and unskilled. We then arrive at the following: total labour content of skill production equals approximately 7,600 hours (rounding up), of which skilled labour makes up around 5 per cent (rounding up again).

The total embodied hours figure quoted above is a first approximation (in fact an underestimate, as we shall see). Let us denote this approximation by TH_0. Using TH_0 we can construct a first approximation to the transmission rate of embodied labour on the part of skilled labour:

$$R_0 = TH_0/AH.D$$

where AH represents the annual hours the skilled worker will work once qualified, and D is the depreciation horizon in years. We can now use R_0 to re-evaluate the total hours embodied (on the assumption that the transmission rate for the teachers and others who supply the skilled input into the production of skilled labour is the same as that for their students, once qualified). If the proportion of TH_0 accounted for by skilled labour input is denoted by SP, our revised estimate of the total embodied labour is

$$(1+R_0)SP.TH_0 + (1 - SP)TH_0 = (1 + R_0SP)TH_0.$$

But this new figure for total hours embodied can now be used to re-estimate the transmission rate, permitting a further re-estimation of total hours, and so on, recursively. The resulting successive approximations to the total labour embodied in the production of skilled labour form a geometric expansion, the nth term of which is

$$(1 + R_0SP + R_0^2SP^2 + R_0^3SP^3 + \ldots + R_0^nSP^n)TH_0.$$

Letting n tend to infinity, we can deduce the final limiting value of the total hours estimate, namely $(1 - R_0SP)^{-1}TH_0$, and the corresponding final estimate of the transmission rate for embodied labour

$$R_f = (1 - R_0SP)^{-1}TH_0/AH.D.$$

Remembering that $R_0 = TH_0/AH.D$, R_f may be rewritten as

$$R_f = TH_0/(AH.D - SP.TH_0),$$

enabling us to calculate the final transmission rate directly. Using the above illustrative figures of $TH_0 = 7,600$, $AH = 1,575$ and $SP = 0.05$ we find that

$$R_f = 0.50 \text{ for } D = 10,$$

$$R_f = 0.33 \text{ for } D = 15, \text{ and}$$

$$R_f = 0.24 \text{ for } D = 20,$$

as quoted in the text. In each case the skilled labour multiplier is simply 1 plus R_f.

CHAPTER 3

Work, Time and Computers

The annual labour of every nation is the fund which originally supplies it with all the necessaries and conveniences of life which it annually consumes (Adam Smith, *The Wealth of Nations*).

In this chapter we argue that rational economic calculation should be based upon an arithmetic of time, specifically of labour time. This is not just conducive to social justice, it is equally conducive to technological progress. We go on to show that a system of costing things in terms of labour time is not just a nice idea, it is also practical using modern computer technology. In the process we introduce the reader to certain concepts from computing that are relevant to the organisation of an economy.

In the last chapter we showed that if people were paid in labour money, so that for each hour that they worked they got paid one hour's labour money, then exploitation would be abolished. This great social gain would, of itself, be a justification for the adoption of labour money. Indeed that was the classic justification for socialism—that it abolished wage slavery and returned to the workers the fruits of their labours. Such justice and fairness are not the only benefits offered by this method of economic calculation. It also encourages technical progress.

Human lifetimes are sadly finite. The amount that people can produce during these lives, and thus the wealth of their society, depends upon how much of their lives they are forced to surrender to the production of the things that they covet or need. The advance of our civilisation is regulated by its economies of time. The greater the time and effort that a society must expend to produce its necessities, the poorer it will be, and the less it will be able to support the comforts, arts and culture we know as civilisation. So it is the ever more rapid adoption of labour-saving devices, economisers of time, that is the root cause of the growing prosperity the industrialised world has experienced these last two centuries.

Economies of time

The fundamental economic justification of any new production technology has to be its ability to produce things with less effort than before. Only by the constant application of such inventions throughout the economy can we gain more free time to devote either to leisure or to the satisfaction of new and more sophisticated tastes. A socialist production engineer must seek always to economise on time. It is as Adam Smith said, our 'original currency', and a moment of it needlessly squandered is lost for ever. Socialism will show itself to be superior to capitalism only if it proves better at husbanding time.

In a capitalist economy, manufacturers are driven by the desire for profit to try to minimise costs. These costs include wages. Firms often introduce new technology in order to cut the workforce and reduce labour costs. Although this use of technology is frequently against the immediate interest of the workers directly involved, who lose their jobs, it is to the ultimate benefit of society. The benefits of technical change are unevenly spread—the employer stands to gain more than the employee—but in the end, it is upon its ability to foster technological improvements that capitalism's claim to be a progressive system is based. The need to accept new labour-saving technology is generally recognised within the trades unions, who seek only to regulate the terms of its introduction so that their members share in the gains.

It is a very naive form of socialism that criticises technical change under the belief that it causes unemployment. The real criticism that can be made of capitalist economies in this regard is that they are too slow to adopt labour-saving devices, because labour is artificially cheap.

Historians have long argued that the reason why the ancients failed to develop an industrial society, despite all the science of the Greeks and the engineering skills of the Romans, was the institution of slavery. Where all industrial production was relegated to slaves, rational calculation of labour costs was discouraged. A slave was not paid by the hour, so the master had no incentive to account for the hours of his servants' labour. Without such calculation there was little incentive to economise on labour time. So, for instance, although the Romans knew of the water wheel, they never moved on to the widespread application of mechanical power (White, 1962).

Capitalism was a clear advance on slavery. The capitalist buys his labour by the hour and is reluctant to waste it. He employs time and motion study to check that he is making good use of what he has bought. But still, he buys his labour cheap—if he did not, there would be no profit in it. Here is the paradox: what is bought cheap is never truly valued. The lower are wages, the greater the profit; but when wages are low employers can afford to squander labour. The capitalist is one step above the slaveholder in rationality, but that step can be a small one.

The railways of Britain were a technical marvel. Broad straight tracks were laid across the land. Hills were made level by tunnels and cuts, valleys by embankments and viaducts.

> Their mark on this land is still seen and still laid
> The way for a commerce where vast fortunes were made
> The supply of an empire where the sun never set
> Which is now deep in darkness but the railway is there yet[1]

. . . and its traces will doubtless remain for millennia to come, like the roads and aqueducts of another empire. The labourers or 'navigators' who built the railways worked with the same tools as the Roman slaves who built the aqueducts. They were built by muscle power, by pick and by shovel. The one great technical advance in two millennia was the wheel barrow, a Chinese invention.[2] The navvies had it, the slaves did not.

The railway was the product of the machine age. It was not beyond the wit of Stevenson or Brunel to design steam-powered mechanical excavators. They did not bother because wage slaves could be had cheap.

Again, in the present century in British docks, dockers laboured to unload ships with techniques that had not changed since the middle ages. Hired by the day, they did the work of slaves without even the security that went with slavery. It took full employment, strong trades unions and better wages to persuade the capitalist class that it was worth investing in bulldozers, JCBs and containerisation.

Both these examples are groups of manual labourers, traditionally the most exploited sections of the working classes. A similar story can be told of any number of sweated trades—garment making, toy making, etc.—where wages are low. In such areas production technology is stagnant and the incentive to innovate is low. As a general rule we can say that the lower wages are, the less likely it is that employers will modernise. We can illustrate this with an example as shown in Table 3.1. The table shows the comparative costs of two methods of digging a ditch in a road. With the old method the contractor hires two men who each work a 50 hour week. Along with the men, he hires a compressor and two pneumatic drills. These are used to break up the road surface which is then excavated using shovels. The wear and tear on the compressor and drills along with the fuel for the compressor amounts to a further 100 hours labour. With the modern technique, the contractor hires a mechanical excavator and one man, who completes the job in 50 hours. In this case the wear and tear on the excavator plus its fuel amounts to 125 hours of labour time. The modern technique needs only 175 hours of direct and indirect labour to complete the job, compared to 200 hours for the old technique.

Table 3.1:
Two ways of digging a ditch

Method	direct labour	indirect labour	labour cost	money cost
Old	100 hrs	100 hrs	200 hrs	£1053
New	50 hrs	125 hrs	175 hrs	£1091.25

Assuming:
Value created by labour   £7.53 per hour
Wage Level   £3.00 per hour

Suppose that, as in 1987 Britain, an hour's labour produces goods that sell for £7.53, and suppose the rate of pay for labourers is £3.00 per hour. If we now work out the money costs of the two techniques, we find the situation is reversed, the old method is cheaper. Because labour is to be had cheap, the older, more labour-intensive technique appears to cost less. It thus pays capitalists to waste human labour.

A good example of this could be seen in the computer industry. In the 1950s IBM developed highly automated machinery to construct the core memories for their computers. As demand grew their factories became more and more automatic. In 1965 they even had to open an entire new production line just to make the machines that would make the computers. Still they could not keep up with demand:

> The situation was becoming desperate. Then a newly appointed manager at Kingston who had spent several years in Japan, proposed that workers in the Orient could be found with sufficient manual dexterity and patience to wire core planes by hand. Taking bags of cores, rolls of wire, and core frames to Japan, he returned ten days later with hand wired core planes as good as those that had been wired by automatic wire feeders at the Kingston plant. It was slow and tedious work but the cost of labor in the Orient was so low that production costs were actually lower than with full automation in Kingston. (Pugh *et al.*, 1991, p.209)

One of the criticisms that the economic reformers levelled at the price and wage structure in the USSR in the 1970s and 80s was that the low level of wages there led to this same sort of waste of labour. In the USSR wages were kept low, and a significant part of people's incomes came in the form of heavily subsidised housing and public services. The enterprises that employ people did not pay for these services. The reformers advocated a change in the price and wage system so that services cost more and wages were raised to compensate. They claimed that the higher price of labour would then act as an incentive for innovation.

The argument is valid, but it does not go far enough. The problem arises because the wage, that is to say *the price paid for labour* rather than *labour time itself,* is used in costings. This means that the outcome of any attempt to compare the costs of different production techniques will be affected by wage levels. If we use monetary calculations, where costs of production include wages, then we cannot arrive at a measure of economic efficiency that is independent of the distribution of income. To avoid this we need some objective measure of the amount of labour used to produce things. This is easier said than done.

Objective social accounting

The market provides firms with price information upon which they can base their costings. This gives some kind of rational basis for firms to choose what seems the cheapest method of production, even though this will be systematically biased towards techniques which waste labour. If we want to get a more objective source of cost data, we need a system of data collection that is independent of the market. This is where computer technology comes in. We need a computerised information system that gives production engineers unbiased estimates of the labour time costs of different technologies.

Market prices are used as a cost indicator in capitalist countries, but they have a certain arbitrary character. An artist dies in poverty. A few decades later his pictures change hands for millions. A sudden panic hits the stock markets. In a matter of hours hundreds of billions are wiped off stock prices. Farmers destroy crops because the prices are too low. Walk through the poor areas of a British or American city and you will see the pinched faces and stunted figures of people for whom food is too expensive.

Market prices are the plaything of supply and demand. Demand does not depend upon human need but upon ability and willingness to pay. This means that the distribution of wealth, whims and fashion all affect demand. Supply is subject to a more mundane constraint: the resources that go into making things.

A new Van Gogh painting requires the man himself. Where is he? The supply of original Van Goghs cannot increase. Their prices, the objects of subjective fancy, have no limit beyond the folly and vanity of the rich.

The supply of tomatoes depends upon labour, land, sun, water, greenhouses, oil, etc. Their costs of production are given by the state of agricultural technology and by the costs of the required inputs. Their supply is subject to objective constraints, which sets a limit to their prices.

We can never hope to have a rational measure of the present cost of a painting by Leonardo, but a socialist economy should have available to it some measure of the objective costs of different products. We could in principle measure costs in terms of any widely used resource. In an industrial economy, we might reasonably price goods in terms of the energy that went into their production. If society faced overriding constraints upon the amount of energy that it could use, perhaps for environmental reasons, then this might be a good way to price things. We advocate using labour time as the basic unit of account because we think that society is about people, and for the moment at least, how people spend their lives remains more important than any one natural resource. We will come back to the environmental arguments against relying too much upon this one measure in chapter 5.

Defining labour content
To cost things in terms of labour we need to define the labour content of a good. If we want to know the labour content of a tomato, it won't be enough simply to measure the number of seconds the tomato farmer spent tending it and plucking it. We also have to take into account the labour indirectly used: the labour of the people who built the greenhouse the tomato grew in, the labour of the oil workers who produced fuel for the greenhouse, and so on. This appears to create a problem of circularity: to know the labour content of each good we need to know the labour content of several more.

re 0.der to deal with this complex interdependence we need what is known as an input-output table, which records how the outputs of industries are used as inputs by other industries. In the example given in Table 3.2 the food industry uses 2,000 barrels of oil, and employs 2,000 workers, to produce 40,000 loaves per week. The oil industry employs 1,000 workers and uses up 500 barrels of oil to produce 2,000 barrels of oil per week. This little economy has

Table 3.2:
A simple input output system

Industry	Inputs		Gross Output
	workers	*oil*	
bread production	2,000	2,000	40,000 loaves
oil production	1,000	500	3,000 barrels
Totals	3,000	2,500	

Net Output

loaves	40,000
Oil barrels	500

net outputs of 40,000 loaves and 500 barrels of oil to distribute as food and fuel to a working population of 3,000.

The relationships shown in Table 3.2 can be used to compute the labour content of oil and loaves. Consider bread first. We wish to find out how much labour time, expressed in person-weeks, goes to make a loaf. One person working one week will be said to create one person-week of value. We know from the table that:

(1) value of 40,000 loaves = 2,000 Person-weeks +
2,000 × value of barrel of oil.

That is, the total labour value of bread production equals the direct labour in this sector plus the total indirect labour represented by the input of oil. Equation (1) can be re-written to give the value of one loaf of bread in person-weeks as:

(1')value of bread =   (2,000 + 2,000 × value of oil)/40,000
= (1 + value of oil)/ 20

Thus if we knew the value of oil in terms of labour we could work out the value of bread in terms of labour. From the table we can see that

(2) value of 3,000 barrels =   1,000 person-weeks +
value of 500 barrels

Thus 2,500 barrels must be worth 1,000 person-weeks and one barrel must be worth 0.4 or two fifths of a person-week. Using result (1') we can now work out the value of bread:

value of bread = (1.40)/20 = 0.07 person-weeks

So the final result is that the labour values of a loaf of bread and a barrel of oil are 0.07 and 0.4 person-weeks respectively.[3]

The problem of scale
In his book *The Economics of Feasible Socialism* (1983), Alec Nove emphasised the importance of the sheer scale of modern economies. He said that the Soviet economy included some 12 million distinct types of product, and quoted the estimate of one O. Antonov that to draw up a complete and balanced plan for the Ukraine would take the labour of the whole world's population over a 10 million year period.

The same argument may apply to computing labour values. It is one thing to solve the equations for our toy example of an input-output table. It would be quite a different thing to solve a system of 12 million simultaneous equations. But it is not enough just to say that calculating labour values for a large economy is complex, we have to know *how* complex it is. The estimate quoted by Nove gives an impression of vast and unmanageable complexity, and seems to close off the question from further discussion. (We should point out that Nove is by no means alone in making this sort of claim. Such arguments are quite routine amongst opponents of socialism. We cite Nove in order to show that even left-leaning economists tend to throw up their hands at the complexity of socialist planning.) But what we need is an account of the laws which govern how long it takes to compute labour values for economies of different degrees of complexity.

It may be impossibly difficult to prepare the plan (or to calculate labour values) by manual methods, but it does not follow that it would be impossible using computers. To decide on this we need to establish quantitative relationships between the scale of the economy to be planned and the amount of computer time that will be required. The time that it takes to perform calculations is studied by a branch of computer science called complexity theory.

The idea of complexity
Complexity theory deals with the number of discrete steps that are required to perform a calculation. These discrete steps correspond roughly to the number of instructions that would have to be executed in a computer program that performed the calculation. As an example consider this problem.

You are given a deck of 99 cards. Each card has a number between 1 and 99 printed on it. The cards are in an arbitrary order. You have to sort them into ascending order. How do you proceed? One solution applies these rules.
1. Compare the first card in the deck with the second. If the first has a higher number than the second, swap them round.
2. Repeat step 1 with the 2nd, 3rd, 4th pairs of cards, etc., till you

reach the end of the deck.

3. If you found that the deck was in the right order, then stop, otherwise go back to step 1.

How long will this take to sort the deck? That depends upon the original order of the deck. The best case would be if the deck was sorted to begin with, then a single pass through the deck, performing 98 comparisons, will be enough. The worst case is if the deck is originally in descending order. You now have to reverse the order. The first card you look at has the number 99 on it. Step 1 moves it to position 2 in the deck, step 1 is then repeated until we reach the end of the deck. Each time, the card with 99 on it is moved along one position. Eventually after 98 repetitions it arrives at the back of the deck.

It follows that a single pass through the deck will move one card into the correct position. We have 99 cards in the wrong position to start with. So we will need 99 passes through the deck. This involves 99×98 comparisons. If we had 50 cards it would take 49×50 steps. The number of operations in the worst case will be about N^2 where N is the number of cards. In computing we say that this technique *is of time order N^2*. This means that the time to solve the problem can, as a rough order of magnitude be assumed to be the square of N.

There is a better solution.

1. Divide the deck into 10 stacks depending upon whether the last digit on the card is 0,1,2 ... or 9.
2. Form a new deck by putting these stacks one behind the other starting with stack 0 and ending with stack 9.
3. Starting from the bottom of the deck, re-divide it into 10 stacks depending upon the first digits on the cards.
4. Repeat step 2. The deck is now sorted.

Using the second method we only have to look at each card twice. The number of steps is thus $2N$ where N is the number of cards. This is clearly a much faster method than the previous one. We say that it is *of time order N*.

Problems of time order N are easier than those of time order N^2. The worst problems are ones that require an *exponential* number of steps for their solution. Exponential problems are generally considered too complex for practical computation except for very small N.

In looking at the problem of economic planning and the feasibility of performing the necessary calculations on computers, we have to determine the time order of the computations involved and the size of the input data (N).

Simplifying the labour value problem

Let us return to the problem of calculating the labour values of all the commodities in an economy. The conditions of production can be represented as an input-output table, and from this table a set of equations can be derived, as in the example above. In principle, these are clearly solvable—we have the same number of equations as we have unknown labour values to solve for. The question is whether the system is practically solvable.

The standard method of solving simultaneous equations is Gaussian elimination.[4] It is equivalent to the school textbook method. This method yields an exact solution in a running time proportional to the cube of the number of equations[5] (see Sedgewick, 1983, chapter 5).

Let us suppose that the number of distinct types of output in the economy to be planned is of the order of a million (10^6). In that case the Gaussian elimination method applied to the input-output table would require $(10^6)^3 = 10^{18}$ (a million million million) iterations, each of which might contain ten primitive computer instructions.

Suppose we can run the problem on a modern Japanese supercomputer such as the Fujitsu VP200 or the Hitachi S810/20, then how long will it take? These machines are capable of performing around 200 million arithmetic operations per second when working on large volumes of data (see Lubeck *et al.*, 1985).[6] So the time taken to compute all of the labour values of the economy would be on the order of 50 *billion* seconds or 16 thousand years. Rather obviously, this is far too slow.

When one runs into a scale problem like this it is often convenient to reformulate the task in different terms. The input-output table for an economy is in practice likely to be mostly blanks. In reality each product has on average only a few tens or at most hundreds of inputs to its production rather than millions. This makes it more economical to represent the system in terms of a vector of lists rather than a matrix. In consequence, there are short-cuts which can be taken to arrive at a result. We can use another approach, that of *successive approximation.*

The idea here is that as a first approximation we ignore all inputs to the production process apart from directly expended labour. This gives us a first, approximate estimate of each product's labour value. It will be an underestimate because it ignores the non-labour inputs to the production process. To arrive at our second approximation we add in the non-labour inputs valued on the basis of the labour values computed in the first phase. This will get us one step closer to the true labour values. Repeated application of this process will give us the answer to the desired degree of accuracy. If about half the value of an average product is derived from direct labour inputs then each iteration round our approximation process will add one binary digit of significance to our answer. An answer correct to four significant decimal digits (which is better than the market can achieve) would require about 15 iterations round our approximation process.

The time order complexity of this algorithm[7] is proportional to the number of products times the average number of inputs per product, times the desired accuracy of the result in digits. On our previous assumptions this could be computed on a supercomputer in a few minutes, rather than the thousands of years required for Gaussian elimination.[8]

High tech and intermediate tech solutions

The computation of labour values for a whole economy is now feasible in a few minutes using modern supercomputers. These computers are expensive, but not prohibitively so. They are already used for weather forecasting, atomic weapons design, oil prospecting and nuclear physics. It would not be unreasonable to give a national planning bureau the same computational capacity as the Met Office. Until recently, supercomputer technology has been within the capability of a only few countries, primarily the USA and Japan. Britain now has the ability to produce machines of this capacity using highly parallel processors; Edinburgh University is building a machine with a capacity of 10,000 million instructions per second. As of 1988, the USSR had several projects underway to develop similar supercomputers, but it seems unlikely that any of them were in series production (see Wolcott and Goodman, 1988).

It is worth pointing out, however, that essentially the same results could be achieved with a considerably lower level of technology. We present a short outline of how this might be done.

The intermediate technology solution requires four components. The first of these is Teletext, familiar to the British public under the trade names Cefax and Oracle. These are public information systems that use spare bandwidth on television channels to transmit pages of digital information about the news, sport, weather, etc. The second component is the public telephone network. The third is the personal microcomputer with an adaptor capable of receiving teletext, the whole costing a few hundred pounds at current prices. The fourth component is the system of universal product coding developed by the retail trade. Universal product codes are the numbers displayed under the bar codes on nearly all marketed goods.

It is already standard practice for all but the smallest firms to perform cost analyses using spreadsheet packages on personal computers. In our hypothetical socialist economy, each unit of production would use such a package to build a model of their production process. Besides being used for internal accounting purposes, this can act as the collector of statistics for planning purposes. The spreadsheet model would have fed into it how much labour had been used over the last week, how much of each other input, and what the gross output had been. Given up-to-date figures for the labour values of the various inputs, the spreadsheet would rapidly compute the labour values of the outputs.

Where will the up-to-date labour values come from? They are broadcast continuously on teletext by the public broadcasting authorities. If there are one million products, then teletext should be able to broadcast revised labour values every 20 minutes. The products would be identified by their universal product codes. The personal computers listen in and update their spreadsheet model in response to any broadcast changes in labour values.

If for any reason the personal computer in a place of work decides that the labour value of the product produced there has changed, it dials up the central teletext computer and informs it of the change. These changes might either be due to some change in local production technology, or a broadcast change in the value of one of the inputs. The whole system would be acting as a huge distributed supercomputer continuously evaluating labour values by the method of *successive approximation*.

Although it uses cheap and simple technology, this approach has several advantages over a centralised supercomputer. It not only performs the computations but also performs data collection, which is notoriously one of the most difficult aspects of any planning system. Secondly it would be a much more robust system. If a few small computers break down, the figures for some labour values may get slightly out of date, but the system as a whole would survive. The only single vulnerable point would be the central teletext broadcasting system, but this would be considerably cheaper than a central supercomputer, which would allow it to be replicated with backup machines.

Using this distributed calculation system each unit of production would have available to it if not up-to-the-minute then up-to-the-hour estimates of the current social labour cost of production alternatives. This is much faster than a capitalist market can achieve.

Notes to Chapter 3

1. Gaston, P., *Navigator*, on 'Rum, Sodomy and the Lash', The Pogues, Stiff Records.
2. The wheelbarrow was introduced to Europe in the labour shortage that followed the black death.
3. This is obviously a very simple input-output table, having only two inputs and two outputs, while a real economy would have hundreds of thousands of commodities. But whatever the scale of the economy the mathematical principles are the same. From an input-output table a set of linear equations can be derived of the form:

$$L_1 + I_{11}v_1 + I_{12}v_2 + I_{13}v_3 + \ldots + I_{1N}v_N = Q_1v_1$$
$$L_2 + I_{21}v_1 + I_{22}v_2 + I_{23}v_3 + \ldots + I_{2N}v_N = Q_2v_2$$
$$L_N + I_{N1}v_1 + I_{N2}v_2 + I_{N3}v_3 + \ldots + I_{NN}v_N = Q_Nv_N$$

where L_i is the amount of direct labour used in the ith industry; I_{ij} is the quantity of industry j's output used in the ith industry; v_i is the per-unit labour content of the product of the ith industry; and Q_i is the total output of the ith industry. We have n equations and n unknowns: the v_i's. Since there is the same number of independent equations as unknowns we can in principle solve for the v_i's. But these are the labour contents of all of the goods, which is what we were looking for.
4. We start off with n equations in n unknowns. These can be reduced to n–1 equations in n–1 unknowns by adding appropriate multiples of the nth equation to each of the first n–1 equations. This step is then iterated until eventually we have 1 equation in 1 unknown. This is immediately soluble. We then back-substitute this result in the immediately preceding system of 2 equations in 2 unknowns, and so on.
5. The intuition behind this is simple. For each of the variables eliminated we must perform n(n–1) multiplications. There are n variables to eliminate, hence the complexity of the problem is of order n^3.
6. It should be borne in mind that computer technology has advanced considerably since the mid 80's. By the mid 1990s manufacturers hope to deliver machines capable of about 1 million million operations per second.
7. The word algorithm is a corruption of the name al-Kowarizimi, the 9th century Persian mathematician who wrote a book popularising the use of the Hindu decimal number system for basic arithmetic. What is now termed school arithmetic was on its introduction to Europe in the middle ages called algorithmics. This was distinguished from arithmetics which used the abbacus and the Roman number, system. The essential point about algorithmics was that it used a small set of simple rules and basic tables of addition and multiplication learned by rote to perform operations on numbers of arbitrary size. Extended to other mathematical problems, an algorithm is a step by step procedure that can be carried out without the exercise of intelligence to arrive at some result. Simple algorithms are those used in long division or in obtaining square roots. It is formally specified as a recursive procedure by which the answer to a problem can be arrived at in a finite number of steps. Any problem that can be expressed as an algorithm can be solved by a machine.
8. Hodgson (1984, p.170) states that the best method for solving an input-output table involves n^2 calculations. While he doesn't give any explanation for this claim, we assume that he must be recognizing the use of an iterative technique (or else the complexity would be n^3), but he fails to recognise that the technical coefficient matrix would be sparse. A better use of data structures reduces the complexity substantially, as argued above.

CHAPTER 4

Basic Concepts of Planning

The idea of economy-wide planning is not fashionable. Surveying the current state of the world, one could easily get the impression that economic planning is an idea whose time has passed. Economic growth has faltered in the USA after Reagan and in the UK after Thatcher, and advocates of the untramelled market have less grounds for self-confidence than they appeared to in the 1980s, but on the other side of what used to be the 'iron curtain' the collapse of the Soviet-style planned economies is all but complete. Even if capitalism is visibly flawed, planning seems to offer no alternative. The self-confidence of socialists is at an historic low.

We are swimming against the tide, but, we believe, with good reason. The 'failure' of economic planning in the traditional Soviet mode was not illusory, but we have two counter-arguments to make. First, the system which has been abandoned in Russia was one particular implementation of planning. It was a system shaped by the needs of military production in a state caught in an arms race, starting from a level of economic development far below that of its enemies—initially Germany then the USA. The arms race and its associated trade embargoes were part of an open and deliberate US policy to bankrupt the USSR. The militarised structure of the Soviet economy was no more an essential feature of socialism than is the militarisation of the economy of Israel an essential feature of capitalism. Other models are possible, and we wish to present the outlines of a system which can be efficient in satisfying consumers' wishes while at the same time guiding the economy towards equality, social justice and a sustainable place in the environment of planet Earth. Second, we see the costs of the new, thrusting capitalism as socially unacceptable, and we expect that more and more people will come to share this view. The skewing of the distribution of income, wealth and economic security towards greater inequality; the neglect of social provision and public goods; the headlong exploitation of the natural environment—all these negative legacies of the Reagan and Thatcher years will have to be redressed. We believe that a new socialist planning system is the most promising form of economy to deal with these deep-seated problems.

This chapter introduces our conception of such a new planning system. We discuss the key features of economic planning in general, and distinguish these from the features of a capitalist economy. The following chapters then set out in detail the planning mechanisms which we see as most likely to be efficient and effective. We distinguish these from the traditional 'bureaucratic planning' in the USSR, and show how our proposed alternative can be made to work by harnessing the remarkable powers of the latest generation of computers.

Planning and control

Planning can be thought of as a branch of control theory, the study of regulating systems. Control theory normally deals with the control of automatic industrial plant. The process of automatic control is conventionally represented by a feedback loop; an example of such a feedback system might be a central heating controller. The goal might be to keep a workplace warm during the hours that it is occupied, say 9am to 6pm. This goal or desired temperature could be thought of as a plan target. The actual temperature of the building is the output of the plant (in this case a central heating system). The current temperature is compared with the goal and an error signal (the gap between current and desired temperature) is fed into the controller. This then controls the flow of fuel into the central boiler to regulate the temperature.

A crude central heating controller would just turn the fuel on or off depending on whether the temperature is below or above target. This would result in an erratic movement of temperature as shown in Figure 4.1.

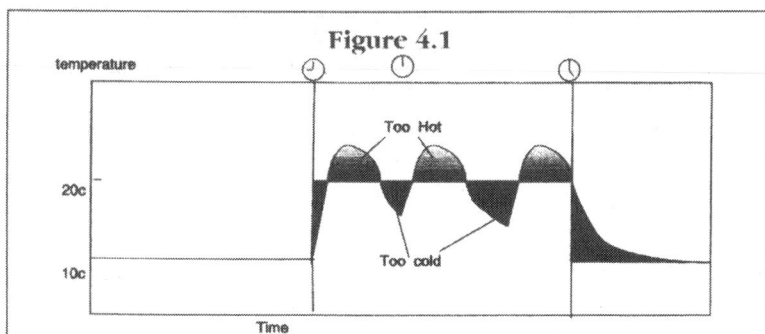

Figure 4.1

In the example the heating is switched on at 9am but the place does not really get warm until 10. It then overheats for a while until the heating turns off. The building then cools down until at 11.30 the heating cuts back in, leading to overheating around 12.30. It goes on fluctuating for the rest of the day. We are all familiar with workplace heating systems like this!

The problem with this type of controller is that it lacks foresight, and does not take into account how the plant will react. A more intelligent control system would know about the plant parameters. It would know the heat output of the boiler, it would know how rapidly heat is lost through the walls and windows as a function of temperature, and it would know the specific heat of the building. Given a heating schedule, it could predict when it would have to turn the heating on to ensure that the place was warm enough by 9am. It would also calculate that by gradually turning down the boiler as the room temperature approached the target it could

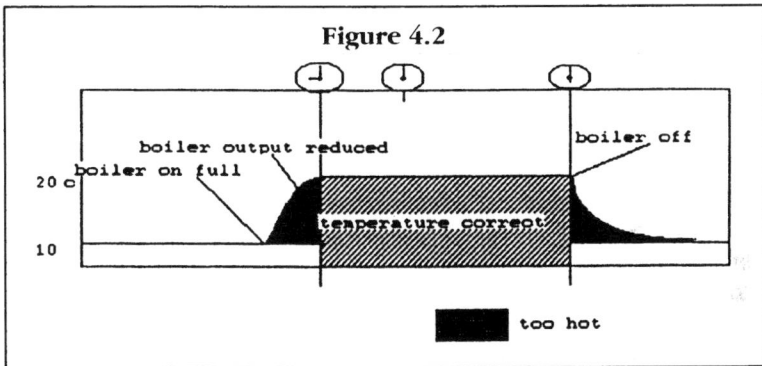

Figure 4.2

prevent the place getting too hot. An intelligent controller might give us a temperature graph as shown in Figure 4.2.

In this case the controller would have to be a more complex device than the simple clock and thermostat combinations in most central heating systems. It would require an internal model of the system to be controlled and a schedule of goals to be met. The controller draws up a plan to meet that schedule subject to what it knows about the system it is controlling. It turns on the heating a couple of hours early to make sure that the room is warm enough, and turns it down in time to prevent overheating. It can do this because it can use its internal model to simulate the way the real system would behave under different inputs. This ability to simulate internally the behaviour and characteristics of the system under control means that it does not operate by the trial and error process of the first controller.

There is an analogy here with the way a market economy operates. Capitalist firms respond to market signals, such as the relationship between price and cost of production. They adjust their production in response to such signals, with the general aim of maximising profit. The control model here is the same as the dumb central heating controller: it is reactive and lacks foresight. Thus there are bound to be economic fluctuations and instabilities. Actually, the situation is worse as there is no reason to suppose that a large number of firms, each responding to different feedback signals, will display any kind of coherent goal-directed behaviour. At least with a dumb central heating system there is some clear overall goal. In a market economy there is no such overall goal. In particular consumers' wishes cannot act as a goal or control input as they are only effective when backed up by the money to purchase things. But consumer purchasing power is an internal variable of the economy, itself subject to fluctuations as a result of unemployment, conditions in the credit market, etc. It is as if the setting on the thermostat were to be affected by the fuel consumption of the boiler.

Adam Smith proposed the powerful metaphor of the 'invisible hand' of market forces. Supposedly the pursuit of private profit by individual firms, and private advantage by consumers, would lead to an outcome 'as if' the system were designed to maximise the welfare of all. Modern general equilibrium analysis has performed the useful theoretical function of showing how restrictive are the conditions required to ensure the Smithian result (see Hahn, 1984). The economic history of the twentieth century—with its episodes of mass unemployment, runaway inflation and environmental destruction—has shown more practically that the play of market forces cannot be relied upon to deliver socially desirable outcomes.

Capitalist goals second order
If consumers' wishes do not act as an external control input for the capitalist system, can government policies play this role? Only in a very limited sense, for the typical economic goals that capitalist governments set themselves are second-order. They are not concerned with the direct satisfaction of peoples' wants and needs, but instead relate to features and deficiencies of the economic system itself. For instance, inflation and the Balance of Payments, two major targets of government policy, do not directly concern human needs. Inflation is a matter of what numbers we associate with goods; it is a problem of measurement. Inflation can occur

under conditions of great material poverty as in China in the 1940s or in times of comparative material prosperity as in Britain in the 1970s. The rate of inflation by itself tells us nothing about the degree to which the economy is satisfying human needs. The Balance of Payments is also a second order phenomenon; it measures the degree to which the citizens and government of a country are becoming debtors or creditors of the rest of the world. This is an aggregate of contractual relations, and again it does not measure the degree to which the population's needs are being met. This is not to say that inflation and the trade balance are unimportant, just that they are second-order problems concerned with the operation of the economic mechanism itself. This is the case with unemployment too.

Unemployment does indirectly affect the satisfaction of needs. The unemployed suffer a decline in their standard of living and, less evidently, so does the population as a whole, due to the loss of the goods that might have been made had the unemployed been in productive work. But again this is a problem that arises because of the institutional structure of the capitalist economy. People may be unemployed while needs are unmet, and while the machinery and equipment needed to meet them stands idle, because firms reckon it is unprofitable to meet these needs.

The only first-order goal that capitalist governments set for the economy is the growth rate. This does concern the aggregate ability of the economy to meet needs, but in the process of aggregation a lot can be hidden. What does a growth rate mean? 'Real growth' is commonly taken to be the growth of the total money value of output minus the rate of inflation. What this really means is another matter. Can it be said that if the economy grows by 5 per cent then human happiness has grown by 5 per cent? What if the growth has been at the expense of the quality of life, or of social equality? What if the price of that growth has been the pollution of the air and seas, and to what extent does the economic output that is being measured make a real contribution to happiness? Does growth in advertising or money-lending really increase the satisfaction of anyone other than those who directly profit from it?

What would be first-order goals?

We favour a characterisation of socialist economic planning which centres on *the capacity of the planning system to impose democratically decided objectives on the course of economic development.* Let us consider the kind of politically decided objectives which a planned economy should be able to sustain.

Historically, the first objective of planning in socialist economies has been to promote a programme of crash industrialisation, itself a means of achieving collective security and an infrastructure capable of supporting rising levels of social provision and individual consumption. According to Paul Gregory's careful investigations (1970), there can be little doubt that the planned economies were able to achieve a faster pace of industrialisation than market economies at a comparable stage of development.

For an already industrialised economy, however, the economic objectives to which socialist planning should be directed include the following.

1. A general rise in the cultural level and living standards of the people, with emphasis on those of the working class for as long as a distinct 'working class' continues to exist. This involves the extension, and improvement in the quality, of social provision (collective consumption); the development of choice and quality of consumer goods; a general reduction in working time and increase in leisure time; and the attempt to make work itself more enjoyable and personally rewarding.
2. The construction of a long term resource-constrained development path, *i.e.* a trajectory of economic development which respects environmental and ecological constraints, and does not store up intractable future problems due to resource-exhaustion or environmental destruction.
3. A change in the economic structure to one that ensures real economic equality between the sexes through the progressive elimination of patriarchal forms of economy.
4. The reduction of class, regional (and in less developed economies town/country) inequalities.

These are obviously rather general goals (although they are more specific than the typical economic goals of capitalist governments). They must be further specified in the course of constructing an operational plan, and the next section examines various aspects of this process.

Levels of planning

Planning decisions may be broken down into three levels: macroeconomic planning, strategic planning, and detailed production planning. The connection between these levels is as follows.

First, a *macroeconomic* plan sets certain general parameters governing the evolution of the economy over time. Specifically, it concerns the breakdown of total production (or as we would prefer to express it, the breakdown of total labour time) between various highly aggregated categories of end use. How much of society's labour should be devoted to the production of consumer goods? How much to the provision of social goods such as health, education or socialised child-care? How much to the accumulation of means of production to augment the future productive capacity of the economy? And how much (if any) to the repayment of foreign debt or the acquisition of foreign assets? A macroeconomic plan must answer these questions. It must also address the question of how intensively the economy's given productive capacity should be exploited. The answer here is not necessarily 'to the maximum', although that will be the answer during wartime. A capitalist government may, for instance, decide to reduce aggregate demand and generate unemployment in order to reduce the rate of inflation—this is macroeconomic planning of a kind. A socialist planning agency will have no interest in creating unemployment, but equally it will not wish to work the population as hard as possible. There is a trade-off between productive labour and leisure time, and the macroeconomic planners will have to take into account the people's preferences in this respect, when calculating how much labour time is available for the various uses.

Second, the *strategic plan* concerns the changing industrial structure of the economy. Given that so much of the available labour-time is to be devoted to public provision, so much to consumer goods and so much to producer goods, which particular sectors should be developed, exploiting which technologies? Which types of goods should be imported, because they can be produced more cheaply elswhere? Which industries should be phased out over the long run? In the context of strategic planning, issues such as the environmental impact of various industries and technologies, and the appropriate criteria for assessing potential investment projects, must be addressed.

Third, within the framework established by the macroeconomic and strategic industrial plans, *detailed production planning* concerns the precise allocation of resources: Which specific types of goods are to be produced in what quantities, using how much labour, and in which locations? Which productive units are to receive inputs from which others? And so on.

Governments in capitalist economies are able to carry out some degree of macroeconomic and strategic industrial planning (outside of wartime, they obviously do not attempt detailed production planning). But since these governments do not have property rights over the principal means of production, their ability to plan is limited, and depends on the co-operation of capitalist enterprises and other private agents. Consider macroeconomic planning.

Governments may, for instance, expand the money supply and lower interest rates with the intention of stimulating investment spending, causing a reallocation of resources in favour of accumulation of means of production. But if capitalist enterprises do not see investment as sufficiently profitable, low interest rates may fail to make much difference. Or again, a government may cut taxes in the hope of increasing total output and employment, but if the consumers who benefit from the tax break choose to spend their gains on imported goods the result may be a trade deficit rather than domestic expansion.

As for strategic industrial planning in a capitalist economy, the striking success story is the Japanese Ministry of International Trade and Industry. The MITI has been able to foster a far-sighted adjustment of the structure of Japanese industry in the face of a changing pattern of world production and competitive advantage. Those industries which, in the calculation of MITI, offered the best prospect of long-run competitive growth were built up with the aid of state-funded research and development. One of the better accounts of this process is contained in Keith Smith (1986). The success of MITI has proved hard to emulate; it depends on the willingness of capitalist enterprises in Japan to co-operate with the Ministry, and a co-operative climate of industry-government relations cannot be legislated into existence.

In principle a socialist government, with property rights over the means of production, should be in a much better position to carry out coherent and effective macroeconomic and strategic industrial planning. The fact that such a government has the power to shape these aspects of the economy does not, of course, guarantee that this power will be used wisely. But if the planning process is open to debate, democratic whenever possible, and systematically calls upon the best efforts of the scientific community, there is good reason to hope that the results will be superior to those of the capitalist market.

The next five chapters develop the concept of planning in various ways. Chapter 5 elaborates the issues involved in strategic planning; chapter 6 sets out the requirements for effective detailed planning. Macroeconomic planning is discussed in chapter 7, and the marketing of consumer goods in chapter 8. Chapter 9 examines the issue of the informational requirements for the planning process as a whole.

CHAPTER 5

Strategic Planning

We use 'strategic planning' as something of a portmanteau term. This chapter examines a number of aspects of planning, mainly relating to the overall structure of the economy, which do not naturally fall under the headings of macroeconomic or detailed production planning (the latter are dealt with in separate chapters). The main topics to be covered here are
1. The planning of the industrial structure
2. Environmental considerations
3. Investment planning and the time dimension of production
4. Planning of the mode of distribution of goods and services
5. Agricultural production planning

1. Planning the industrial structure
There are a number of areas where long term *politically* determined objectives for production can be realistically envisaged: housing, transport, energy supply, communications, tourism, industrial restructuring. In each of these cases, 'lumpy' decisions have to be taken. For instance, the shape and form of new housing developments are properly a matter for democratic debate and decision. Or consider the case of personal transportation.

Whether a country relies upon private cars or upon public transport is a decision which has huge long-term effects upon a society. And this is a case where the sum of individual private decisions does not necessarily correspond to a socially optimal result. When transport in great industrial cities relied upon the train and the tram, speeds of travel through city centres were higher than they are now. For those who could afford them, the new private cars offered a speed advantage over the tram, since cars did not stop to pick up passengers. But as more and more cars came onto the roads congestion increased, and both cars and public transport got slower as a result. At all times the private car continued to offer a speed advantage over public road transport, so each individual retained an incentive to go by car. Rising car use took trade away from the buses and trams and services became worse. The end result is dangerous and congested roads, air pollution and longer journey times. Here is an example where a social decision on the shape of the economy may produce results far superior to the aggregate of private decisions.

A decision either to extend or restrict the use of cars has major industrial implications. In a big country, the car industry may directly and indirectly employ millions of people making cars, making components, providing petrol, servicing, building and repairing roads. The layout of cities and the forms of retail trade are also influenced by the level of car ownership. Strategic planning should be able to take these ramifications into account in a systematic way. If a decision is made to restrict the use of private cars, the plan must call for the redeployment of the labour associated with the car industry.

The above example concerns a technology which is already well-understood. A different issue for strategic industrial planning arises with new technologies. Looking back at past industrial development we can see a series of waves in which different industries played the leading role: textiles, railways, heavy engineering, chemicals, automobiles, consumer durables, electronics. The success of each industrial economy has depended upon its ability rapidly to develop these pioneer industries. The first two waves brought Britain to prominence, the third and fourth Germany, the mass production of automobiles and consumer durables was pioneered in the USA, and with electronics the lead has shifted to the Far East.

Newly industrialising economies have a comparatively easy task: they start off without an established industrial base and can put all their efforts into building up the latest industries. The USSR from the '30s to the '50s achieved remarkable growth rates by expanding heavy industry; forty years on Taiwan and Korea achieve similar results with the electronics industry. This type of initial industrial development is well suited to planning since the planning authorities can copy the industrial structures of the existing world leaders.

It is much more difficult for an already industrialised country to restructure and play a pioneering role. In this case there is nobody to copy. Old industries must be run down in favour of industries that may become possible on the basis of technology that has yet to be developed. This requires foresight; plans must be drawn up that project the results of present scientific research into a future in which whole new industries will rest upon them. The knowledge, technology and skills that will be required must be identified, and the research and development organisations brought into being that will convert science into technology. Education and training must be reorganised to produce a labour force that will be able to operate these new technologies. Final consumer products using these technologies must be conceived and designed. Manufacturing processes must be invented. Production equipment and components supplies must be developed, production lines created and put in motion.

If an economy is not to stagnate, this sort of restructuring must be carried out repeatedly, with restructuring plans drawn up to cover 10 or 15 year periods. It is not clear to what extent this level of planning can be democratic. The knowledge of which technologies are likely to be relevant in 10 to 20 years time will initially be concentrated in a small research community, and it is difficult for people without specialist knowledge to make judgements on the matter. It may be possible, however, for the technical specialists to draw up a number of feasible options for future industrial development, which could then be canvassed in public debate.

The composition of the planning bureau responsible for drawing up strategic plans must be determined according to the time-scale of the plans involved. The longest-term plans would have to be formulated by small committees of economists with research scientists on secondment from their usual work. For plans with a 5 to 7 year perspective, larger numbers of economists would have to be supported by production engineers. Shorter-term plans would have to be drawn up on the basis of a much wider input from product designers and industrial managers.

A crucial element in the sucess of strategic plans is their ability to harness innovation. This is an inherently paradoxical issue, since innovation, by definition, cannot be known about before it happens. However, the process of moving from a new concept to its regular industrial application takes time. Although the innovation process may be impossible to plan at the start, planning becomes more and more possible as it progresses. Any modern industrial economy needs a regular process by which the unknown is made knowable, and the knowable becomes the used. Scientific research and development become branches of the social division of labour, which, at a technical level, are relatively independent of the dominant form of ownership in the economy.

This is not to say that social relations have no bearing upon the process of innovation—clearly they do. But whether the economy is socialist or capitalist seems less important than a whole series of other factors. Innovation is a branch of the division of labour in which an economy may or may not specialise. There are many capitalist countries and they have very varied records when it comes to the industrial application of new technology. Britain is as notorious for the laggard pace of its technological innovation as Japan is acclaimed for its speed. The reasons defy simple explanation, and certainly cannot be reduced to the simple formula: The greater the market freedom, the greater the degree of innovation. Incalculable elements of national psychology and culture—a society's attitude to the new—seem to enter into the equation.

Alongside these imponderables, identifiable objective factors play their parts: how good is a society's education system, how much of the national income is spent supporting research, how much is spent on development? Out of the research and development budget, how much goes on civilian and how much on military research? Does the society have within it institutions that are capable of integrating all aspects of the development cycle from 'blue skies' research to finished product?

There are demonstrable links between the amount a society spends on education and civilian R&D and its rate of innovation. The institution of a democratic planning system, in which major divisions of the national budget like defence, education and R&D were subject to an annual popular vote, would not guarantee that society would choose to spend a large amount on R&D. The citizens might decide to give it a low priority with consequent effects for their economy, but this would be the result of a deliberate choice freely taken rather than a side effect of the narrow private decisions of company accountants.

For R&D to be effective there must be a transmission belt that spans the stages of pure research, applied research, product development, and mass production. The economic performance of Asian capitalisms seems to indicate that the later stages on the transmission belt are particularly crucial. Western capitalism has had more publicly funded pure research, but an excessive portion of the applied research and product development has been oriented towards arms production. The resulting fighter aircraft and rockets have been marvels of sophistication but the capacity to innovate in the production of civilian goods has all but vanished. The UK and the USA were no better at applying new technology to video recorders, motorbikes or cameras than the USSR. The arms industry was the only one in which publicly funded applied research and product development led through into production. For a socialist economy to use science to improve civil industry an absolute priority would be to create a collection of civil institutions to replace those of the military-industrial complex.

2. Environmental considerations and natural resource constraints

In chapter 4 we made reference to the need for a socialist economy to adopt an environmentally sound growth policy. This section discusses some of the specific implications of this goal, and assesses the relative merits of market and planned systems with regard to environmental issues. Some further relevant points will be developed in chapter 14, where the focus is on the kind of property relations required to ensure the careful husbanding of natural resources.

Up to this point, we have assumed that the cost of producing any good or service is adequately captured by the total human labour-time expended in its production. In a recent critique of socialist planning, Don Lavoie (1985) raises once again an old objection concerning the inadequacy of labour values for dealing with the costs of non-reproducible natural resources. The argument is that a costing in terms of labour values fails to deal with natural or non-labour inputs. In a market system, natural resources have a price-tag and enter into costs of production; under the labour theory they are free. Thus, it is argued, the labour theory will underestimate the cost of goods produced from scarce natural resources.

A serious issue is at stake here. But this argument, which originated with von Mises, can be turned against the advocates of the market, as the rational use of natural resources is capitalism's weakest point and (potentially) socialism's strongest.

How is the 'free market' price of natural resources determined? The classical answer is that it comes from differential ground rent. In that case the marginal land or oilfield or forest comes free and the cost of production at the margin[1] comes from the labour (and in neoclassical theory, capital) inputs. But the oil from the marginal well is a depletable resource too, and in a market system *this depletion has no price*. There is only a finite amount of oil, but this is not recognised in its market price. Indeed what we have seen with capitalism has been a reckless destruction of natural resources wherever the resource has been at the margin. Here it is worth recalling the point that Marx makes about the American frontier, where the quality of land improved as colonists moved out of the coastal states and onto the plains. As the marginal land in geographical terms became the most productive land (which moreover could be had free as it was stolen from the Indians), all constraints on natural resource exploitation were removed. Hence agricultural practices (absence of crop rotation, monocultures) were adopted which led to rapid soil exhaustion. These characteristics, in the most market-oriented of economies, led to the catastrophic soil erosion of the dustbowl. The same holds for timber exploitation at the margins. Timber stolen from native peoples by capitalist companies is treated as a free resource on the West coast of North America or the jungles of Amazonia and Borneo, and forests that have taken thousands of years to develop are cut down in a few decades.

The only circumstance in which a market system will lead to a husbanding of land and preserve its fertility, is if there is a landowning class that derives its revenue from ground rent and has a vested interest in preserving that revenue. Technically, this presupposes a differential rent arising from diminishing returns at the margin. Politically, it presupposes that the landowning class is rich, politically sophisticated and backed by the state power. This combination only occurs under specific historical circumstances. In most parts of the world during the capitalist era the land has been held by poor peasants or hunter-gatherers with little access to political power. Their natural resources have been simply expropriated. Moreover, whether it is rational for landlords to husband a resource or to mine it, destroying soil fertility etc., will depend upon the discount rate. At any positive discount rate[2] it makes sense to deplete non-renewable resources. At low and stable discount rates it may be economically viable to carry out investments that enhance the quality of the land, as was done by the 18th century British landlord classes, but here we are dealing with slowly renewable resources rather than non-renewable ones.

In sum, the market will in all cases waste resources at the margin whether returns are increasing or diminishing. It will husband slowly renewable resources at low discount rates in combination with diminishing marginal returns. It will always deplete non-renewable resources.

The introduction of imputed rents[3] into a socialist economy, as was advocated by Soviet 'reformers', is equivalent to performing calculations of labour values using marginal rather than average costs and assuming diminishing returns to labour. But given the arguments above, imputed rents under socialism will be no more effective in husbanding resources than real rents are under capitalism. We would argue the more radical point that ecological destruction is the result of any 'economic' decision mechanism, *i.e.* any decision mechanism based upon a single objective function. Any decision procedure based upon prices fails to convey information about the ecological and environmental consequences of a course of action, since these are complex and not reducible to an accounting entry. Any non-qualitative assessment of environmental impact is misleading. The environmental consequences of a course of action have to be determined by scientific investigation and resolved by political struggle. Examples of this have been the campaigns waged by the scientific community in the USSR to stop industrial development on the shores of Lake Baikal and to halt the plans to divert Siberian rivers south to irrigate Central Asia.

There is no guarantee that wise decisions will be taken on these issues. The most that can be asked for is that political conditions exist to allow free and informed debate on the issue, along with freedom of scientific investigation and publication, and that a final decision is taken by a free vote. In a capitalist country such decisions are almost invariably arrived at to suit the commercial interests of big companies who are able to buy political influence. In a socialist democracy major environmental issues should be settled by referendum after a prolonged and open debate in the media. If a hydroelectric scheme is proposed that will flood a valley which is both a beauty spot and a unique habitat it is pointless to search for some economic formula that will decide if the project should go ahead. The problem is political, not economic. That is to say, a decision requires a deliberate judgement of priorities, and cannot be reduced to a comparison of simple numbers, whether expressed in labour time or money.

The question of resource depletion is paradoxical because policies of rapid depletion and extreme conservation lead to similar results. If we use up North Sea oil in one big boom lasting a few years then future generations are deprived of it, but if we leave it in the ground permanently then again we are all deprived of the use of it. The prudent alternative is to plan to use up the oil at such a speed and in such a way as will enable us to develop substitutes before it runs out. There is little evidence to show that the market is doing this. On the other hand there was some evidence of this being done in a systematic way in the USSR. For the last thirty years the Soviets consistently devoted considerable resources to thermonuclear fusion research in the hope of developing a replacement for fossil fuels. Western machines like the Joint European Torus (JET) derive from the Soviet *Tokamak* designs. And in the course of 1987 with the launch of the new *Energy* heavy lift vehicles it transpired that a major objective of the Soviet space program was the development of solar energy.[4] Projected uses of these vehicles include the placement of orbiting mirrors to provide illumination of arctic work sites during the winter months, and the construction of orbiting solar power plants to transmit microwave power back down to earth. This sort of long-term project can be undertaken by a socialist economy as part of the normal planning mechanism. The market mechanism can never do it. Capitalist countries can only compete in this area insofar as they set up special state agencies that mimic socialist planning—NASA or the CEGB.

3. The time dimension of production

In our discussion of the use of labour values we have up to now assumed that a day's work tomorrow counts for the same value as a day's work in 10 years' time. It may be objected that this is unrealistic and that such a system of calculation would lead to the adoption of projects that are excessively capital intensive. We can illustrate this with a concrete example. It has been proposed that a barrage be built across the estuary of the river Severn in order to generate electric power and provide a motorway link between England and Wales. This project would, once constructed, produce electricity at a very low labour cost, since the 'fuel' comes free in the form of an unusually high tidal oscillation of some 7 meters. But the massive civil engineering involved in the construction would cost more than the construction of coal-fired stations of equivalent output.

This is notionally shown in Figure 5.1, which compares the labour that would have to be expended over 5 year periods on the two projects. Over the whole 30 years the total labour expended to produce the same amount of electricity from coal would be greater than from the tides. But for the first 10 years of the project, during construction, the cost of coal-powered stations would be lower. If we decided how to generate electricity just on the basis of minimising labour costs then the tidal system would be a clear winner. In fact the English electricity generating board has chosen not to build the tidal station because the interest it would have to pay on the money borrowed to build the barrage would outweigh the savings in fuel in later years. At a lower rate of interest the choice would be different. A costing of the two alternatives using only their labour content, *i.e.* in terms of pure labour values, is equivalent to using a zero interest or discount rate.

A zero discount rate could be argued against on both subjective and objective grounds. On the principle that jam today is better than the promise of jam tomorrow, it may be better to save effort this year even if that entails more work in the future. A subjectively determined discount rate could conceivably be set politically (with people being allowed to vote every few years on whether they wanted the discount rate raised, lowered or left the same). But a

Figure 5.1
Effect of 9% discount rate on relative costs of two power schemes

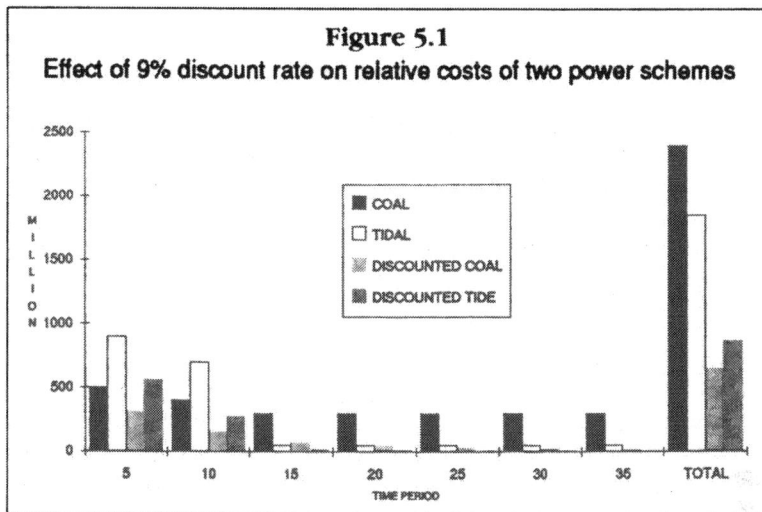

more objective approach is possible: one could use the average growth rate of productivity as the discount rate. The rationale for this is that if labour productivity doubled every decade then one hour of labour now would be equivalent to half an hour's work in ten years' time. Since we can never accurately know the future, it would be necessary to estimate future productivity growth on the basis of recent history. It may be noted that on this basis the decision of the electricity board not to proceed with the Severn barrage was economically irrational as the discount rates used in their calculations were well above the actual average rate of growth of productivity in the economy. This instance strengthens the argument that rational economic calculation will only really become possible in a socialist state.

In capitalist economies the discount rate is determined by contingencies in the money market which are quite divorced from actual production possibilities. It is driven by speculative movements of international capital combined with undemocratic decisions of the monetary authorities; it is unstable and fluctuates from month to month. The use of such a variable in economic decision making is indefensible either on grounds of economic efficiency or democracy.[5]

4. Market and non-market distribution
One strategic decision, relating to the overall shape of the economy, concerns which goods should be allocated directly by the plan, and which should be 'marketed' in some sense. We envisage a fully

planned allocation of producer goods, alongside a market in consumer goods. The precise nature of the latter system is spelled out in chapter 8; as we shall show, it is quite distinct from the market in capitalist economies, in that it is subordinated to a planned allocation of social labour time. But we still face the question of where exactly to draw the line between market and non-market distribution, or rather what principles to apply in deciding this point.

Four main points are relevant to this issue. We discuss these under the headings of rights of citizenship, freedom of choice, coping with scarcity, and costs of metering.

Rights of citizenship
The first principle is that those goods and services which are basic prerequisites for full participation in the productive and communal life of the society should be provided as of right, and financed out of general taxation. Prime examples here would be education, health care and child care (we shall also argue in chapter 13 that televisions equipped with electronic voting machines should be provided as a right of citizenship, to permit full participation in political democracy). In order to function as an active, productive member of society one must be well-educated, healthy and free of the need to stay at home with dependent children all day. These goods are necessary to give individuals the 'positive freedom' to control their own lives.[6] In addition, it is in the interest of society as a whole that each of its members be educated, healthy and productive; the benefits of education, health care and child care are not confined to the individual. (In the parlance of economics, there is an external benefit or 'positive externality' here, and it is widely recognised that markets do not produce optimal results where externalities are important.) Who will fall ill when is unpredictable and the cost of treatment cannot generally be met by the sick whose income earning capacity has been diminished by disease. Health care is a matter of need rather than whim or fancy, and as such is more equitably and efficiently distributed when the medical profession allocate it free on the basis of need, rather than sell it at a profit to the highest bidder.

Freedom of choice
The second point is that, once the basic prerequisites of citizenship are provided, individuals (or families, or communes) should have maximum freedom to decide in what form they want to enjoy the fruits of their labour. State allocation or rationing is poorly adapted to this end; we need some form of 'market' on which people are able to spend their labour tokens. (As mentioned above, we

describe such a market in chapter 8.) This mode of distribution would be used for food, drink, entertainment, books, clothing, holiday travel and so forth—goods where 'externalities' are absent or unimportant. While it does not make sense for society to allow its members to fall into ignorance or unnecessary disease, or to be trapped at home with young children, it makes perfect sense to allow them to choose between caviar, wine, books, shirts or trips to the highlands.

Coping with scarcity

Our third point concerns goods which are in relatively fixed supply, and where the demand exceeds the supply at a price of zero. Take the example of a congested stretch of motorway. New roads can be built, or an old road widened, but that takes time and may be objectionable on environmental grounds; let us suppose for the moment that the supply of motorway is effectively fixed. If no price is placed on the use of the road, it becomes so congested that nobody is able to travel fast. In this case a toll makes good sense. It is a way of 'rationing' the use of the scarce resource. People for whom fast individual travel is important will pay the toll, while others may decide to use public transport instead.

Tolls of this kind also provide useful information for planners. Suppose the construction of new motorway is under consideration. The construction will be costly in terms of labour time. If the existing road is overcrowded when no toll is charged, that does not of itself mean that new construction is cost-effective, but if a toll related to the cost of new construction is levied and the existing road is *still* overcrowded, then there may be a case for building more road (unless there are strong environmental considerations to the contrary).

The general point here is that opposition to capitalism need not imply blanket opposition to 'market solutions' to problems of scarcity—there may even be good grounds for putting prices on some goods which happen to be supplied 'free' (*i.e.* financed out of taxes) in the present society.

Costs of metering

We suggested above that consumer goods which do not carry any important external effects should be marketed in exchange for labour tokens. This principle has to be qualified in some cases to allow for basic economic rationality. That is, there is no point in charging people individually for a good if the costs of metering their consumption and billing them exceed the revenue to be gained, when the good is priced at its cost of production net of these latter costs. In this light, ideological considerations apart, the privatisation of water in Britain is probably irrational. Water is a very low-cost product, and it is not at all clear that the costs of metering and billing are justified. (If clean water were to become a scarce and costly commodity, the situation would be different.)

5. Agriculture
Free markets in agriculture are almost unknown in the developed world. The western governments which advocate the adoption of the free market as the solution to the food problems of Poland strenuously resist any attempt to impose it on their own countries. Food markets are strongly regulated in Japan, the European Community and the USA. The purpose of such regulation is both to ensure stability of supply, and, more importantly, to cushion the politically influential farming lobby from the rigours of the market. The methods adopted differ in detail, but the general effect is to hold food prices above free-market levels to protect farmers' incomes.

The predictable effect of this is to encourage overproduction. Excess food is produced, which is then bought up at subsidised prices and accumulated in warehouses and grain silos. The disposition of these surpluses poses a conundrum. The simple answer would be to sell them off cheaply to consumers, but this is ruled out as it would undercut prices and harm farm incomes. Special gimmicks are resorted to. Butter is distributed to pensioners at Christmas. At Salvation Army offices squalid scenes develop as old people queue and scramble to obtain their free pound of butter. Even worse, food is destroyed. Stocks of potatoes are deliberately contaminated with purple dye to make them unfit for human consumption. Farmers are paid incentives to leave their land idle rather than grow food.

At the same time, high prices encourage farmers to put marginal land under the plough. Water meadows, hedgerows and woods vanish beneath grain prairies. At subsidised prices it becomes worthwhile to douse the land with chemicals, contaminating food, killing wildlife and poisoning water supplies with nitrates and pesticides. We reach the ultimate absurdity when landowners have to be paid not to destroy sites of scientific interest by planting conifers, which they would never have considered in the first place were it not for the incentive payments for planting trees.

What exists now in the West is a crazy amalgam of public regulation and private self-interest, all in effect devoted to the enrichment of the landowner. Despite this, apologists for this system can point to the East and say: 'At least we don't have food queues like they do in Russia.' The popular picture of communist agriculture involves permanent shortages, Russian queues and Polish meat riots.

Before the collapse of Communism in the East there were wide divergences in agricultural systems. Poland had predominantly private agriculture while the Czechs across the border had socialised agriculture. Poland had butchers' shops with bare shelves while state shops in Prague were piled with salamis and sausages.[7] The USSR had predominantly socialised agriculture but was also notorious for shortages.

As these examples show, it is not a simple matter of private farms being better or worse than socialised farms. Other factors—pricing policy, the distribution system, and the cultural level of the countryside—all play their part. Moreover, whether shops are full or empty is a poor measure of the effectiveness of an agricultural policy. If prices are high enough, shops will always be full. There are plenty of countries in the world where full shops go alongside hungry people. Conversely, if you hold prices artificially low, shops will sell out.

A better way to judge a system of food production and distribution is to look at the nutritional standards of the population as a whole, and at the ecological effects the system produces. There is now an immense body of scientific knowledge relating to diet. Even before the second world war, nutritionists had worked out the quantities of proteins, fats, carbohydrates and vitamins needed for a balanced diet. This knowledge was put to good use in setting wartime food rations. Although traditional sources of supply were dislocated, the rational planning and allocation of what remained meant that health and nutritional standards for the population as a whole actually increased.

Some of the nutritional advice of the 1940s may seem a little dated now. Epidemiological studies into diet and heart disease have led to modern recommendations prescribing somewhat less butter and animal fats and more complex carbohydrates. But the same general principle applies: if the population as a whole consumed a diet in conformity with the latest scientific wisdom then the general standard of health would improve. It would no longer be a matter of preventing diseases like rickets or tuberculosis fostered by chronic undernourishment, but of curbing the great modern killers—cancers and heart diseases—brought on by a poor diet.

This suggests that food supplies not only can be, but ought to be, planned. For a given size and age-structure of population, total food requirements can be readily calculated. This can then be obtained from three sources: imports, socialised farms and fisheries, and private farms and fisheries. We will assume that food imports are regulated by long-term supply contracts with various producer-nations, which, barring major climatic catastrophes, provide a reliable base supply of those foods that cannot be economically produced at home.

This leaves a known target for domestic production. If we assume that the agricultural sector is made up of a mixture of state farms, co-ops and family farms, then the problem is how to achieve the target level of output from these sources. Agriculture is more affected by the weather than other industries. Its output fluctuates from year to year, and exact annual planning is impossible. But over a period of several years these fluctuations even out, and by holding buffer stocks, regular supplies can be maintained. It would be reasonable to set three or four year moving targets for agricultural output. Family farms and co-ops could be asked to tender for the supply of fixed quantitites of crops over a three year period. They would be asked to specify what inputs they intended to use in terms of machinery, energy, fertilisers and so on, plus how much value-added they were going to ask for their labour. The supply contracts could then be awarded according to a formula that takes into account both the cost (in terms of direct and indirect labour) and the environmental effects that would be produced by applying the specified quantity of chemicals and fertilisers.

A tendering system would avoid the overproduction that plagues Western systems of agricultural planning. It places the needs of the consumer and the environment before that of the producer. It would encourage efficiency, and hasten the closure of marginal, uneconomic farms. The farms which win contracts would be rewarded with long term stable prices and markets.

Notes to Chapter 5
1. The concept of the margin and of marginal returns have their origin in the theory of ground rent. Here the margin represented the literal edge of cultivation. Marginal land was the last, worst land to be brought under the plough.
2. A discount rate is an abstraction of the notion of a rate of interest. If, in a capitalist economy I am promised a £1000 postal order in a year's time, this has a present value to me of somewhat less than £1000. If I want to spend the money now, not in a year's time, I must take out a loan which I promise to repay in a year. Suppose that the credit company charges me 25% interest, then by borrowing £800 now I would be able to pay back the loan plus the £200 interest when the postal order arrives. A future income of £1000 would have discounted present value of £800. The possibility of doing this is obviously an effect of the existence of credit institutions, but capitalist economics abstracts the idea from its institutional framework and advances it as a general principle of economic calculation.
3. An imputed rent in a socialist economy involves the state acting as if it were two private individuals: a landowner and an industrialist. The state as landowner charges the state as industrialist a rent for the land used by industry. Since the

state owns both the land and the industry this is a purely internal accounting operation.

4. See *The Times* 10/8/87.

5. It must be emphasized that the use of a discount rate in a socialist plan in no way implies the existence of a money market, loans, or the payment of interest on loans. It is merely a parameter used in the computer programs that evaluate the social costs of different production alternatives.

6. On the concept of positive freedom, see Partha Dasgupta (1986).

7. Bulgarian agriculture was on the Czech pattern. One of the authors visited Bulgaria during the height of the Polish Solidarity agitation during the early 1980s. His large well-fed Bulgarian hosts were openly contemptuous of the Poles: "No wonder they're in a mess, they privatised agriculture back in '56."

CHAPTER 6

Detailed Planning

In chapter 4 we introduced the idea of planning as a case of feedback control. Figure 6.1 recapitulates the basic idea. This general concept can now be extended to take into account the specific points we have made about socialist planning up to this point.

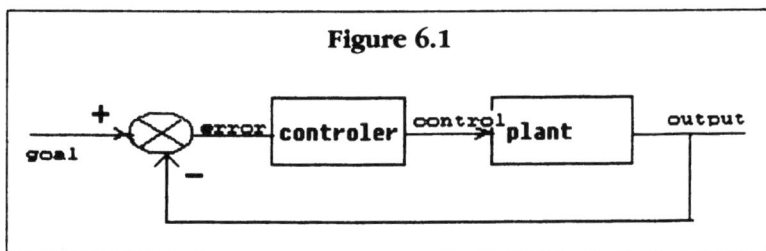

Figure 6.1

As we have seen, strategic planning deals with the general shape of the industrial structure of the economy. In this chapter we are concerned with detail planning, which deals with just how much of each individual product must be produced to meet these general objectives. The strategic plan may stipulate that 7 per cent of national income will be allocated to electronic consumer goods. The detail plan will have to say what this means in terms of quantities of TVs of each model, numbers of each type of amplifier etc. And in order to achieve these output targets the plan must specify the numbers of each type of component required to build the amplifiers and TVs: 500,000 colour mask tubes of 14" diagonal, 300,000 of 20" diagonal, 12.5 million of 10 micro-farad ceramic capacitors, and so on.

Figure 6.2 displays the inputs into detail planning. *Simulation and scheduling* involves constructing a detailed model of the operation of the economy in order to predict how much of each intermediate input will be required to produce the final combination of outputs. *Marketing*—which feeds into detail planning

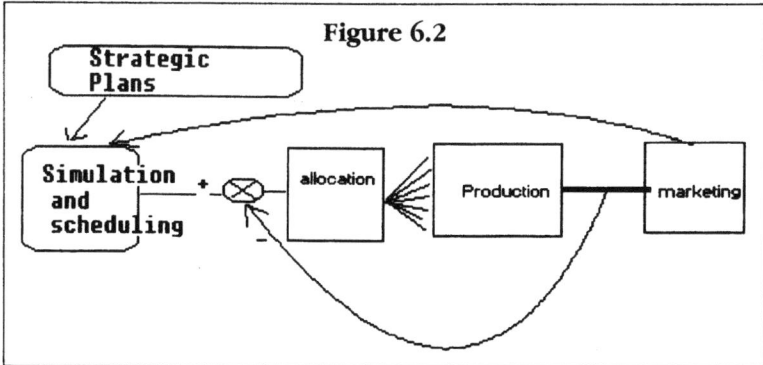

Figure 6.2

indirectly—returns information on whether the price people are willing to pay for a product is high enough to justify its continued inclusion in the plan. If people are not willing to pay as much in terms of labour time as the labour time required to produce it, then that particular product should be cut back or discontinued and resources shifted to a different one. The details of our proposed marketing feedback mechanism will be set out separately in chapter 8; for the moment we will concentrate on simulation and allocation.

We introduced input-output tables in chapter 3, in the context of calculating the total labour content of commodities. This method of representing the economy is also very useful for formulating and understanding the problem of detailed planning. An example input-output table is shown in Table 6.1. The reader may also wish to refer back to the example shown in Table 3.2. Recall that the input-output table or matrix records the flows of product from each industry to every other industry. Each industry appears twice, occupying one row and the corresponding column. In the presentation we employ here, along a given industry's *row* there appear the quantities of that industry's product that are supplied as inputs to all industries. For instance, if row 1 refers to the oil industry, the numbers in that row represent the quantities of oil supplied to the oil industry itself, to the electricity-generating industry, to the truck-manufacturing industry, and so on. Down each industry's *column* we find the quantities of all products that are required as direct inputs to the given industry. For instance, if column 3 represents the truck-manufacturing, then reading down that column we will find the quantities of oil, electricity, and so on required to make trucks.

Some basic terminology is useful for understanding what is going on here. First of all, the gross output of an industry refers to the total output of that industry, regardless of the use to which it is put. Gross

Table 6.1:
Portion of an input-output table

	oil	*electricity*	*trucks*	*etc.*
oil	1,000	50,000	800	. . .
electricity	50	20	40	. . .
trucks	30	10	20	. . .
etc.	.	.	.	

— Rows show where the output of each industry goes.
— Columns show the inputs required by each industry.
— Figures in the table should be thought of as in appropriate physical units (e.g. barrels of oil, kilowatt-hours, and number of trucks worn out; all on a per-year basis).

output is sub-divided into *intermediate* output and *final* or *net* output. Intermediate output is that portion of the industry's product which is destined to be 'used up' within the productive system itself (for instance, the coal used in the steel industry, or the steel used in the personal computer industry). Final or net output is the remaining portion of the product, available for final uses (either consumption—individual or collective—or net investment designed to build up the economy's productive base).

Some products are more or less pure intermediate goods. For example, aside perhaps from a few metal-working hobbyists, consumers simply have no interest in sheet steel, so that virtually the entire output of sheet steel will figure as intermediate product, entering the production process in various industries. On the other hand, some goods are pure final goods, with no intermediate uses (no industry uses toothpaste as an input). But some goods have both intermediate and final uses. Natural gas is used by households for cooking and heating, as well as by various industries as an input to production.

One more term is important: the *technical coefficient* for an ordered pair of industries tells us how much of the one industry's product is needed (directly) in order to produce one unit of output of the other industry. For instance, if it takes 10 kilograms of steel tubing to make one bicycle, then the (steel tubing, bicycles) technical coefficient is 10, if steel is measured in kilos, or .01 if steel is measured in tonnes. Note that the total direct input requirement for steel tubing in the bicycle industry can be found by multiplying the total output of bicycles by the relevant technical coefficient. With a coefficient of .01, the production of 2,000 bikes would require 2,000 times .01 = 20 tonnes of steel tubing.

We are now ready to address the structure of the problem facing the planners in a socialist economy. What people are ultimately interested in is the bundle of *final* goods that the economy produces. Suppose we have a set of targets for such goods.[1] Meeting these targets requires that the appropriate amounts of *intermediate* goods are produced. The PC industry can turn out the number and type of PCs that are wanted only if it receives the right amounts of plastic, steel, silicon, etc. from its industrial suppliers, which in turn requires that those other industries receive the intermediate products *they* need, and so on, in a highly complex web of interdependence.

So here is the problem: Starting from a list of desired *final* outputs, how can we compute the *gross* amounts of every kind of product that are needed to support the final output targets? In principle, the answer can be found directly, as follows. (Those who find mathematical notation excessively daunting might skip a few paragraphs to the conclusion, but we use only the simplest of algebra.) Consider a simple little system with only two distinct industries. Let G denote gross output, I intermediate output, and F final output. Subscripts denote the industries, 1 and 2. Since gross output equals intermediate output plus final output, we can represent our toy economy with the following two equations, one for each industry.

$$G_1 = I_{11} + I_{12} + F_1$$
$$G_2 = I_{21} + I_{22} + F_2$$

In the double subscripts against the intermediate outputs (I), the first number represents the *source* of the product and the second represents its *destination*, so that I_{12}, for instance, denotes the amount of industry 1's product used in industry 2. Spelled out in English, the first equation says that the gross output of the first industry is the sum of three components: first, the intermediate output of product number 1 required within the first industry itself (as, for instance, the oil industry consumes some oil—though for any industry which does not consume any of its own product this term will be zero); second, the intermediate output of product number 1 needed in industry 2; and third, the final or net output of product number 1.

Now perform this simple trick: write each intermediate output quantity (I) as gross output (G) times the relevant technical coefficient. This is just as in the case of the bicycles and the steel tubing discussed above, where the intermediate use of steel tubing in the cycle industry was equal to the gross output of bikes times the steel-tubing-per-bike requirement. If the technical coefficients are denoted by a's, we will have the following:

$$G_1 = a_{11}G_1 + a_{12}G_2 + F_1$$

$$G_2 = a_{21}G_1 + a_{22}G_2 + F_2$$

Without going through all the steps, we can now see how the problem may be solved. After replacing the I's with the a-times-G terms, we have reduced the problem to a matter of two equations in two unknowns, namely the gross outputs of the industries. Simple but tedious algebra should yield the desired result: equations specifying the gross output of each industry as a function of the final outputs and the technical coefficients alone. And once the gross outputs are found, the intermediate outputs flowing into each industry are easily found too—again, as in the bicycle example.[2]

The mathematics of the problem have been well-understood since the pioneering work of Wassily Leontief and John von Neumann in the 1930s and 40s, and the solution is not hard to find if the system is reasonably small. But if one is dealing with a whole economy, the only way to make the system 'small' is to express it in highly aggregated terms. The rows and columns of our spreadsheet might refer to, say, 'consumer electronics', 'motor vehicles', 'oil and gas', and so on. This is acceptable for some purposes, but it is not good enough for practical socialist planning. If the planners are to provide a blueprint which can effectively guide production, ensuring that that all economic activities mesh properly, they must be able to specify the outputs and inputs in exact detail. But in that case the input-output table will be colossal, with millions of rows and columns and therefore thousands of billions of technical coefficients. Solving the resulting system of simultaneous equations is not a trivial task. In addition a prodigious amount of detailed information must be gathered (e.g. in the form of the technical coefficients) before calculation can even begin.

Information gathering, and the mathematical processing of that information—both of these issues are important. We will begin by examining the task of calculation, assuming the necessary data to be 'given' (the economists' favourite little phrase); in chapter 9 we shall return to the problem of obtaining the data.

The mathematical issues which arise here are essentially the same as for the computation of labour values, discussed in chapter 3. In principle, the problem could be solved directly via Gaussian elimination, but, as we saw in chapter 3, this is simply not feasible for extremely large systems. As with labour-value computation, the way to proceed is to exploit the sparse nature of the input-output matrix or 'spreadsheet'. Since the table, when specified in full detail, has a huge number of zero entries (representing the toothpaste that is *not* used in making sausages, the timber that is *not* used in making spectacles, and so on), we can better represent the conditions of production in the form of linked lists, and then seek an iterative solution.

The two main iterative techniques available (known as the Jacobi and Gauss-Seidel methods) will accept input data in the linked-list form. These methods do not directly calculate the answer to the problem, but they produce successively closer approximations to the answer. For the economic input-output application it can be shown that if there is a unique solution to the problem—which could in principle be calculated directly—then these iterative methods will produce results which converge on that solution (Varga, 1962).

The working of the iterative method in this application can be explained fairly simply. The required data input comprises (i) the target final output list, (ii) the (non-zero) technical coefficients and (iii) some initial guess at the required gross output of each product. These starting values for gross output are then fed through the set of technical coefficients, and the quantities of each product needed as inputs are calculated. On this basis, a new set of gross output figures is calculated. This new set is then used as the input for another round, and so on. If the algorithm[3] is convergent (i.e. if the problem has a unique solution in the first place), then after a while the change in the gross output numbers from round to round will get smaller and smaller. The algorithm terminates once all the approximate gross outputs change by less than some pre-set 'small' amount.

The choice of starting values for the gross outputs is not crucial, as the convergence property of the algorithm is independent of initial conditions: if *some* starting values will work, then so will *all* starting values (again, see Varga, 1962). Nonetheless, convergence on the solution will be quicker if the initial guesses are reasonably close to the correct values. The planners can rely on past experience, where applicable, to select starting values of the right order of magnitude.

The time order of the Jacobi iterative method is given by the number of outputs times the average number of distinct *direct* inputs needed in each production process, times the number of iterations required to produce a satisfactory approximation. If there are, say, 10 million products with an average of 200 direct inputs each, and 100 iterations are needed, then 2×10^{11} calculations must be performed. Suppose each of these requires 10 computer instructions. In that case we have a total of 2×10^{12} instructions, and a computer with a speed of one billion instructions per second could do the job in 2×10^3 seconds, or a little over half an hour.

Planning in the USSR

Two sorts of questions suggest themselves at this point, concerning the relationship between the argument we have just been through and the experience of planning in the Soviet Union. First, one might ask: If the calculations required for consistent detailed planning are so vast and complex, how on earth did the Soviets manage before high-speed computers were available?

In fact it is rather remarkable that the Soviets should have been so successful, during the pre-computer days of the 1930s, in building up their heavy industrial base using centralised planning methods. The economy was, of course, much less technologically complex at that time, and the plans specified relatively few key targets. And even so, there are many tales of gross mismatches between supply and demand during the period of the early 5-year plans. A huge expansion of the inputs of labour and materials meant that the key targets could be met despite such imbalances.

In addition, we should note that the early Soviet plans were not drawn up in the way we have described. Working backwards from a target list of final outputs to the required list of gross outputs, consistently and in detail, was quite beyond the capacity of Gosplan, the state planning agency. Often, instead, the planners started out from *targets that were themselves set in gross terms:* so many tons of steel by 1930, so many tons of coal by 1935, and so on. This early experience arguably had a deleterious effect on the economic mechanism in later years. It gave rise to a sort of 'productionism', in which the generation of bumper outputs of key intermediate industrial products came to be seen as an end in itself. In fact, from an input-output point of view, one really wants to *economise* on intermediate goods so far as possible. The aim should be to produce the *minimum* amounts of coal, steel, cement, etc., consistent with the desired volume of final outputs.

The second sort of question that arises here is in a sense the reverse of the first: If the mathematical and computational techniques we have discussed are well known, how come the Soviet planners weren't doing much better by the mid-1980s, when fast computers had become available?

We have pointed out part of the answer to this, in discussing the first question above. The necessarily rather crude planning methods of the 1930s left their mark on the system that evolved in later years. Given the peculiar ideological sclerosis of the late Stalin years—interrupted by the Khrushchev 'thaw' but then resumed under Brezhnev—new approaches to planning were generally regarded with suspicion. There is a suggestion in the literature on Soviet economics that the very idea of starting the planning process from final output targets (the procedure we have advocated above) was seen by the official guardians of orthodoxy as somehow 'bourgeois'.

In addition, interest in novel computer-based planning methods in the USSR came 'out of phase' with the real technological possibilities. The types of computer system available to Soviet planners in the 1960s and even 70s (when the improvement of the planning system was a live issue) were primitive by today's Western standards. Soviet economists were well aware of the potential benefits of the use of consistent input-output techniques, but the equipment at their disposal permitted the analysis of only 'small', highly aggregated input-output systems. While these were of some use for inter-regional planning exercises (investigating the interdependence of the regions of the USSR), they could not be used for routine detailed planning. For the most part, input-output analysis remained an academic exercise, and the overall impact of the computer on Soviet planning disappointed the early expectations.[4]

It is important to note that the unavailability of super-fast central computers was not the only or even the most important constraint. As we explained in chapter 3, in the context of calculating labour values, it would be possible to accomplish the same results using a large distributed network of much more modest personal computers, linked by an economy-wide telecommunications system. Such equipment was also unavailable in the years when Soviet economists were thinking seriously about improving the planning system. Cheap PCs are a relatively recent development, and besides the telecommunications system in the USSR is notoriously backward (as anyone who has tried to make a phone call between Moscow and Leningrad knows).

Further, as we shall see in chapter 9, effective detailed planning requires a standardised system of product identification, which in turn demands sophisticated computer databases. In the USSR, the planners continued to work with the system of so-called 'material balances'. This system, which involved drawing up 'balance sheets' showing the sources of production and the planned uses for each product individually, represents a sort of crude approximation to the input-output method. Not only were the planners unable to calculate effectively the interactions amongst these balances, but in addition the classification of products was incomplete and inconsistent.

A political point is also relevant here. Our planning proposals absolutely require a free flow of information and universal access to computer systems, and this was politically impossible in the USSR under Brezhnev. Even access to photocopying equipment was strictly controlled for fear of the dissemination of political dissent.

Finally, of course, computerisation is no panacea. There were many problems with the economic planning mechanism in the USSR which would have had to be tackled before the application of extra computer-power could be expected to yield much of a dividend. (One example: the irrational and semi-fossilised pricing system, with the prices of many goods stuck at levels which guaranteed shortages and queues.)

Effective detailed planning of a complex economy, it would appear, requires the sorts of computer and telecommunication technology available in the West as of, say, the mid-1980s. By this time, however, the ideological climate in the Soviet Union had shifted substantially in favour of market-oriented 'reforms'. It would seem that Soviet economists—or at any rate, those who had the ear of the political leadership under Gorbachev—were little interested in developing the sorts of algorithms and computer systems that we have discussed. They had apparently lost their belief in the potential of efficient planning, perhaps partly in response to an earlier, premature overselling of the benefits of computerisation, and partly in response to the trend in favour of free market economics in the West.

A further point is that any introduction of labour value accounting would immediately have highlighted the issue of the surplus product, how large it was and on what it was being spent. Neither the old bureaucracy nor the new soviet bourgeoisie would have wanted this issue raised too openly. Only politically conscious workers would be likely to have raised it, and to do so they would have had to have rediscovered long submerged roots of the communist movement.

Detail planning and stock constraints

To return to the main line of our argument, we have claimed that it is now quite feasible for a planning agency to work backwards from a list of final target outputs to the list of gross outputs which will balance the plan, even when the input-output table accounts for the relations between industries in minute detail. But this does not complete the calculations necessary for the detailed plan. It may not be possible to produce the quantities of all products that are called for by the gross output computations, because of 'external' constraints in the form of stocks of means of production and labour supply.

The planners may calculate that satisfaction of the plan targets calls for the generation of x tera-kilowatt-hours of electricity. The balancing of the input-output system will have ensured that sufficient oil, coal, or uranium is called for to meet that electricity requirement, but is there enough generating capacity in the form of power stations? The economy's ability to produce over any given period is limited by the availability of stocks of durable capital goods which take a long time to build. And then there is labour: is there enough labour available to meet the gross output requirements of the plan?

These questions can be answered fairly quickly once the gross output numbers are generated. The planning system can forward to each industry its gross output requirement, and the individual industry computers (which need not be super-fast machines) can then calculate their needs for means of production stocks and labour, exploiting their knowledge of the per-unit means of production and labour coefficients for their own sector. These industrial needs can then be fed back to the central computers, summed up, and compared to the central records of the stocks of means of production of different types, and to the central calculation of labour supply respectively.

If the constraints happen to be met—i.e. if the industries are calling for no more of each type of means of production, and for no more labour, than is available economy-wide—well and good. Note, though, that even if the overall constraints are met there may still be a need for a reallocation of resources between industries: the central planning agency would have to optimise this reshuffling and issue instructions accordingly. But if the overall constraints are violated at this point, some adjustment of the plan is needed. The original target final output cannot be achieved (unless the 'external' constraints can somehow be relaxed), and the planners must think again. Those final output targets which have the lowest social priority can be reduced, and the whole calculation repeated. Since the complete process is likely to take hours, or at worst days, a number of repetitions are possible within a reasonable time-frame for plan construction.

The importance of this last point—that is, the presence of constraints on production other than those taken into account by the system of input-output flows—really depends on the time-frame of the planning decision. If the plan is sufficiently long term, then stock constraints become less relevant. If more electricity-generating capacity is called for, then it can be built up accordingly. In the limit, the only 'external' constraints on the economy's input-output system are the supply of labour and the availability of non-reproducible natural resources. In that case, adjusting the target levels of final output in conformity with the external constraints should be relatively simple. But conversely, the shorter the time-scale of the plan, the more important the 'external' stock constraints become. Any means of production that take longer than the plan period to construct must be reckoned as stock constraints; and if the time-scale is very short, the state of inventories of materials becomes important too. One of the authors has been investigating a computer algorithm suitable for plan-balancing in the latter situation, an algorithm which differs substantially from the standard input-output approach outlined above. The theoretical basis for this alternative algorithm is presented in the next section.

A new plan-balancing algorithm

Suppose we start off with a shopping list of annual outputs that we want to achieve for 100,000 different consumer goods. These targets may be conservative, in which case resources would be left idle, or they may be excessive and beyond what could be achieved with current resources. We would like to know whether the targets should be scaled up or down to make efficient use of resources, including the economy's existing stocks of machinery of various kinds. It is unlikely to be a matter of making an x per cent change in the quotas for all consumer goods. Quotas for some goods will have to be adjusted up or down more than others.

If we have a limited number of sheep and spare capacity in the chemicals industry, we want to know what this implies for quotas of wool and acrylic jumpers. Should targets for wool garments be cut? And what does this imply for production of acrylic ones? How many knitting frames should be switched from producing wool to acrylic?

Suppose the free knitting machines could be allocated to any one of a thousand lines of knitwear. All the spare capacity could be poured into increasing production of a particular line of flourescent blue jerseys with 'St Tropez Sport' written accross the front in pink, but it is doubtful if such a solution would please consumers. What is required is a set of rules by which computers can decide what are likely to be sensible adjustments to the plan targets in the light of resource constraints. We have developed a computer program which will make such adjustments based upon the economic principle of diminishing marginal utility. A full account of the algorithm can be found in Cockshott (1990).

The harmony function

The algorithm uses techniques developed for neural net simulations (a sub-field within Artificial Intelligence). Researchers in this area have proposed that neural systems can be analysed using thermodynamic concepts. A nervous system consists of a large population of entities loosely coupled to one another, and as such it falls into the abstract category of problems treated by statistical mechanics. It has been found that thermodynamic concepts like energy, entropy and relaxation can be usefully applied to neural models. Each neurone, like an atom in a solid, is linked to and reacts with a subset of the total population. In both cases we have large populations developing under stochastic laws[5] subject to local interactions. One can define a suitable analogue of energy for a neural net—broadly how closely its behavior corresponds to the desired behaviour. It can be shown that if one introduces into the behaviour of the neural net a computational analogue of temperature, then by a relaxation process one can cause the net to stabilise around the desired behavior pattern.

Again arguing by a process of analogy, neural nets and crystals are, at a certain level of abstraction, rather like an economy. In an economy industries are linked to one another by local interactions. In this case it is the relationship of supplier to user rather than synaptic connections or electrostatic forces that we are dealing with, but there is an abstract similarity.

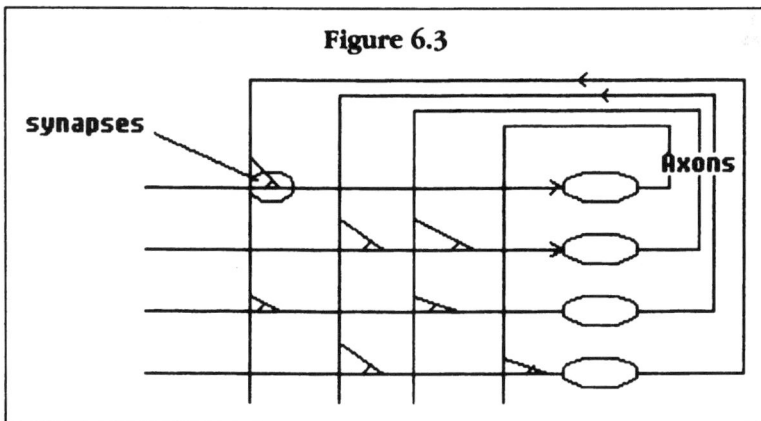

Figure 6.3

Note the similarity between the neural net in Figure 6.3 and an input-output matrix. The columns in the diagram represent the outputs of the nerve cells on the right. The synapses drive the inputs to the cells which are represented by rows. The rows act to sum the level of excitation on their inputs. The level of excitation on the inputs in turn determines the level of output on the axons. We can make an analogy with the columns of an input-output table representing the levels of activity of an industry. Let us label the synapses S_{ij}, where i ranges over the rows and j ranges over the columns. The strength of the connection on S_{ij} represents the amount of output of the ith industry used to produce one unit of the jth industry. Neural net theory predicts that such a net will settle into a pattern of excitation that is consonant with the weights on the synapses. The resulting levels of excitation on the cells would represent the relative intensities with which the industries should be operated. Neural nets can be modelled mathematically. The implication is that we should be able to balance an economy by the same sort of mathematical techniques of relaxation as are used in modeling neural nets. What we have to do is find some analogue of energy which we can minimise.

People working with neural nets often pose the problem in the inverse sense—instead of trying to minimise the energy of the network they maximise what they call its *harmony*. Formally this is just the inverse of energy, but it has a greater intuitive appeal. A neural net is set to be in a state of maximal harmony when it has learned to give the 'right' responses to external stimuli.

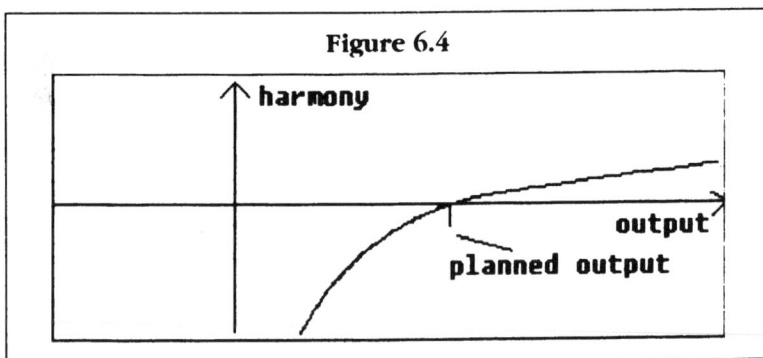

Figure 6.4

We can apply this notion of harmony to an economy. We define a harmony function over each industry of the form shown in Figure 6.4.

As can be seen the harmony becomes rapidly negative if the net output (output after allowing for consumption of the product by other industries) of a product falls below the target. The harmony gradually becomes positive if we exceed the target. This is to indicate that the problems caused by shortages are more serious than the benefits obtained from surpluses. An illustrative function with these properties is shown in algorithmic form below:

let u = (output – goal)/goal
if u < 0 then harmony = – u²
otherwise harmony = √u

The idea is that people get diminishing satisfaction from each additional unit of a particular good they consume. The first time your relatives give you a teapot for Christmas your gratitude is heartfelt; the fifth time round it is a little forced. The implication of this is that the additional social satisfaction that comes from exceeding output targets tends to fall off rather sharply, and people will be more upset about shortages than they will be pleased by superfluity. We can model this with what we term a harmony function as shown above.

When output of a good is at target level we define the harmony for that good to be zero. If output is in excess of the target the harmony is positive and when output is below target harmony is negative. This harmony function is used by the computer as a guide to adjusting outputs. Our objective is to maximise the harmony of the entire economy, to bring it all into balance.

Stages of the algorithm
1. Randomly allocate resources to the industries. This is a notional random allocation, taking place within the computer. No real allocation of goods in the economy takes place at this stage. We specify a random allocation, since if our relaxation technique is valid then any starting point is as good as any other.
2. For each industry determine which of the resources currently available to it is the rate-limiting factor, that is to say the resource that acts as a bottleneck on production.
3. Each industry gives up non-critical resources (*i.e.* those which are surplus to requirements, given the rate-limiting factor) and allocates them to a common pool. This by definition does not reduce production and thus leaves harmony unaltered. Note that this reallocation takes place only within the computer's memory; there would be no reallocation in the real world until the whole algorithm terminated.
4. Work out harmony of each industry.
5. Work out the mean harmony for the whole economy.
6. Sort industries in order of harmony.
7. Starting with those industries with highest harmony, reduce their output until their production level is such that their harmony is equal to the mean harmony. This is easy to do since the harmony

function is invertible (that is, we can work backwards from harmony level to the corresponding output just as easily as from output to the corresponding harmony). Resources thus released go into the common pool.

8. Starting with the industries with lowest harmony, assign to them resources from the 'pool' and increase their output until they are producing at a level equal to the mean harmony.

9. Work out the new mean harmony. If it is significantly different from before go back to stage 6.

This algorithm has the effect of equalising the harmony of the different industries. After as few as a dozen iterations mean harmony will change by less than 1 per cent with successive iterations. By itself, however, it has the drawback that it only brings the economy to a *local* maximum of harmony. In computer experimentation, one often finds with the algorithm in this form that there are unused resources left over and that the overall level of output is lower than it could be. Intuitively we can understand this as being due to the very strong tendency of the algorithm to settle in the region of whatever mean harmony it starts out with.

This can be overcome by introducing a bias towards increased output. In step 7, instead of reducing output of high harmony industries to the mean, we adjust their output until it is equal to (mean + B) where B is the bias. At the start of the program we set B high then reduce it with each iteration. The effect of this is that only industries with very high initial harmonies reduce their output at first, but the industries with low harmonies continue to increase their outputs. In consequence the mean harmony tends to rise with each successive iteration, and the system eventually stabilises around a maximal mean harmony.

Provided one chooses one's data structures carefully this algorithm is approximately linear in running time. In other words, a problem with 100 industries will take 10 times as long as one with 10 industries. As with the conventional input-output analysis discussed above, one important point is not to represent the input-output table as an array, but to take advantage of the fact that it is a very sparse matrix and represent it using linked lists. The time order of the algorithm will then be roughly nm where n is the number of industries and m the mean number of inputs per industry. The algorithm is reasonably simple, and has been used to simulate a plan for about 4,000 industries on a Sun workstation in about 300 seconds. A Sun workstation executes about 3 million instructions per second. Since it is linear in its time requirement the program should take something like a million seconds (less than 2 weeks) on a 68020 (a popular microprocessor) to balance the plan for an economy with 10 million products. It would also require something like a thousand megabytes of store. This requirement is not excessive; it is equivalent to a thousand PCs and would cost about half a million pounds at current prices.

A British company Meiko has developed a multiprocessor that uses up to 1024 micro processor chips to gain speed. The proposed use of this machine is in particle physics simulations, and it is capable of 10,000,000,000 instructions per second. If we could run the problem on a Meiko computing surface with 1024 transputer chips, each with 4 megabytes of memory, the plan for a major economy would be computable in about 10 minutes.

In addition to arriving at a feasible set of target outputs, the algorithm would also produce as a side effect the correct allocation of capital goods and raw materials between industries. This is exactly the detailed information that one needs for a plan.

We have argued that there exist computational techniques that would allow the detailed planning of an economy in terms of physical units without any reference to money or prices. These techniques are computationally tractable, and could be accomplished on the sorts of high performance computers that are currently available for things like particle physics and weather forecasting. They can be viewed as simulating beforehand the sort of equilibration process that an idealised market is supposed to achieve.

Economic cybernetics in Chile

One of the most interesting experiments with computerised planning and control of the economy was undertaken in Chile under the Allende government in the years 1972 to 1973. The system was designed by Stafford Beer and is described in his book *The Brain of the Firm*.[6] Beer's objective was to provide real time decentralised control of the economy. Since his system provides a practical example of the general type of regulation mechanism we are proposing, it may be useful to outline its characteristics.

With the conventional statistical methods available to Western governments, economic statistics are often many months out of date by the time they arrive on the desks of decision makers. In consequence, decisions may be made to try to resolve a crisis some months after the crisis actually occurred. Since the policy instruments available to the government are also slow-acting, decisions may be taken whose effects are the opposite of what was intended. After the stock market crash of 1987, the British government feared a recession and in 1988 introduced tax cuts. By the time these came into effect demand was already accelerating anyway, so by 1989 the result was accelerating inflation. Lags in the availability of data meant that completely inappropriate action was taken (although in this case there was also a strong ideological commitment to tax cuts, regardless of the macroeconomic conditions).

Such perverse effects, in which feedback induces worse oscillations in the system, can be avoided if controllers are provided with up-to-date information and have the means to take immediate appropriate action. In Chile a computer network was established to do this in only four months, to the great surprise of sceptics who had argued that such a network would take years to set up. The task was accomplished with the computer technology of the early '70s and the very limited telecommunications capacity of a poor country like Chile. A combination of microwave and telex links joined all the key industrial centers to computers in the capital. Within these limits it was possible to provide the government with economic information that was no more than a day old. More modern equipment could do better.

Information was presented in iconic form. Large screens in an 'Opsroom' displayed annotated flow graphs of the interactions between subsections of the economy. The graphics displays avoided using figures. The magnitudes of the flows between different sectors were indicated by the widths of the lines flowing between them. Industries and sectors were shown as blocks with bar graphs inside them telling what proportion of the industry's capacity was being used. The room provided seating for seven people, this being the largest number who can effectively participate in a discussion. Large buttons on the arms of the chairs could be used to control the displays, and highlight different features.

The notion of the Opsroom was taken from wartime experience in air defence. As in war, real-time information was displayed for immediate decisions. Decisions could be tested using computer simulations which showed what the effects would be if a given course of action were taken. In the event it was used like a wartime headquarters in the struggle to break the anti-government boycotts imposed by private lorry companies. The computer network enabled the government to mobilise all its available transport resources to keep goods flowing.

It was intended that an Opsroom would be provided in each industry, and indeed in each plant. Sophisticated statistical programs analysed the data flowing up from lower levels of the system to search for any significant changes. Human decision makers were insulated from information overload, and just presented with significant data on which decisions were needed. The Opsroom for a plant would be provided with warnings as soon as anything unusual occurred. If the computers detected a crisis, they alerted the Opsroom and started a clock running. If the Opsroom had not responded effectively within a certain time period, the next higher Opsroom in the tree was alerted. This gave each unit the freedom to act locally within its competence without endangering the viability of the social organism. It was envisaged that the Opsroom at factory level would be run by local workers' committees. The democratic presumption was that modern visual and computing aids would allow people to manage their factories without sophisticated training.

With the bloody coup that established Pinochet in power, and prepared the way for Friedmanite monetarist economic experimentation in Chile, all this was swept away. The Opsroom perished with Allende and democracy in the burnt out ruins of the presidential palace.

Notes to Chapter 6
1. Where these targets are to come from is another matter. We have made some relevant points already, in chapter 5, and will have more to say in chapters 8 and 13 in particular.
2. With many equations, it is more economical to represent these equations in matrix form. The matrix counterpart of the equations in the text, in their second form, is
$$g = Ag + f$$
where g denotes the (n × 1) vector of gross outputs, f denotes the (n × 1) vector of final outputs, and A denotes the (n × n) matrix of technical coefficients. (n is the number of industries in the system). This system can be solved thus:
$$g = Ag + f$$
$$\Rightarrow \quad (I–A)g = f$$
$$\Rightarrow \quad g = (I–A)^{-1}f$$
(In this context, I represents the n × n identity matrix.) In words, the conclusion says that we can determine the answer, the list of required gross outputs, by finding the inverse of the Leontief matrix (I–A) and multiplying this into the final output vector, f.
3. The word algorithm means a procedure for calculating something by a well defined sequence of steps (see note 7 to chapter 3). If one is to instruct a computer to solve a problem one has first to define an algorithm or sequence of steps capable of producing the answer. The steps are then written down in a computer language as a program. A convergent algorithm is one which gets closer and closer to the right answer with each step that is done.
4. For an assessment of the Soviet experience with computers with computers in planning through the 1970s see Martin Cave (1980).
5. Stochastic laws means subject to the laws of chance, unpredictable in detail but with predictable average behaviour.
6. See also the afterword to Beer (1975).

CHAPTER 7

Macroeconomic Planning and Budgetary Policy

As we indicated in chapter 4, macroeconomic planning concerns the overall balance of the economy with respect to the different broad categories of final use of the product. The macro plan must ensure that these components of the product are mutually consistent and add up to the desired total. To develop the idea of macro planning we need a consistent accounting framework. The three aspects of macroeconomics—theory, policy objectives, and accounting system—are closely related. For instance, the development of the modern system of National Income accounts in the capitalist economies was motivated by the seminal macrotheoretical work of J.M. Keynes in the 1930s. In turn, the availability of reasonably reliable and coherent national accounts was a precondition for the application of Keynesian policies during the post-war years. The Soviet-type economies employed a different national accounting system, which had its theoretical roots in a rather narrow interpretation of Marx's distinction between productive and unproductive labour. The type of planning we propose requires a system of national accounts based on labour-time as the social unit of account. This concept also has marxian roots, but is rather different from the traditional practice of the socialist economies.

This chapter begins with a discussion of the general implications of labour-time accounting at an economy-wide level. It then develops in parallel the policy issues facing socialist macroeconomics, and an accounting system within which these issues can be tackled. Once this basis is established, some more specific questions relating to saving, credit and tax policy are examined.

Macro accounting in labour-time

Let us define the Gross Value Product, of the socialist economy, as the total labour content of the goods and services produced within the economy over a given period, say a year. The Gross Value

Product can be broken into two components according to the source of the labour-content. The larger component is the input of current labour, *i.e.* labour carried out within the given accounting period. We shall call this Current Labour. In addition, there is past labour 'transferred' from goods produced in previous periods. These may take the form of stocks of materials produced last period but used up this period, or of durable means of production (machinery, plant and equipment) which gradually wear out and/or become obsolete over time. We refer to this transfer of past labour as a whole as Depreciation. This breakdown gives us our first macro accounting identity:

$$\text{Gross Value Product} = \text{Current Labour} + \text{Depreciation} \quad (1)$$

We shall also define the Net Value Product, as the labour content of those goods and services produced over and above the amount required to make good the consumption of the products of past labour (Depreciation). Hence our second identity:

$$\text{Net Value Product} = \text{Gross Value Product} - \text{Depreciation} \quad (2)$$

Now the basic principle of distribution in our system is that *workers should receive labour tokens in direct correspondence with the amount of labour they perform* (see chapter 2). We recognise certain qualifications of this principle on an individual basis, but economy-wide it holds good: the total issue of labour tokens per period equals the total hours of labour performed. Letting Current Labour Tokens denote the current issue of labour tokens in exchange for work rendered we have a third identity:

$$\text{Current Labour Tokens} = \text{Current Labour} \quad (3)$$

Taking identities (1) to (3) together, it follows that

$$\text{Current Labour Tokens} = \text{Net Value Product}.$$

Suppose for a moment that workers were able to retain all of Current Labour Tokens as 'disposable income'. And suppose they wish to spend all of this income on consumer goods. It is also a principle of the system we propose that consumer goods should have *a price in labour tokens equal to their total labour content*, at least as a first approximation (the details of this proposal will be spelled out in the next chapter). It follows that if workers spend all of Current Labour Tokens, their consumption will exhaust the Net Value Product. According to the above equations, the workers cannot consume the whole of the Gross Value Product, since their income (Current Labour Tokens) falls short of Gross Value Product by the amount of Depreciation, thus ensuring that the resources are available to make good the consumption of previously produced means of production. But even so, the exhaustion of Net Value Product by workers' consumption is untenable for two reasons.

First, there are important final uses of the social product other than personal consumption: social provision (health, education etc.); net accumulation of means of production to enhance the economy's future productive capacity; and, possibly, lending to other economies. Abbreviating these three uses of resources by Social, Accumulation and Trade (for trade surplus) respectively, and denoting personal consumption by Consumption, we have:

$$\text{Net Value Product} = \text{Consumption} + \text{Social} + \text{Accumulation} + \text{Trade} \quad (4)$$

Equation (4) shows the breakdown of the Net Value Product into its four basic uses. If the plan calls for positive levels of social expediture and accumulation, it is clear that consumption must fall short of Net Value Product, and therefore must also fall short of Current Labour Tokens, the issue of labour tokens for current work. One way to arrange for this is to tax the labour-token income of the workers. It may not be necessary to collect tax equal to the full difference between Current Labour Tokens and the plan's allowance for consumption, because the workers may decide to save some of their labour token income, and to the extent that they save they are 'freeing up' resources for uses other than consumption. We shall return to these points.

Second, a part of the plan's total personal consumption allowance must be made available to non-workers—retired people, the disabled, people moving between jobs. If the only way to purchase articles of personal consumption is using labour tokens, then some quantity of tokens must be made available to non-workers via the state's budget. To preserve equality between the issue of labour tokens and work performed, these tokens for non-workers cannot simply be 'printed up' (this would be inflationary); rather, they must be taxed away from the workers and transferred to the non-workers.

Before turning to the substantive issues of taxation and saving, it will be useful to put the above ideas into the context of a 'flow of funds' account. This will enable us to check their consistency. Let us divide the economy into two sets of agents, labelled the *household sector* and the *state sector.* The household sector includes individuals, families and communes, while the state sector comprises all economic units outside of the 'household'. We assume there is no private property in the means of production, so there is no separate corporate or financial sector to take into account. Our procedure will be to determine exhaustively the sources and uses of funds for each of the sectors.

Starting with the household sector, the basic source of funds is the issue of labour tokens in exchange for work performed currently, Current Labour Tokens. In addition, as mentioned above, we have an issue (transfer) of labour tokens to non-producers, which we will denote by Transfers. These funds can be used by the household sector in three ways. They may be paid to the state in the form of tax; they may be spent on consumer goods (Consumption); or they may flow into the net saving of this sector (Net Savings). If this reckoning of sources and uses is comprehensive the two totals must be equal, hence

Current Labour Tokens + Transfers = Tax + Consumption
+ Net Savings (5)

Turning to the state sector, its basic source of funds is tax revenue. In addition, in its capacity as 'financial institution' (of which more below), the state sector will collect the Net Saving of the household sector. The state sector uses its funds for making transfers of labour tokens to non-producers (Transfers), for social provision (Social), accumulation (Accumulation), and lending to other economies (Trade). Again, if these sources and uses are comprehensive we have

Tax + Net Savings = Transfers + Social + Accumulation + Trade (6)

Equations (5) and (6) can be reorganised in various ways. One simple change is to consolidate taxation and transfers. Let us define Net Tax as taxation minus transfers of labour tokens (Tax-Transfers). This is the net amount of labour-token 'revenue' available to the state for 'financing' activities other than consumption. With this modification, we can rewrite (5) and (6) as follows:

Current Labour Tokens – Net Tax = Consumption + Net Savings (5')

Net Tax + Net Savings = Social + Accumulation + Trade (6')

Adding two equations yields a third equation. If we add (5') and (6'), Net Tax and Net Savings cancel out and we are left with

Current Labour Tokens = Consumption + Social + Accumulation
+ Trade (7)

But since Current Labour Tokens equals Net Value Product we have in effect arrived at equation (4) again, hence demonstrating the consistency of our labour-time accounts.

We have found it useful to borrow the terminology of capitalist monetary accounting in the above demonstration ('revenue', 'financing', 'funds' and so on). But to get a proper understanding of the macroeconomics of a planned economy we have to look behind this language. In this system, labour tokens are used purely for the acquisition of consumer goods by the household sector. The state sector issues labour tokens in direct exchange for labour performed in the national economy (*i.e.* outside the 'household'), but does not need them to acquire goods, essentially because the state is presumed to own all goods other than those it sells to consumers. Suppose a hospital is built: the state pays all the labour involved at a rate of one labour token per hour, but does not 'in addition' have to pay anything for materials, or for the completed building. The state can never run short of 'money' (there is no money in the system). And it can never really run short of labour tokens either, since these are simply accounting entries created in the name of the workers (or possibly in the name of the commune of which the workers are members—see chapter 12).

There is, however, a real issue of macroeconomic balance. If sufficient consumer goods are to be available to meet the demand forthcoming, without an inflationary depreciation of the labour token, the state must ensure that it claws back (in effect, cancels out) the right proportion of the tokens it issues to the workers in the first instance. For example, suppose the overall macroeconomic plan calls for 55 per cent of the Net Value Product to be made available in the form of consumer goods. Also suppose, for simplicity, that the consumers do not choose to save any of their income. In that case the state must 'cancel out', via net taxation, 45 per cent of the basic issue of labour tokens. If net taxation falls short of this, the flow of labour tokens into consumer spending will exceed the quantity of social labour devoted to the production of consumer goods. The result will be 'labour token inflation' (or shortages and queues if prices are held steady). If net taxation is excessive, on the other hand, the flow of labour tokens into consumer spending will fall short of the labour-value of consumer goods produced, causing either labour token deflation or the piling up of surplus goods.

The above example relied on the simplifying assumption that consumers do not carry out any saving. Clearly, if some saving does take place then the requirement for a balanced tax policy becomes more complex. The next section deals with the issues of saving and borrowing on the part of the household sector, after which we return to examine some of the details of tax policy.

Household saving and credit

Why do people save? For some, saving, like virtue, may be its own reward, but the economists demand that people have rational motives for their actions and present us with a hierarchy of motives for saving.

At the lowest level there is saving for consumer goods. Here we have the thrift of the poor and lower middle classes who put aside money for that big purchase: the car, the bicycle or the holiday. Those with the money pay for such things out of current income. Then there are those who look beyond consumption to save for when they will no longer be able to work. The most exemplary of savers are those who think not of themselves but of those yet to come, and put money into trust funds to provide their offspring with private education or leave bequests to their heirs.

Beyond this nice social and temporal hierarchy, are those who like Pharaoh save against lean times to come: unemployment, serious illness, early death of the 'breadwinner'. On the other hand, some save *faute de mieux*, where current consumption is simply regarded as adequate without exhausting income or there are no goods which tempt the consumer to additional spending. This category speaks either of comfortable bourgeois prosperity or conversely of consumers in Eastern Europe and the USSR where desired consumer goods are not available, resulting in 'forced saving'.

Socialism is likely to weaken some of these reasons for personal saving. For example, the upgrading of free public education (even if private education is not proscribed) and a reduction in income differentials would weaken both the desire for, and the ability to sustain, educational trusts. An adequate state pension would reduce the necessity for private saving. If you do not fear penury in your later years why not spend your money now when you can enjoy it? You may never live to see retirement.

With full employment and steady economic growth the need to provide against loss of income through unemployment goes away. If you are confident of your children's future, and if there is anyway no chance of them living off property income, you are less likely to save in order to leave them a bequest.

Now let us consider briefly the main reasons for personal credit under present conditions. As regards short- to medium-term credit, this is mainly geared to shifting forward in time purchase of durable goods for which consumers would otherwise have to save—particularly for young people who expect their incomes to rise in future. On the other hand, the main reason for long-term personal credit is clearly to finance the purchase of houses.

These reasons are likely to persist under socialism, although there is undoubtedly an element of 'loan-pushing' relating to consumer credit under present circumstances, with individuals being encouraged to take up unserviceable debt positions. This would be stopped. Also, the existence and scale of saving for house purchase depend on the forms of housing tenure available, and a well-run state rental sector would reduce the incentive for house ownership.

Despite the fact that socialism is likely to reduce some of the motivations for personal saving and credit, these phenomena are unlikely to disappear completely. The basic reason for such saving and credit is people's desire to plan the time profile of their *purchases* relatively independently of the time profile of their *incomes*. From the individual point of view, saving represents consumption deferred while credit permits consumption to be brought forward.

But there is an important distinction here between what is feasible for the individual and what is feasible for society. In a pre-market society saving is simple to understand. Grain is hoarded ready to be consumed in time of hardship. Pharaonic Egypt or Maoist China could save in a very physical sense. When Mao advised the Chinese to 'dig tunnels deep, store grain, prepare against war or natural disaster', he was talking about deferred consumption quite literally. In Aesop's fable the wise ant saves up grain against the coming of winter while the cricket eats, sings and makes merry.

In modern society individual savers may still have this simple view of their thrift; money has replaced grain, but it is still 'put aside for a rainy day'. Insurance companies use umbrellas as their emblems. But there is a paradox in the hoarding of money that does not arise with grain, a paradox that the ancients recognised in the parable of Midas. You can't eat gold, or money. It is no use saving up money unless there is something to buy with it. The individual who hoarded gold would probably survive a famine, for in any famine the price of grain goes up, and only those with ample cash can eat. But society as a whole is not fed by the cash savings of hoarders. Only real stocks of grain prevent starvation, so in a famine the rich get what little there is and the poor die.

Those who save in banks are even further removed from 'natural thrift' than the peasant with his trove of gold Napoleons. In times of war, natural or economic disaster they are likely to see their savings vanish in hyperinflation or bank crashes. When the destruction of actual combat, or the dislocation of war reparations, deprives an economy of marketable goods, this real shortage reflects itself in the depreciation of the currency; those who end up clutching bundles of depreciated banknotes in the aftermath of military defeat learn Midas's lesson the hard way.

More generally, the savers of today can only realise their wealth tomorrow out of tomorrow's income. Somebody saving for retirement thirty years hence may think that he is deferring consumption, but would not be pleased to have to live off 30-year-old loaves in his old age. In practice there are no longer any goods whose consumption is deferred. Instead savers acquire a legal title that, granted the survival of the financial system, allows them to claim part of the future product of society. Retired people are actually supported not by their savings, but by the work of the younger members of society. The material burden of an ageing population is not avoided by the mechanisms of life insurance or fully funded pension plans. The young will still be the only support for the old; the shift from filial piety to mutual funds did not alter this reality, which will remain whatever the social system.

In this respect savings are a contract with the future—a strange contract in which one party, the one who has to provide the final goods, may not yet have been born. And such a contract with the future is an uncertain thing. The younger generation may renege on it. They may pursue inflationary wage increases that threaten retirees on fixed incomes. They may start a revolution and ruin the stock market.

Nonetheless, in the context of a planned economy, there is a sense in which today's savers may be able to contribute to the flow of real income tomorrow. By saving today, people relinquish a part of their current command over output. They thus 'free up' resources which would otherwise be required to produce consumer goods. In a capitalist economy there is a considerable danger that the resources thus released will just lie idle. When a consumer decides to save part of his or her monetary income, this act of 'non-consumption' does not of itself transmit to firms a message that certain consumer goods will be wanted in certain quantities at a definite future date. At best, the increase in saving may convey, via a fall in interest rates, the general message that production geared towards future sales is now more profitable. But Keynes argued that even this channel is highly unreliable (see Keynes, 1936, chapter 16, or for a good recent discussion of the point Axel Leijonhufvud, 1981). So the result of an increase in saving may be to depress the aggregate demand for goods, causing a recession.

In a planned economy, on the other hand, there is no reason why the resources released by saving should not be put to work building means of production, and in that case they will enhance the productivity of labour in future. In the economy we envisage, the minimum overall rate of accumulation of means of production will be decided democratically. One of the inputs into the accumulation decision would be demographic; faced with the prospect of an increase in the proportion of retirees in the population, the rate of accumulation should be raised, other things being equal, so as to raise labour productivity sufficiently to meet the future demand on the output of productive workers. This must obviously be at the expense of the current level of consumption. But given this basic collective decision, there may still be a case for allowing individual preferences to influence, at the margin, the breakdown between consumption and accumulation. What mechanisms will permit reasonable latitude for personal choice, while respecting the constraints of the overall plan? Here are some suggestions.

1. Current labour tokens may be freely exchanged for some kind of *retirement asset* (e.g. one which pays out an annuity starting at a specified future date or contingency). Such transactions would be conducted through a unified state-run 'financial system' so that their aggregate volume can be monitored by the planning agency.

   As we have argued above, the real counterpart to this saving is the release of current labour from the production of consumer goods, and the appropriate response is for the planners to allocate the 'freed' current labour to net accumulation of means of production (over and above the minimum rate of accumulation decided socially). This will then permit a higher output of consumer goods in future. There is clearly no guarantee that the planners will use the labour-time 'freed' by saving to gear up production of precisely those articles that the savers will, at some future date, prefer to consume. This depends on the effectiveness of the strategic planning process, and perfect foresight can hardly be expected of any economic system. Nonetheless, the planners will be able to take central account of the flow into savings, and to ensure that the labour-time thus released is used productively.

2. To permit a shorter-term flexibility, current labour tokens might also be exchangeable for *consumer saving deposits*, from which labour tokens may be withdrawn at a later date in order to purchase various consumer durables, vacations etc. If the inflow into such deposits is greater than the outflow per period, the balance may used to 'finance' consumer credit. If desired, the terms of such credits, in particular their rate of repayment, could be used to equalise the demand for such credit with the supply forthcoming from the net acquisition of saving deposits. In that case the net result would simply be a re-shuffling of consumption among individuals, with no impact on the general macroeconomic balance of the economy.

3. Aside from the above recognised forms of saving, individuals are not able simply to hoard labour tokens. Hoarding, which would disrupt the labour allocation plan, is avoided by having the labour tokens expire after a specified date, much as the banks refuse to honour personal cheques after a specified period in the current system.

These points on saving and credit can be brought into the context of our flow of funds accounting, developed in the first section of this chapter. There we noted that net household saving (Net Savings) appeared as a *use of funds* on the part of the household sector, and as a *source of funds* to the state. We can now unpack the details of net saving. Gross saving is the sum of the household sector's gross acquisition of retirement assets (Retirement Asset Acquisition) and its gross acquisition of consumer saving deposits (Saving Deposit Acquisition). To derive net saving, we must subtract the disbursements which households receive from their retirement assets (Retirement Asset Disbursement), the withdrawals they make from their consumer saving deposits (Withdrawals), and the net amount of new consumer credits extended (New Credit). In equation form we have

Net Saving = Retirement Asset Acquisition
      + Saving Deposit Acquisition
        − Retirement Asset Disbursement
        − Withdrawals
        − New Credit.

Or, bracketing together the terms dealing with retirement assets and the terms dealing with consumer deposits and credits:

Net Saving = (Retirement Asset Acquisition
        − Retirement Asset Disbursement)
      + (Saving Deposit Acquisition
        − Withdrawals
        − New Credit).

Focussing on consumer saving—other than retirement assets—and credit, note that the quantity (Saving Deposit Acquisition − Withdrawals − New Credit) functions as a net source of funds for the state. This term represents the net inflow of funds into the consumer saving/credit system. It was suggested above that this flow might be deliberately set to zero, by varying the terms of consumer credit so that the demand for such credit just exhausts the net inflow of deposits. Whether this policy makes good sense probably depends on the terms which are required to achieve such balance.

Consider a situation in which the personal sector shows a strong tendency to save and a relatively weak tendency to take up consumer credit. In that case the balancing referred to above might require 'giveaway' terms for consumer credit—possibly even a negative interest rate. The use of all of the net deposit inflow for this purpose then looks like a less than optimal policy: part of that flow could be treated instead as a 'source of funds' for accumulation, where it could presumably earn a higher social rate of return.

The potential problem with this solution is that while consumer saving deposits are quite liquid, and short- or medium-term consumer credits are fairly quickly self-liquidating, the means of production which might be constructed using these funds will not be 'liquid'.[1] Faced with an unanticipated outflow of deposits from the system before the accumulation projects 'mature', the state could then be obliged to create excess labour tokens, raising the possibility of labour-token inflation which would undermine the system of calculation we are proposing.

This is essentially the problem diagnosed by Keynes, where savers wish to save in the form of liquid assets, while their funds are used to acquire illiquid capital goods. But the problem is solvable in a state-monopoly financial system: the state is in a position to tell savers that they cannot have their cake and eat it. If the consumer saving deposit/credit system is tending to run a surplus the state can announce that the liquidity of these deposits is conditional, and potentially subject to rationing, rather than creating an inflationary excess of labour tokens if a big demand for the liquidation of deposits should occur.

Similar issues arise if the consumer saving/credit system tends to run a deficit, even when the terms of consumer credit are made very stringent. Is there then a case for using 'funds' from other sources (eg. a surplus on the retirement asset account) to 'finance' extra consumer credit? Or should consumer credit be rationed?

A current surplus on the retirement asset account indicates the accumulation of claims to future output on the part of future retirees, and the safest way of ensuring that such claims can be met is to deploy the surplus in accumulation of means of production. This argues for a strict separation between the retirement asset account and consumer credit. On the other hand, to the extent that consumers take out current credit on stringent terms (which are nonetheless assessed as realistic for the borrower—this would obviously be a condition for the granting of such credits) they are committing themselves to diminishing their own claims to future output, relative to their future receipts of labour tokens. But this reduction should then 'accommodate' the claims of the retirees. The best policy here might be cautious flexibility: while not operating a complete separation of accounts, rationing could be used to avoid excessive deficits (or surpluses) on the saving deposit/consumer credit account.

Interest on savings?
One question which arises from the above is whether interest should be paid on the savings of the personal sector. Let us first examine the consequences of a zero 'nominal' interest rate on such savings, so that people are able to withdraw from the system over time exactly the cumulated sum of the labour tokens which they have previously contributed. Note that as the productivity of labour grows over time, and the labour content of specific goods falls, labour tokens will in effect become 'worth more': there is a form of implicit interest on labour-token savings. It is reasonable that people should be able to collect this 'interest' on their long-term saving, since their non-consumption makes possible an accelerated accumulation of means of production which in turn helps to bring about increased labour productivity, but there is no call for any additional payment.[2]

In the classical, full-employment model of capitalism the function of interest on savings is to induce a sufficient supply of saving in order to finance investment, but in the system we envisage investment is socialised and the basic source of 'funding' for accumulation is taxation. To the extent that the retirement and deposit/credit accounts run a current surplus, personal saving may make some contribution to the 'financing' of accumulation, but this is secondary. There is no need to encourage individual saving, since the basic social rate of 'saving' (that is, non-consumption) is decided democratically when the plan for accumulation and taxation is drawn up.

Tax policy
Regardless of the precise arrangements for dealing with household saving, tax policy will play the important role of balancing the macro plan. In what form or forms should the state tax the earners of labour tokens? In the Soviet-type economies, the bulk of tax revenue was traditionally raised through the 'turnover tax'. With this tax, the state drives a wedge between the price charged to the purchaser of a good and the price credited to the seller, with the difference flowing to the state treasury. Such a tax is inconsistent with the system we propose, as it would involve systematically pricing consumer goods at values greater than their true labour content. As implied above, we favour an income tax; we shall also suggest

that the state appropriates differential ground rent as a supplementary tax.

What should a socialist income tax look like? Socialists and social democrats in the capitalist economies have typically supported a progressive income tax (one in which those with larger incomes pay a higher percentage tax rate), on the grounds that the well-off can afford to bear a larger share of the tax burden. In effect, a progressive income tax is seen as a way of reducing the inequality of pre-tax incomes under capitalism (although whether the tax systems of real capitalist economies have achieved this objective is debatable). But if the distribution of personal incomes is basically egalitarian in the first place, as we have proposed, the case for a progressive tax falls. The fairest system is probably a flat tax, so many labour tokens per month or year per earner.

A flat labour-token tax carries the following message: each able-bodied person of working age is obliged to perform a basic amount of work for the commonwealth. In exchange for this labour contribution, people are supplied with their basic collective needs. If people want an additional, disposable income with which to acquire consumer goods, they will have to work more than this basic minimum. We envisage maximum flexibility over hours of work, so that the individual can choose his or her working time, and if a worker chooses to work long hours, she can enjoy the benefits of this without paying any extra income tax.

A flat tax also carries the advantage of relatively high predictability of tax revenue. The revenue from a proportional income tax depends on how much people earn (*i.e.*, in this system, how much they choose to work), but the revenue from a flat tax depends only on the number of workers. This predictability will be helpful in ensuring that the plan for social provision and accumulation is met. Suppose that the planners have allocated X million hours of social labour time to uses other than personal consumption: the flat tax can then be set at a level which will produce $X - Z$ million labour tokens in revenue, where Z million tokens is the forecast level of net household saving.[3]

It is worth contrasting this with the proposal of the Green Party in Britain, that all citizens should be paid a guaranteed social income whether they work or not. This social income would presumably be met out of general taxation, including an income tax. In a sense this is the mirror image of our proposal, since a flat tax such as we propose can be considered as a negative social wage. The Greens' proposal is quite feasible, and has the great merit over the present system of means-tested benefits that it removes the notorious 'poverty trap'.[4] Nonetheless, we have two criticisms of the guaranteed social income proposal. First, it seems to imply an acceptance that unemployment is inevitable. Given that there must be unemployment, the Greens wish to deal with it in the most humane way. We do not accept this. We contend that an economy can be run at full employment. The combination of egalitarian incomes, full employment and a flat tax removes the poverty trap, along with the disincentive to work, more effectively than the Greens' scheme. For the second criticism is that the guaranteed income system needs a high rate of income tax to fund it, with implicit disincentive effects. We envisage a zero marginal rate of income tax, in other words a flat poll tax on those in employment. Combined with flexible working hours, this allows individuals to decide for themselves when the benefit flowing from an extra hour's work balances the effort it entails. In a full-employment economy the Greens' scheme, which effectively allows people to choose subsidised idleness, is likely to be resented by the working majority who would have to support the idle.

Ground rent

We refer elsewhere to the system of property relations required to support our conception of the socialist economy (see chapter 14). This involves state ownership of land. While we do not rule out the private ownership of part of the housing stock, the state should retain ownership of the land on which the houses stand. Home owners should be liable for a ground rent based upon the current rentable value of the land used for their house. Under these circumstances somebody who buys a house is just buying the fabric of the building, and the price paid for a house of similar size and standard of repair in London should be the same as that in, say, Bradford. Over and above the price, the occupier pays a rent or land tax to the state, reflecting the difference in convenience or amenity of the house they are using. Such rents could make a significant contribution to the finances of the state.[5]

If these rents are to perform the macroeconomic function assigned to taxation within the system discussed above, they clearly have to be assessed in labour tokens. Payment of labour-token rents then constitutes one exception to the general principle that these tokens buy only the products of labour, priced according to their labour content.

Excise tax

A final point on taxation may be worth mentioning. We have said that consumer goods should in general be priced in labour-tokens according to their labour content. But there may be an argument for exceptions to be made in certain cases. In capitalist economies, excise taxes are levied on goods the consumption of which the state wishes to limit for some reason, generally because 'excessive' consumption of these articles is reckoned to have undesirable social consequences (alcohol, tobacco, etc.). Short of proscribing such goods, the socialist state may wish to pursue a similar policy. Note that this would *not* be a general sales tax or VAT, but a specific charge on selected consumer goods.

Taxation and Accumulation

In western economies accumulation of new means of production is split between the private sector and the public sector. Private sector accumulation is the result of the autonomous decisions of companies and is mainly financed out of retained profits, but with some element of the recirculation of savings into accumulation via the financial institutions. Public sector accumulation has traditionally been financed by borrowing.

In socialist economies on the Soviet pattern, the situation was the reverse. Public sector accumulation was financed mainly through the turnover tax on state enterprises, with recirculated savings playing a secondary role. As stated earlier, we also envisage that taxes would be the major source of funds for accumulation but with the proviso that all tax levels must flow from democratic votes.

A key criticism of Soviet socialism was the fact that decisions about the rate of growth, and thus the rate of accumulation, were taken by a political elite. This lent to socialist accumulation a partially alienated character. To avoid this, alternative proposals regarding the percentage of national income to be devoted to accumulation should be submitted to plebiscite. If it is agreed that investment should total 15 percent of GNP, the state would then be entitled to levy taxes to finance this. Given that there are other sources of funds for accumulation—*i.e.,* savings and rent—the full costs of accumulation would not be born in taxes, but the power to vary taxes would provide the degree of freedom necessary to balance the social budget.

Notes to Chapter 7
1. Such deposits might be governed by regulations similar to those on existing savings accounts, with a formal right on the part of the state to make depositors wait for their funds, which nonetheless could be waived under normal conditions.
2. It is more debatable whether even this implicit interest should be available on short-term savings in consumer deposits. The setting aside of tokens in such deposits will not, under the scheme suggested above, make more than a marginal contribution to accumulation. To remove the implicit interest, labour tokens in savings deposits would have to be devalued at a rate equal to the growth rate of

labour productivity. But insofar as the acquisition of these deposits makes funds available for consumer credit, for which consumers are willing to pay interest, there may be a case for the non-devaluation of labour tokens in saving deposits.

3. This illustration assumes for simplicity that the flat tax on labour-token earners is the only tax. Actually, we argue that the state should exploit a further source of revenue, ground rent, as discussed below.

4. With means-tested welfare benefits, people on low incomes face very high effective marginal tax rates. If you take a job and start earning, you become liable for national insurance and income tax, and also lose all or part of your welfare benefits. This makes it very difficult to raise your effective income and acts as a disincentive to work.

5. For a fuller discussion of rent in a socialist economy, including the payment of rent in agriculture, see chapter 14.

CHAPTER 8

The Marketing of Consumer Goods

A criticism commonly levelled at the Soviet-type economies—and not only by their Western detractors—is that they were unresponsive to consumer demand. It is therefore important to our general argument to demonstrate that a planned economy can be responsive to the changing pattern of consumer preferences—that the shortages, queues and surpluses of unwanted goods of which we hear so much are not an inherent feature of socialist planning. This chapter develops our concept of a socialist market in consumer goods.

One way into this issue is to return to the general account of planning offered in chapter 4. We distinguished three levels of planning: macroeconomic, strategic and detail. Within the parameters of the macro and strategic industrial plans, detail planning is concerned with selecting the precise target pattern of final output, and ensuring that sufficient resources are available to meet that target. But how are the final output targets for consumer goods to be determined? What sort of mechanism is needed for modifying these targets in the light of feedback from consumers?

The basic principle of our proposed scheme can be stated quite simply. All consumer goods are *marked* with their labour values, *i.e.* the total amount of social labour which is required to produce them, both directly and indirectly. (The practical calculation of these labour values was discussed in chapter 3.) But aside from this, the actual *prices* (in labour tokens) of consumer goods will be set, as far as possible, at market-clearing levels. Suppose a particular item requires 10 hours of labour to produce. It will then be marked with a labour value of 10 hours, but if an excess demand for the item emerges when it is priced at 10 labour tokens, the price will be raised so as to (approximately) eliminate the excess demand. Suppose this price happens to be 12 labour tokens. This product then has a ratio of market-clearing price to labour-value of 12/10, or 1.20. The planners record this ratio for each consumer good. We would expect the ratio to vary from product to product, sometimes around 1.0, sometimes above (if the product is in strong demand), and sometimes below (if the product is relatively unpopular). The planners then follow this rule: Increase the target output of goods with a ratio in excess of 1.0, and reduce the target for goods with a ratio less than 1.0.

The point is that these ratios provide a measure of the effectiveness of social labour in meeting consumers' needs (production of 'use-value', in Marx's terminology) across the different industries. If a product has a ratio of market-clearing price to labour-value above 1.0, this indicates that people are willing to spend more labour tokens on the item (*i.e.* work more hours to acquire it) than the labour time required to produce it. But this in turn indicates that the labour devoted to producing this product is of above-average 'social effectiveness'. Conversely, if the market-clearing price falls below the labour-value, that tells us that consumers do not 'value' the product at its full labour content: labour devoted to this good is of below-average effectiveness. Parity, or a ratio of 1.0, is an equilibrium condition: in this case consumers 'value' the product, in terms of their own labour time, at just what it costs society to produce it.

This is the general idea of our 'marketing algorithm'; the rest of this chapter will expand on the idea in various ways. First, we consider the question of whether the establishment of market-clearing prices is always desirable. Second, we show the relationship between the marketing algorithm and the macroeconomic planning discussed in the previous chapter, and in the process give a more formal account of the algorithm. Third, we examine the relationship between our proposal and the profit mechanism under capitalism. Finally, we fend off a criticism made by Alec Nove of the idea that labour values can play a useful role in socialist planning.

Market-clearing prices

Market-clearing prices are prices which balance the supply of goods (previously decided upon when the plan is formulated) and the demand. By definition, these prices avoid manifest shortages and surpluses. The appearance of a shortage (excess demand) will result in a rise in price which will cause consumers to reduce their consumption of the good in question. The available supply will then go to those who are willing to pay the most. The appearance of a surplus will result in a fall in price, encouraging consumers to increase their demands for the item.

When a particular good is in short supply relative to consumer demand, an alternative to raising the price is rationing. This can be done formally (with ration books, as during wartime) or informally, simply by letting queues or waiting lists emerge, in which case the goods go to those who are willing to get in line early and wait. Our marketing algorithm relies upon setting prices at market-clearing levels in each period, and then using the gap between these prices and labour content as a signal for increasing or reducing production in the next period. But are there cases in which rationing is a fairer way of dealing with a shortage? And on a related point, our algorithm presupposes that the equilibrium price of a good ought to equal its cost of production, as measured by its labour value. But are there cases where goods ought to be subsidised, *i.e.* where the product should be made available to consumers, even in the long run, at a price below its cost of production?

The answer here depends on the distribution of income in society. Our views on the appropriateness of various pricing and rationing policies are shown in Table 8.1. Rationing is the best way of ensuring that scarce goods are fairly distributed if incomes are unequal, since it prevents the rich cornering the market. Take the case of food for example: formal rationing will ensure that everyone can get enough to survive. If there is ample food to go round but poverty prevents some people from being able to feed themselves adequately, then some kind of food subsidy is a rational policy, though it is not clear that holding the price below cost is the best way to proceed: the issue of food tokens to those most in need is probably more effective. If food subsidies in the form of reduced prices are attempted when food is scarce, the available supply will disappear from the shops and queues will form whenever new supplies come in. This is true irrespective of whether incomes are equal or unequal. The policy of the EC, which artificially raises the price of food to benefit private farmers, and of the USSR, which subsidised foods in scarce supply, are both unsound. (In both cases strong political pressure inhibits changes.)

The basic point is that *if incomes are equal*, the distribution that would obtain at market prices is likely to be fair, and there is no justification for subsidies. We can envisage extraordinary cases

Table 8.1:
Cases for rationing

Supply of Good	Income Distribution	Best Policy
Scarce	Unequal	Rationing
Plentiful	Unequal	Subsidies
Scarce	Equal	Market Prices
Plentiful	Equal	Market Prices

where formal rationing might be desirable, in order to ensure access to necessities under conditions of severe but temporary disruption of supply. But in general we see the establishment of market-clearing prices as the best policy in a socialist commonwealth with a basically egalitarian income distribution.

Consumer goods and the macro plan

In the last chapter we discussed the issues arising in connection with the distribution of social labour between different end-uses. In that context we denoted the total social labour devoted to the production of consumer goods by Consumption. Let us now denote the total *expenditure* of labour tokens on consumer goods by Token Consumption. The macro plan aims at holding Token Consumption and Consumption as close to equality as possible. This involves jointly (a) setting the level of taxation and (b) forecasting the saving behaviour of households. The planners do have some means of influencing net household saving, but some element of forecasting is likely to remain, and this means that exact equality of Token Consumption and Consumption is unlikely to be achieved. If net saving falls below the forecast, then Token Consumption will exceed the pre-determined level of Consumption. In that case the planners may respond in the next period by raising taxation, encouraging more net saving in one way or another, or increasing the allocation of social labour to consumer goods. Or, if the planners reckon that the sub-forecast saving was a temporary 'blip', they may choose not to respond. Exactly parallel reasoning applies in the case where saving is above the forecast level.

This means that although equality of Token Consumption and Consumption is a target, which should be realised 'on average' over time, the precise ratio of Token Consumption to Consumption is liable to fluctuate somewhat around 1.0 from period to period. Note that this ratio can be thought of as an aggregate price level of sorts: it represents the average number of labour tokens required to purchase the product of an hour's social labour, in the market for consumer goods. Now the marketing algorithm discussed above uses as an indicator for the reallocation of resources the ratio of market-clearing price to labour value for each consumer good. In the first presentation of the idea we assumed that the average of this ratio, across all consumer industries, should be 1.0. We can now see that this is a slight over-simplification. If we form a weighted average price-to-labour-content ratio across all goods during one period—weighting each commodity by the proportion of the total Consumption which the commodity accounts for—this average will identically equal the macroeconomic ratio of Token Consumption to Consumption, which, as we have just seen, may diverge from 1.0 to some extent.

In the light of this macro consideration, we can reformulate the consumer goods marketing algorithm more precisely as follows:

1. The central marketing authority (CMA) places orders with the producers of consumer goods of various types, subject to the constraint that the orders have a total labour content of Consumption$_t$, the overall consumption allowance for period t.

2. The CMA receives the output it ordered and sells it to consumers at market-clearing prices.

3. The ratio of market-clearing price to labour content is calculated for each product, and the total expenditure of labour tokens, Token Consumption, is recorded. Then for each product the following decision rule is applied:

   If price / value > Token Consumption/Consumption then increase orders for good.

   If price / value = Token Consumption/Consumption then maintain orders for good.

   If price / value < Token Consumption/Consumption then reduce orders for good.

   Increased resources will therefore be devoted to lines of production where the price/value ratio is above average, while resources will be withdrawn from the production of goods having a below-average price-to-value ratio.

4. Go back to step number 1.

Some of the steps in this algorithm stand in need of elaboration. Step 2 requires that the marketing authority sets market-clearing prices for all consumer goods. This is easier said than done. It is easy enough to specify a rule for moving *towards* the market-clearing price: raise the price if there is an excess demand for the commodity; lower the price in case of an excess supply. But how big a change should be made? Absent the economists' theoretical fiction of the 'Walrasian auctioneer', it is not possible directly to determine the set of prices which will clear all consumer goods markets. Strictly, we should say that prices are set at *approximately* market-clearing levels. The planners must work by trial and error, informed by the results of statistical analysis of demand elasticities, much as capitalist firms with market-power (and hence able to set the price for their own output) do at present. Further, it is not clear that movement to 'perfect' market-clearing prices (which exactly balance the flow demand with current production) would be desirable, even if it were possible. This might give rise to excessive price fluctuations. For any storable commodity, changes in inventories provide a means of damping market price fluctuations. Excess demand can be met in part by a rundown of inventory, rather than putting all of the adjustment onto the price.

Some more detail on step 3 of the algorithm may also be useful. This step calls on the planners to increase or reduce production of the different consumer goods depending on whether they show a price-to-value ratio higher or lower than the social average. The objective here is to produce just enough of each commodity so that its market-clearing price equals its labour value (a ratio of 1.0). Just as with finding market-clearing prices each period, this must be an (informed) trial and error exercise. Finding the output level which will make the market price assume some specific level is the inverse of the problem of finding the price which will clear the market given some pre-determined level of supply. The problem can be solved directly only if one knows the demand equations for all goods in exact detail, including the spillover effects whereby change in the price of any one commodity affects the demand for others. A second complication is that the labour value itself may be a moving target: altering the scale of output of a given product may alter its labour content per unit. If economies of scale predominate, the labour value of a commodity will tend to fall as output of that commodity is increased; if diminishing returns predominate, labour values will increase with increased output. For these reasons, we should think of the consumer goods marketing algorithm as always moving *towards* the price = value condition, rather than achieving a static state with prices equal to values throughout.

In this context one special feature of the algorithm deserves attention. The fact that each good is marked with both a labour value and a market price may induce some degree of stabilising speculation, limiting the fluctuations of market prices. The point is that the current labour value of a commodity gives some guide to its probable long-run price. Suppose that a particular good is currently trading at a price substantially above its labour value. Seeing this, consumers may decide to postpone consumption of the item, in the anticipation of a lower price in future. Conversely, if a product is selling for much less than its labour value, that will suggest to consumers that it is a temporary bargain, which may increase the current demand. Such speculative shifts in demand will tend to limit the divergence of market prices from values, by damping the demand for items with above-value prices and stimulating the demand for items with below-value prices.

Comparison with capitalist markets

How does our proposed marketing algorithm relate to the economic mechanism of a capitalist market system? There are similarities as well as important differences. In a capitalist economy, the production levels of marketable goods are adjusted over time in response to differential *profitability*, with additional resources flowing into industries showing above-average profits, while resources are withdrawn from the production of goods showing below-average profit. Our ratio of market price to labour value obviously performs a somewhat similar role to profitability. In each case a comparison is made between what consumers are willing to pay for each commodity and its cost of production (measured in some way or other).

In a standard argument in favour of the capitalist market system, market prices are said to register the 'votes' of consumers for the various goods available. Price will be high (relative to production cost) where an item is highly valued by consumers, and the resulting high profitability will lead to an expansion in the production of those items which are most highly valued. The obvious objection to this argument under capitalism concerns the inequality of consumers' incomes. The rich have many times the 'votes' of low-income consumers and hence the structure of production will be skewed towards satisfying the demands of the former (however frivolous), while the real needs of the poor will go unmet if they fail to register in the form of monetary demand. But if the distribution of income is basically egalitarian this objection falls and the voting analogy has some force.

Aside from the difference in the distribution of consumers' incomes, how does our consumer market differ from the capitalist system? Let us focus on the contrast between our 'success indicator'—the ratio of market price to labour value—and the capitalist success indicator of profitability. The profit on the production of a commodity under capitalism is the difference between its market price and its (monetary) cost of production. This 'cost of production' is in turn formed by multiplying the market price of each input to the production process by the quantity of that input required per unit of output. That is, the calculation of production cost in the capitalist sense presupposes markets in the inputs to production ('factor markets' in the jargon). It is on these markets that the monetary prices of labour, materials, machines and so on are formed.

In the planned economy we envisage, there are no 'factor markets' of this type. Were markets to exist for labour and means of production, then what you would have would be a system of generalised commodity production structurally indistinguishable from capitalism. There is a market in consumer goods, the 'signals' from which are used to guide the reallocation of resources among the various types of consumer goods. But once the pattern of final output of goods is decided, the allocation of inputs to support this pattern is computed centrally, and the required means of production and labour are allocated by the planning agency (see chapter 6). The individual enterprises are not subjects of right, capable of possessing, buying or selling means of production (for more on this point, see chapter 14). While the typical capitalist enterprise finds the prices of its inputs given by the terms on which its suppliers are willing to part with their goods, the socialist production project faces no such 'givens'. In the socialist economy, 'cost of production' has to be calculated socially, and (as we have already explained) we believe that the total direct plus indirect labour content ('labour value') is a reasonable measure of social cost.

Apart from its applicability in the absence of factor markets, the adjustment algorithm we propose has a distinct advantage from the socialist point of view. Profit, the 'success' indicator for capitalist enterprises, depends in part on the degree of exploitation of labour within the enterprise. For instance, if two enterprises are producing the same product and employing the same technology, higher profits will accrue to the enterprise which manages to pay lower wages or enforce a longer working day. Our proposed ratio of market price to labour-value, on the other hand, is not sensitive to the degree of exploitation within the enterprise. An enterprise can show a particularly 'successful' performance (high price-to-value ratio) only by (a) producing products which are attractive to consumers and for which consumers are willing to pay a premium (hence raising market price), or (b) using efficient production methods which depress the labour content of the product. Enterprises will not be 'rewarded' for paying below-average wages or imposing longer hours of labour.

Conclusion

The arguments presented in this chapter, while not worked out in full detail, support the point that a socialist planned economy need not be unresponsive to consumer demand. We have outlined a mechanism which is capable of adjusting the pattern of output of consumer goods in conformity with a changing pattern of demand. While this mechanism relies on a market of sorts, it is quite distinct from the capitalist mechanism. It depends neither on private property in the means of production, nor on the formation of market prices for the inputs to the production process.

Having established our basic points, let us consider Alec Nove's (1983) critique of the use of labour values in socialist planning. Nove, in company with many other economists, argues that whatever merits the marxian labour theory of value may have in the analysis of capitalism, it is irrelevant to the planning of a socialist system. Suppose that labour values provide an adequate measure of the social *cost* of production—even then, says Nove, they are misleading, since they totally fail to take account of the valuation of different commodities by consumers.

In the light of our discussion in this chapter, we can see that this objection is not so much false as misplaced. True, the fact that a particular commodity requires 3 or 300 hours of social labour for its production tells us nothing, by itself, about the usefulness or attractiveness of that commodity to consumers, or about the appropriate scale of production of that commodity. Simply, this objective, production-side information must be complemented with information relating to demand. If we know that, at the current scale of production, a given commodity has a labour content of three hours *while its market-clearing price is three labour-tokens,* that tells us that its scale of production is about right. If the market-clearing price is substantially above three labour tokens, that tells us that its scale of production is too small, and if the price is much less than three labour tokens then its scale of production is too large. The planners can then make suitable adjustments. Arbitrarily setting prices equal to labour values might well produce undesirable results,—as Marx and Engels pointed out in their critiques of nineteenth century suggestions to this effect[1]—but that is not the only possible use of labour values in a socialist planning context.

Note to Chapter 8
1. See in particular *The Poverty of Philosophy* (Marx, 1936). For further discussion of this point see Cottrell and Cockshott (1993a).

CHAPTER 9

Planning and Information

We are proposing a system of computerised planning which involves the simulation of the behaviour of the economy in great detail. To make this feasible the central computers must be supplied with copious amounts of technical information, for instance lists of the products being produced and regular updates on the technology used in each production process. Other computer systems will have to record the available stocks of each type of raw material and every model of machine so that these constraints can be fed into the planning process.

The problem of information has a social as well as a technical aspect. We need the right hardware and software, but we also need the right measures and incentives, so that it will be in people's interest to supply accurate information. In this chapter we examine both aspects of the issue. (Material relating to this topic can also be found in the last section of chapter 3, where we discuss the information-exchange involved in the calculation of labour values, and the last part of chapter 6, which outlines the cybernetic system established in Allende's Chile by Stafford Beer.)

Information and property

It is clear that a precondition for effective centralised planning would be a national telecommunications network able to support the transmission of digital information. Most developed capitalist countries already have this. (The networks in the erstwhile socialist countries are some way behind.) But just having the communications networks is not enough. Commercial secrecy has influenced the way data-communications systems have developed, and it would be quite impossible to gather the information required for production planning in a present-day capitalist country. The details of production techniques are available only to the managements of private firms. Although the telecommunications agencies in capitalist countries have laid the cable networks that would be needed for planning, and although the necessary production data are already held in the filestores of company computers, these computers are not set up to make the information accessible to anyone outside the company.

A major concern in Western countries is what is called Data Protection or Computer Security. Computer firms devote millions of pounds to researching and perfecting mechanisms for restricting access to computerised information. Data on a computer can be electronically labeled in such a way that only certain authorised people in the company hierarchy can get access to it. Users of the computer can be assigned different *privileges* which regulate their *access permissions* to computer files. This cult of secrecy is so ingrained and habitual that it is never questioned in the computer profession. Indeed one of the textbook examples in database design is to set up a system that will allow managers to find out the salaries of employees, but prohibit employees from finding out what their managers earn.

All this effort is necessary because information is treated as private property. It is a strange sort of property in that it can be stolen and remain where it is intact at the same time. Indeed it could be argued that information is not by nature suited to be property since it is so easily copied and is so difficult to protect. Nonetheless the computer industry has grown up around the notion of protecting and hiding information. To establish the free and open flow of information demanded by a rational planning system will require not only the legal abolition of commercial confidentiality, but also the redesign of most of the installed computer software currently in use.

Requirements of a statistical service
Let us consider what is needed in the way of a national statistical service for planning, and how it could be built by technically feasible means. (By technically feasible means, we do not mean items one could could go out and buy immediately, but technologies which could be implemented within the current state of the art.)

Product coding
Computers deal with symbols; they can only simulate the external world if the world can be given a symbolic representation. If we want to write a computer program that works out how resources are to be allocated to different production processes we will need some means of identifying these resources. When writing the program it may be convenient to follow the economic theorists and simply tag all the types of resources with index numbers from 1 to n, but if the program is to have any real world referent then these numbers must somehow be associated with real products. The

planning process will involve many computers that have to communicate information and instructions, and it would cause confusion if these machines used different identification numbers.

At present, each company has its own stock control code numbering system. The same product may be assigned three different and incompatible codes by the initial manufacturer, the wholesaler and the company that uses the product. The planning process would be greatly hampered by such a multiplicity of codes. This points to the need for a universal product coding system: each type of product would be assigned a specific ID number that would be used in all computerised exchanges of information.

The advantages of a standardised numbering system are so evident that there is strong pressure even within capitalism to have it adopted. In recent years there has been a growth in the use of bar codes to identify products. A bar code for a product type has most of the attributes required for computerised planning. It has a standard length (12 digits), it is machine-readable, and each code uniquely identifies a type of product. It has certain drawbacks, in that identical products from different companies are assigned different codes, but this is a matter of practice which can easily be altered.

Unified stock control

This leads on to the second requirement: a standardised system of stock control. It may be desirable to extend the barcode system with extra digits so that a given code would identify not only a precise type of product, but also its origin and/or location. This would allow a network of stock-control computers to keep track of the movements of each individual product through the economy. One of the theoretical presuppositions of our planning method is that resources can be switched between alternative uses, but this is possible only if the planning system knows exactly what resources are currently in use at each plant, and can issue unambiguous instructions as to which objects are to be reallocated.

Standardised message formats

The planning system presupposes the routine exchange of messages between different computers. Information would have to be exchanged concerning the movement of goods, the state of stocks, the best available production technologies etc. This requires that the techniques of information-exchange be standardised. The international telecommunications agency CCITT currently lays down standards for the exchange of documents and images by electronic means. One would need a comparable set of standards for the exchange of economic data.

Obtaining technical coefficients
It should be clear from the preceding chapters that effective planning depends upon having good data on production techniques. There are both technical and social obstacles to collecting these data. The technical problem concerns the sheer quantity of data that must be gathered; we shall deal with this point first. The social problem, arising from deliberate attempts to supply incorrect information, will be discussed in the next section.

Although it may seem an immense task to gather information about every production technique used in the economy, we should recognise that *this information is already being recorded.* It may be recorded formally in internal company plans or informally in the form of the purchase orders that a company makes. A company's purchases form an image of its technology. Since most firms are now computerised, their purchase orders are already recorded in machine-readable form. Production planning in larger firms is already done using computer-aided manufacturing techniques. Given appropriate standardisation, this information could be extracted for planning purposes.

Smaller firms do much of their planning using computer spreadsheets. At any one time a few standard spreadsheet programs dominate the market. One can envisage a situation where all production planning is done using a few packages that have as part of their specification the ability to transmit details of current technology to the planning network. The data that are captured in the process of elaborating the technology at the plant level would then be used to draw up the national plan.

Information: social problems
In the Soviet-type socialist economies there was a problem of enterprise managers systematically misrepresenting data in their statistical reports to the planning authorities. To the extent that enterprise managers wish for 'an easy life', there will be a temptation to underestimate the productivity of the technology currently in use. This corresponds to an overestimation of the technical input-output coefficients. If these overestimates are accepted at face value by the planning authorities, the enterprise will tend to be allocated more resources than it strictly needs to produce a given target output, giving the enterprise some 'slack' and making fulfillment of the plan somewhat easier. (This outcome may, of course, be seen as in the short term interest of the workers

employed in the enterprise too.) When it comes to the assessment of investment projects, on the other hand, enterprise managers may be interested in maximising their command over resources ('empire building'). In that case they will tend to prepare over-enthusiastic accounts of the benefits of further investment in their sphere of operations.

This kind of distortion should be minimised by using a single procedure for recording technical details about both current production and future investment. Suppose we have a system by which production engineers *register* possible technologies with the planning computers. They would give details of the inputs required and the predicted output. On the basis of a central evaluation of the different production technologies, the planning system would choose the intensity with which each technology was to be used. The production project could then be asked to begin manufacture using a particular registered technology. Since the proposer of a given technical process might later have to implement it, there would be an incentive to be as accurate as possible in stating its required inputs and expected outputs.

Information, performance measures and incentives
To take this issue further, a comparison with the situation in a capitalist economy may be instructive. The tendency noted above—for managers to seek an easy life by overestimating their current input requirements, while at the same time overstating the benefits of long-run expansion in their fiefdom—may well apply to the subdivisions of a large capitalist firm. To the extent that these divisions are integrated through internal corporate planning, rather than via the market, the same considerations apply as under socialist planning. But when it comes to the relations among independent capitalist firms, these tendencies are kept in check by the forces of competition (assuming that the market in question is in fact competitive).

From time to time, capitalist firms may well seek an easy life; but if they do, and if entry to their particular market is not too difficult, there will be an opportunity for more aggressive firms to come into the industry, and, by producing closer to the limits of the available technology, to undercut the existing firms. Then the original firms will be forced to produce more efficiently, on pain of loss of market share, reduced profitability, and ultimately extinction. With regard to over-ambitious investment plans on the other hand, the obvious check is that capitalist firms have to pay interest on the funds they borrow for investment purposes, so that it is suicidal to over-borrow. There is a strong incentive to attempt a realistic appraisal of the prospective profitability of investment projects. (Nonetheless, of course, serious investment errors do take place routinely in capitalist economies.)

Is it possible and desirable to emulate these types of check on the self-interested behaviour of enterprise managers (and perhaps workers too) in a socialist economy? Two issues emerge as we try to answer this question: how should the performance of enterprises be evaluated, and what kind of rewards and sanctions are appropriate?

Evaluating the performance of enterprises

On the evaluation of performance, chapter 8 spelled out a market-related criterion for consumer goods (quite distinct from profitability in the capitalist sense), namely the ratio of the market-clearing price of the product to its labour value. It was argued that a high ratio signals 'success', and should lead to the direction of more resources to the enterprises concerned. For enterprises producing consumer goods, this should deter the overstatement of input requirements, since overstatement would result in a higher labour value, and hence a lower ratio of market price to value, compared to the correct statement of input requirements.

We wish to emphasise this point, as the choice of an suitable measure of performance is crucial for economic rationality. Even if managers are socially responsible and wish to advance the public good, the imposition of ill-conceived performance measures will generate crazy results. Nove (1977) points to horror stories about Soviet enterprises being rewarded for maximising their inputs (*e.g.* using as much steel as possible) as an effect of badly chosen targets.

This particular criterion—the ratio of market price to labour value—is *directly* applicable only for goods or services with a market price (*i.e.* in our proposed system, personal consumer goods alone). But the same principle may be extended indirectly, by imputation, to those goods and services which enter the production of consumer goods. The latter products will not have a market price (if they are not themselves consumable), but information on the prices of the consumer goods to which they are inputs can be relevant in assessing their 'social effectiveness'.

Statistical assessment for producer goods enterprises

Consider the measure, market price of a product x minus labour value of product x. For reasons explained in chapters 7 and 8, we would expect that the *average* value of this measure across all consumer goods ought to be close to zero. For any particular consumer good, however, there will be a host of independent forces acting to push this difference away from zero: various shifts in the pattern of consumer demand, along with both short- and long-term changes on the supply side (changes in technology, availability of materials, etc.). The principle known to statisticians as the Central Limit Theorem tells us that the sum of a large number of independent random influences tends towards the 'normal distribution', a smooth symmetrical bell-curve with well-known statistical properties. It therefore seems reasonable to suppose that across the population of all consumer goods, the difference (market price minus labour value) will follow an approximately normal distribution, with a mean of zero. For some goods the difference will be positive, for some it will be negative, and the likelihood of any given absolute deviation from zero will diminish in a predictable fashion, the larger that deviation.

Now consider a given product which does not itself enter personal consumption, but which is used in the production of a number of different consumer goods. The relevant subset of consumer goods can be thought of as a *sample* from the whole population of such goods. If we draw a random sample from a normally distributed population with a mean of zero, we expect on average to obtain a sample mean of zero also. And provided we can determine the standard deviation of the population (a measure of how widely dispersed the elements of the population are, around their mean value), the tabulation of the normal distribution allows us to make probability statements concerning the average of our random sample. For instance, there is a 95 per cent chance that the mean of a random sample will lie in the range zero plus or minus two times the population standard deviation divided by the square root of the size of the sample.

This then provides a clue for judging the social efficiency of the production of the various inputs to the consumer sector. Suppose we take one such input, say a particular type of machine tool. We record the difference between market price and labour value for each of the consumer goods in the production of which this machine tool is employed, and compute the sample mean of these differences. Let's say this mean turns out to be greater than the 'expected value' of zero. This could just be the luck of the draw, but by applying the statistical reasoning alluded to above we should be able to assess the likelihood that this is just a random event. The alternative hypothesis is that the above-zero average is not just due to chance, but reflects the fact that our machine tool is itself produced with above-average social efficiency (it may be particularly well-designed for the job, its construction might be of particularly high quality, and/or it might be produced with a minimum of wastage of labour and materials). So this socially efficient input is contributing to the generation of a positive mean difference between market price and labour value for the various consumer goods with which it is associated.

Using the same reasoning, the planning authorities should be able to identify inputs where there is a suspicion of inadequate social effectiveness. An input falls into this category if we find a significantly negative average figure for market-price-minus-labour-value among the consumer goods employing it. (In this context, 'significant' means that the difference from zero is greater than could plausibly be accounted for by chance alone.)

The suggestion, then, is that all of the inputs to the production of consumer goods be routinely assessed on this basis. Being probabilistic, this method does not yield definite conclusions; it is always possible, if unlikely, that a particular product obtains an apparently 'good' or 'poor' score by chance. But the results of this procedure might reasonably be taken as grounds for further detailed study of enterprises which appear, on the face of it, to be doing particularly well, or badly.[1]

Against monopoly

Some goods and services are neither consumable directly, nor do they figure directly as inputs to the production of consumer goods. These goods do not have market prices, nor can the market prices of consumer goods readily be used to assess them indirectly. But even here, the calculation of labour values should be helpful. So long as there is more than one producer of a given product, the planning authorities can compare the calculated labour values of the same product from various different enterprises; and unless there is good reason for above-average labour value in some cases, the high-cost producers can be made to shape up. In other words, there is merit in 'competition', though this need not take the capitalist form, and a socialist economy should beware of creating a monopoly supplier of any given product,[2] unless the specific arguments against duplication of production facilities are strong and cogent.

Rewards and sanctions?

We have stressed the need for rational measures of economic performance, measures which will make it in the interest of enterprises to supply correct information, and generally to cooperate with the central planners. The question arises: How, if at all, does the measured performance of an enterprise affect the fortunes of its workers? What stake do the workers have in the 'success' of the enterprise in which they are engaged?

The idea that monetary incentives are a pre-eminent human motivation is an outgrowth of commodity producing society rather than a universal of human nature. It is an idea particularly prevalent in Western economic ideology; but its parochial nature even within the capitalist world is evident when we consider the success of Japanese industry, where company loyalty rather than individual incentive is to the fore.

One need only think of non-mercantile professions, to see the importance that can attach to other criteria of success: glory for the soldier, relief of suffering for the nurse, esteem for the scholar, fame for the actor, to realise that there can be rewards every bit as potent as money. Though the poor may have no choice but to desire money for survival, the wealthy desire it primarily because it is the mark of success, status and standing.

The fervour with which our conservatives hold onto their belief in the efficacy and necessity of salvation through monetary motivation has still to be explained though.

For capital the measure of success is its self-expansion, this indeed is its *raison d'être*. Its criterion of success is of necessity monetary. For the individual capitalist, and his theoretical expression the vulgar economist, all appears reversed: money seems the necessary incentive or reward for action. In fact, the psychology that gives such prestige to the pursuit of money is itself called forth by, is a mental reflection of, the inner imperative of capital. As capital's agents, managers and entrepreneurs are obliged to see money as the ultimate driving force of human motivation.

Paradoxically, of course the profits of a capitalist are determined not by his hard work, but on how hard his employees work for him. For the majority in capitalist society, any hard work will enrich others long before they benefit. It is on the self-denying altruism of these philanthropists that the capitalists' ultimate successes rest. Were the sermons preached to the East by Western *laissez faire* economists, on the necessity for self motivation, to be taken at face value, one would be forced to conclude that capitalism was impossible. For how could so many millions be voluntarily persuaded to devote themselves to the good of their employers?[3]

We do not, therefore, recommend bonus payments linked to, say, the enterprise's price-to-value ratio. This would conflict with the principles of distribution laid out in chapter 2. It's true that a high price-to-value ratio in a particular sector signals the need for expansion in that sector. And enterprises could develop a high ratio by coming up with a product that people like very much, or by exploiting a particulary efficient production method—in either case, commendable behaviour. But we can also expect variations in the price-to-value ratio that have nothing to do with the merits of the workers involved. These may be due to factors beyond the control of the enterprises, and perhaps not even foreseeable by them, whether it be shifts in the pattern of demand, in production technologies, or in the cost and availability of certain resources. It is not always easy to distinguish between hard-earned success and good fortune, or between lackadaisical performance and bad luck. Under capitalism this is not an issue: good luck and good judgement are equally rewarded, bad luck and poor work equally punished. But we wish to keep such arbitrariness out of the socialist distribution of income.

Even if we avoid personal pay bonuses linked to enterprise performance, the incentive to be efficient is still there. In a sense, virtue is its own reward. As a result of the consumer goods marketing algorithm, enterprises showing an especially effective use of social labour will be assigned additional resources and labour, hence increasing the opportunities for the workers involved (better promotion prospects, the chance to participate in and shape a growing operation). Enterprises showing persistent below-average effectiveness will find themselves shrinking, their workers assigned elsewhere. For this mechanism to operate properly, it is important that workers do not have the right to permanent employment in any particular enterprise or industry (although they do have the right to employment as such). We return to this point in chapter 14, when discussing the set of property relations required to sustain our model of socialism.

Notes to Chapter 9

1. Monitoring of a similar general type was implemented in Chile by Stafford Beer. Beer was not concerned with the measurement of labour time, but his system was similar to what we are proposing in that it involved real-time data-collection along with a smart statistical filter to screen out uninteresting random variation. For more on this see chapter 6.
2. Soviet planners often created only one plant producing a particular product, in these circumstances it was difficult to tell if alternative production techniques would have been more efficient. Note that the statistical technique advocated in the previous section would have helped even in these circumstances.
3. Capital has its means of trying to ensure compliance, ably documented by Braverman in his account of the modern production process.

CHAPTER 10

Foreign Trade

Two men can both make shoes and hats, and one is superior to the other in both employments; but in making hats he can only exceed his competitor by one-fifth or 20 per cent., and in making shoes he can excel him by one-third or 33 per cent.;—will it not be for the interest of both, that the superior man should employ himself exclusively in making shoes, and the inferior man in making hats? (Ricardo, *Principles of Political Economy and Taxation*, p.136.)

The socialist movement lacks a definite theory of foreign trade. Marx intended to write a volume of *Capital* on international trade, but he died before starting the task. On most questions to do with how to run a socialist economy, specific prescriptions from Marx are hard to come by, but at least he provides conceptual tools from his analysis of capitalism that can be re-applied to the new subject matter of the socialist economy. With international trade we do not even have this.

Marxian economic theory was generally derived from the theories of Ricardo, and in the absence of any specific Marxian theory of trade, the obvious starting point must be Ricardo. Ricardo proposed the idea that trade between nations arose from the differing comparative advantages that nations enjoyed in the production of commodities. It is important to understand what is meant here by comparative advantage. At first sight it seems that an advanced nation with highly productive industries stands to gain little through trade with less developed countries.

The German clothing industry can probably produce garments with less labour than the Chinese clothes industry. The German car industry can certainly produce cars with less labour than would be needed if they were made by backstreet workshops in Shanghai. In both cases Germany has a productivity advantage over China, but it is nonetheless economical to export Mercedes to China and to import cotton goods to Germany. This arises because of the greater *relative* productivity of the German car industry. Compared with hand assembly, the highly automated car factories of Mercedes may give, say, a fivefold improvement in productivity; with the rag trade the scope for improvements in productivity is not so dramatic. Although a German clothing firm might be more efficient, the advantage would not be so great as for the car industry. It thus pays Germany to concentrate its labour force in those engineering industries where it has the greatest advantage.

Suppose that a Merc can be made with 1,000 hours of labour in Germany and that a woman's blouse can be made with 1 hour. In China let us suppose that a similar car would take 5,000 hours to build and that a blouse could be produced in 2 hours. Based on the simple labour theory of value, the relative exchange values of Mercs to blouses in Germany would be

$$1 \text{ Merc} = 1,000 \text{ blouses,}$$

while in China the relative values would be

$$1 \text{ Chinese luxury car} = 2,500 \text{ blouses.}$$

Given free trade, a capitalist who buys Mercedes in Germany, ships them to China, and brings back blouses will make a substantial profit. He will be able to undercut the more efficient German garment producers. The formation of a world market tends to equalise the relative prices of exportable commodities: the import of Chinese garments will tend to depress the price of clothes relative to cars on the German home market, and cheapen the price of luxury cars on the Chinese market. The specialisation associated with trade means that the total world production of both garments and luxury cars can be increased.

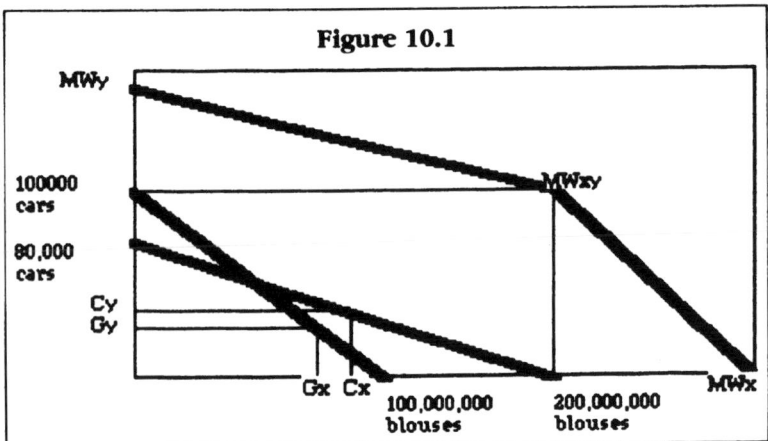

Figure 10.1

Suppose that the Germans have 100 million hours of labour that they can use either on car production or on the production of blouses, and that the Chinese have 400 million hours. Figure 10.1 shows that without engaging in trade with China, Germany can either have 100,000 cars or 100,000,000 blouses or any combination of these two constrained by the formula:

total labour = (cars × German labour per car) + (blouses × German labour per blouse)

China on the other hand can independently choose any combination of blouses and cars constrained by the formula:

total labour = (cars × Chinese labour per car) + (blouses × Chinese labour per blouse)

The world as a whole (if these are the only two countries) is constrained by both these relations so that

world car production = German + Chinese car production, and world blouse production = German + Chinese blouse production.

As a result of these constraints we have:

1. Maximum world production of cars (MW_y) = Chinese + German maximum production = 180,000.
2. Maximum world production of blouses (MW_x) = Chinese + German maximum production = 300,000,000.

In addition, focus on the point MW_{xy} which represents production of 200,000,000 blouses plus 100,000 cars. This is the combined world production which occurs when Germany produces nothing but cars and China nothing but blouses. It can be shown that there is no way in which so many blouses *and* cars can be produced if each country produces some of both goods. From a starting point with both countries completely specialised, let Germany decide to produce 90,000 cars and 10,000,000 blouses, and let China decide to produce 10,000 cars and 175,000,000 blouses. Total world production of cars will be unchanged at 100,000 but world production of blouses will fall from 200,000,000 to 185,000,000. Any such move away from complete specialisation diminishes production of at least one of the goods. This is the essence of Ricardo's argument in his parable about the shoemaker and the hatter. It is a particular example of the class of problems that can be solved by the mathematical technique of linear programming.

International trade allows an increase in total world production as a result of specialisation. This additional production constitutes a source of profit that does not depend upon the direct exploitation of workers. Mercantile capital was able to tap this source of profit in the ancient and medieval worlds when direct production was under the control of classes of agrarian slaveholders or landowners. The ability of the trader to appropriate a share of the surplus was the foundation of the wealth of trading states like Rhodes and Venice.

The labour theory of value developed by Smith, Ricardo and Marx, assumes that the equilibrium prices of goods within a country will be in proportion to their labour content.[1] What can it predict about world prices? Let us consider first the situation where the two countries have not yet fully specialised. In this case the limits to the relative prices of the two goods will be set by their national labour values. In the previous example the price of cars expressed in blouses will be somewhere between 1,000 blouses (as in Germany) and 2,500 blouses (as in China). It should not fall below 1,000 or rise above 2,500. Because both goods will be produced in each country, the less economical domestic product will be competing with a cheaper import, so the relative price of cars falls in China and the relative price of blouses falls in Germany. The existence of two different price ratios is what gives rise to the international traders' profits.

It is unlikely that both countries will specialise totally and fix output at the point MW_{xy} in Figure 10.1. It would be quite fortuitous should this output ratio for the two goods correspond to the ratio in which they are demanded. It follows that the equilibrium condition is likely to be one in which *one* country specialises totally, but the other continues to produce both goods. Under these circumstances the labour value theory predicts that the exchange ratios of the goods in both national markets will be determined by the ratio of their labour values in the country that is not fully specialised. Hence if aggregate demand for cars was greater than 100,000 whilst aggregate demand for blouses was less than two hundred million, Germany would specialise completely in car production and China would produce some cars and some blouses. In this case the Chinese domestic price ratio would determine the world price ratio. German car producers would then earn excess profits through being able to sell their cars at the higher Chinese price.

In the Ricardian theory an essential role in the maintenance of balanced trade between nations was played by monetary movements. Suppose that Germany ran a trade deficit with China. In order to pay for imports German merchants would have to make payments to their Chinese suppliers in Chinese currency. This currency could be obtained by exporting German goods, but if these were not being exported in sufficient quantity, Chinese currency would have to be purchased with gold or silver bullion. In meeting imports, a portion of Germany's stock of gold and silver coin would have to be exported. This would cause a shortage of currency on the domestic market and lead to lower prices. Domestic deflation would make imports relatively dearer and bring trade back into balance.

Suitably generalised, this form of argument is not really limited to international trade—it is applicable to regional trade within a state. If Scotland runs a trade surplus with England, then there will be a net flow of currency north of the border. This will lead to local inflation (higher house prices etc.), but it will also prompt a higher level of consumption which will tend to eliminate the internal trade imbalance. If there is a single set of prices for goods that are nationally traded, then on the same argument as for international trade one would expect regions to concentrate on the production of those commodities for which they have the greatest relative advantage.

The classical theory of foreign trade is a very abstract account, and does not take into account many details of the modern world market. For instance, world monetary systems are no longer based on the gold standard as in Ricardo's day. Consequently, the elimination of trade imbalances by means of movements in gold or silver cannot operate. Credit money and speculative movements in response to changes in interest rates now allow chronic trade imbalances. When Ricardo was writing, international indebtedness with its systematic distortion of trade flows was unknown. Further, the idea of comparative advantage tells us little unless we have some idea why these comparative advantages arise.

Technological development the primary determinant of trade patterns

Although the Ricardian theory does give us some useful information about causes of trade flows it abstracts from the origins of comparative advantage. Why are some countries better at producing particular goods? A major component of trade flows is obviously explained by climate and the distribution of mineral resources. That Saudi Arabia exports mineral oil and Greece olive oil is explained by the endowments of nature. But we can not explain the Japanese export of silicon chips by the easy availability of sand in Japan.

With the uneven development of technology, only a few advanced countries may have any ability to manufacture certain goods. It does not make much sense to compare the comparative advantages of Indonesia and the USA in producing jumbo jets and leather goods, when the USA has an effective world monopoly in jumbos. The analysis could be forced into a Ricardian framework (by working out how much labour it would cost Indonesia to produce its own jets), but this would obscure the more significant factor of very uneven technological development. The structure of trade among the industrialised countries is largely determined by the areas of their technological expertise. An advanced technology helps a country in two ways:

1. It raises the general productivity of labour in a country and thus its overall standard of life.
2. It provides specialised products which the country can export to obtain products which it is less able to produce.

Trade deriving from technical advances is unstable. Advantages are temporary, for in time technologies become common knowledge. Leading industrial countries constantly develop new comparative advantages by introducing new branches of production based upon the results of scientific research. To this extent the products they sell represent the embodied value of their scientific and engineering research. The particular products that they export change from year to year, so that vis-à-vis the less industrialised counties what they are 'specialised' in is the ability to develop new things.

Competition between low wage and high wage economies

A topical issue in the developed capitalist countries is the decline of traditional industries in the face of competition with the newly industrialised countries. This industrial decline has hit the working classes of the USA and Western Europe over the last decade or two, causing large scale unemployment. This has led to political demands for protectionism to prevent job losses. Unlike the situation which prevailed prior to the second world war, when the leading industrial powers tried to protect their home markets, bourgeois governments have resisted this pressure and pushed for even greater free trade. They have used the classical argument that free trade will lead to greater production and higher overall living standards than protectionism. It has been left to trade unions and political parties drawing their support from working-class voters to argue for protectionism. They have argued that unemployment in the developed world is a consequence of competition with the low-wage economies of the third world. Although this issue does not relate directly to our subject matter—foreign trade policy in socialist economies—it is indirectly relevant since socialist parties campaigning for power in capitalist countries have to address it.

In its baldest form, the issue is whether free trade between a low-wage and a high-wage economy will undermine the industries of the latter. Intuitively it seems obvious that cheap goods from the low wage country will flood in and cause unemployment, but the Ricardian theory claims that this intuition is false. In order to isolate the effect of low wages, other differences between the countries must be eliminated. We must assume that they have the same labour productivity and that neither has any natural advantages due to mineral reserves and the like. Under these circumstances the relative prices of commodities in the two countries will be the same. If the amount of labour required to produce cars, and the amount of labour required to produce washing machines, is the same in each country, then the relative prices of cars and washing machines will be the same in each national currency. But in that case there is no profit to be made in international trade, and far from imports flooding in to the high-wage country there will be no international trade at all.

An exception to this occurs when a government systematically overvalues its currency, in which case all imports appear cheap and they will flood in causing domestic unemployment. But there is no necessary link between an overvalued currency and wage rates. Countries with either high or low wages may overvalue their currency for short periods. The labour theory of value predicts that the capitalists in the country that pays low wages will enjoy higher profits, but that they will not threaten the workers in the high-wage economy.

One reason that this contrasts with intuition and experience is that high- and low-wage economies often have different technologies. Activities like textile production and heavy engineering are among the first that newly industrialised countries move into. These are therefore the ones in which they have the greatest comparative advantage, and it is this comparative advantage rather than low wages that explains their exports. The low wages paid in the Indian aircraft industry have yet to threaten the jobs of aerospace workers in Seattle.

Another reason why the Ricardian predictions seem unrealistic is that we have focussed on free movement of commodities alone. If we take into account *capital movements* the previous conclusions no longer hold. Now the capitalists in the high-wage economy will move their capital to where it will earn more profit. This movement of capital from the high- to the low-wage economy will cause industrial unemployment in the high wage economy.

Subsequently the capitalists who exported capital will start living off their overseas earnings. The flow of repatriated profits will strengthen the metropolitan country's currency, enabling it to finance an excess of imports over exports. The combination of an excess of imports with a decline in industrial employment then leads people to think that the former led to the latter. The implication of this argument is that it is much more important for a socialist government to impose controls on the movement of capital than to impose import controls. It is only when capital can flee abroad that the low wages paid in newly industrialised countries threaten the overall living standards of workers in the developed world. Free movement of goods will not by itself affect the internal income structure of countries, although it may cause structural shifts between branches of production.

Advantages of trade deficits

Upon the final analysis do you find that you have gained anything by your policy of always selling to foreigners without ever buying from them? Have you gained any money by the process? But you cannot retain it. It has passed through your hands without being of the least use. The more it increases the more does its value diminish while the value of other things increases proportionally. (Mercier de la Riviere, *L'Ordre Naturel et Essentiel des Societes Politiques*, 1767)

The classical economists developed the labour theory of value in a struggle to understand the underlying workings of the economy. They wanted to know what was going on in the real economy beneath the 'veil' of money. One of their objectives was to produce arguments against the dominant mercantilist theories which justified restrictions on imports as a way of preventing money flowing out of the country. The classical economists argued that this concern with monetary flows was spurious and that it was of no benefit to a country to run a trade surplus. For what did a trade surplus mean but that a country had exchanged useful commodities for gold which was of no use at all? A country that continually runs a trade surplus is giving over to the rest of the world a portion of its annual product for which it gains nothing in return. A trade surplus, far from being desirable, actually impoverishes a country.

This insight has been lost on British Labour governments who seem to have attached some mercantilist virtue to a trade surplus. But in this they were not alone. Across the world, capitalist governments proclaim trade surpluses to be *a good thing*. Like many good things they can be gained by devout hopes and by sacrifices. The sacrifices in this case come in the form of austerity packages that cut working-class living standards to release resources for exports.

According to the classical economists this is all being done in pursuit of illusory gains, but an illusion so persistent and stubborn is not to be explained by the stupidity of the deluded; it must have its origin in real social pressures.

In the case of debtor nations that pressure is plain. They are driven to seek a trade surplus in order to be able to pay off their debts. Where indebtedness is particularly high, the trade surplus may all go on paying the interest on foreign debts. In these cases the deleterious effects of trade surpluses are strikingly evident: the proletariat of debtor nations is driven to the verge of starvation as wealth streams out of the country to benefit Wall Street and the City of London.

With creditor nations there is no such external pressure, but they too can only run trade surpluses at the expense of domestic consumption, so the pressure for trade surpluses must express the interests of some internal groups who will benefit. The principal groups who benefit are the manufacturing capitalists and the financial institutions. It can readily be shown that trade surpluses augment the money profits of domestic manufacturers.[2] The total income (I) generated in the capitalist sector is made up of wages (W) plus various property incomes all of which we will call profit (P). Hence:

$$I = W + P$$

But this income is derived from sales (S), and sales can be divided into three parts: sales to workers (S_w), sales to proprietors (S_p), and net sales to foreigners (the trade surplus, S_f). Hence:

$$I = S = S_w + S_p + S_f$$

If we assume that sales to workers do not exceed wages, $W \geq S_w$, it follows that

$$P < S_p + S_f$$

In words, profits are bounded by purchases by proprietors and the trade surplus. The trade surplus allows higher money profits. This monetary profit is over and above what the proprietors spend on consumption and investment (S_p), and via the mediation of the financial system, accumulates as holdings of overseas assets.

International trade in context of socialism

To talk about socialist international trade, in the sense of the international trade of socialist states, presupposes the existence of distinct nation states. At present this is partly a justified assumption, though it is worth remembering that some socialist states such as the USSR, Yugoslavia and China were not nation states but federations of several nations. It may be better to think in terms of interstate trade rather than international trade. This interstate commerce occurs in three forms: capitalist state to capitalist state as analysed by classical political economy, socialist state to socialist state, and between states of different social systems.

We will first look at socialist trade with capitalist states. Since the Ricardian justification of international trade rests upon differing relative labour productivities between states, comparative advantage is still a valid motive for international trade. If there are different relative labour productivities amongst capitalist states, then it follows that no socialist state can have a set of relative productivities identical to all capitalist states. There will thus be some capitalist states with whom trade will bring advantages.

If trade with the capitalist world is to take place this raises a number of policy issues. Should a socialist state seek a trade surplus, trade deficit or a balanced trade with the capitalist world? Should it seek to balance trade on a bilateral basis or a multilateral basis? What should be its foreign exchange policy? What indeed is the meaning of foreign exchange if money is in the process of being eliminated?

State demand for foreign currency

Socialist states traditionally have gone to great lengths to acquire capitalist currency. Their motivation is the wish for funds to pay for imports of both producer and consumer goods. The state plan generally included a budget for imports of capital equipment and for articles destined for final consumption. One of the problems that planners faced is that they were unable to predict what the prices of imports will be by the time that they are purchased. There is an element of uncertainty in all planning, but at least for a domestic plan it is in principle possible to pre-compute the requirements and outputs of different industries because these industries are subject to centralised control. Foreign suppliers are outside the planning system and the prices that they will demand in 3 years time are unknowable. In some cases it may be possible to negotiate long-term fixed-price supply contracts, but these will be the exception. If trade with capitalist countries becomes too large, the uncertainties this introduces into the planning process can start to undermine economic stability. This is especially the case if the plan comes to depend upon imported industrial equipment which later becomes unavailable due to shortages of foreign exchange.

Any country can obtain foreign exchange through exports of goods and services, tourism, or loans from other governments or banks. The main difference in a socialist country is that all these activities are controlled by public agencies rather than private agents. In principle this gives the public authorities greater control over the balance of trade than is possible with capitalism. Since the state has a monopoly of imports, it can curtail these in the event of shortfalls in planned export earnings. Similarly it can control financial flows. If, for example, foreign loans can only be taken out by the state bank, then the sort of uncontrolled trade deficits financed by private borrowing that have occurred in the US and the UK in recent years will not occur.

But *ad hoc* controls on imports may have considerable disruptive internal effects. If certain factories rely upon imported components, then curtailing imports may hold up production. Even though it may be possible to order priorities so that industrial inputs come first and consumer goods second, this inevitably means cuts in living standards when the terms of trade move against a country. The combined unpopularity of such consumer shortages and fear of economic dislocation from component shortages led certain socialist governments[3] (Poland and Hungary in particular) to rely heavily on loans during the late 1970s. These loans were undertaken at a time when Western banks, trying to recycle oil money, were very willing to lend. Subsequent rises in interest rates and a general deterioration of the terms of trade of the CMEA countries caused the loans to become a crippling burden on the people of these countries. In order to pay the interest the state is turned into an agency for world capital, extracting surplus value from its citizens by reducing real wages and diverting products onto the export markets.

In the light of these dismal experiences it seems wiser for socialist countries to follow Mao Zedong's policy of maintaining balanced trade and refusing to borrow money from capitalist banks. In the long run a country can only obtain imports by exporting the products of its own labour. Either it exports them now, or it will be forced to export even more in the future to pay off loans plus interest. The international banks are not charities; they lend in the knowledge that their money will be reborn, that debts will be repaid many times over.

Alternatives to foreign exchange
The Soviet socialist pattern ·was to maintain an inconvertible currency which did not circulate abroad, and to pay for imports in dollars or marks. We are proposing an internal economic system in

which money as a means of payment is phased out in favour of non-circulating labour credits. These labour credits are not money in the normal sense, in that they can only be used by citizens to pay for publicly produced goods and services; they cannot circulate or be used as capital. When this approach is applied to the problem of overseas trade, it implies a system in some ways diametrically opposed to foreign exchange policy on the Soviet model. These countries paid for their foreign trade in hard currency and often restricted the export of their own currency by means of exchange controls. From the 1940s to the '60s the British government followed a similar policy.

In outline what we propose is the reverse of this: imports from the capitalist world are paid for in labour credits; labour credits may be exported and can circulate abroad but not at home; and the import of foreign currency is outlawed. We wish to prevent the formation of money capital as a social relation within the domestic economy, which is why labour credits are not allowed to circulate domestically. In the capitalist world money capital already exists so there is no objection to labour credits of the socialist commonwealth[4] circulating between foreign capitalists. A capitalist firm that supplies the commonwealth with imports will be given an account with the ministry of foreign trade and credited with a certain number of hours of labour. The firm may then obtain a transferable certificate of credit from the trade ministry.

These certificates of labour credit would then serve as non-interest bearing negotiable instruments which the holders could sell on the financial markets for whatever currency they wished. The demand for such instruments would come from companies who want to buy commonwealth exports. It is unnecessary for the commonwealth trade ministry to establish an exchange rate, that is a private matter for the capitalist financial markets. Since both exports and imports are evaluated (and international transactions settled) in labour vouchers, the dollar or yen price of these on the world market can be ignored when deciding what to export or import. All that matters to the socialist economy is the product of the foreign currency price of goods and the exchange rate.

Viewed in this way foreign trade is just a specialised branch of production that produces imported goods and consumes exported goods. It is then possible to integrate it into the general planning model. It follows that decisions as to which goods are to be imported and which exported should be the responsibility of the planning authorities, since they have databases on the relative labour costs of different production techniques. Given a target level of production of some commodity they can determine whether it is optimal to import it or produce it domestically. Goods are only offered for export if the (labour voucher) price yielded is *above* the labour input required to produce them. Imports are only purchased if the labour price at which they are being sold is *lower* than the amount of labour that would be needed to produce them domestically. If these conditions are satisfied it is self-evident from the labour theory of value that foreign trade will yield an overall saving in effort to the country.

Table 10.1:
Labour time balance of payments

Good	Domestic Cost	Price offered	Decision
Oil	1 million hrs	1.5 million hrs	export
Cars	2 million hrs	1.5 million hrs	import
Deficit	*1 million hrs in domestic units*		

An interesting consequence of this is that the commonwealth will always run a trade deficit when measured in domestic labour units. For example, consider a Norwegian commonwealth that exports oil and imports cars (see Table 10.1). The Norwegians export oil that took 1 million hours to produce and get back cars which would have taken 2 million hours had they been made in Norway. Hence in domestic terms they import twice as much as they export, although in terms of prices actually paid trade is balanced. When things are computed in terms of labour costs it is clear that a country makes no net gain unless it runs a trade deficit. This is an expression under socialist property relations of the mercantile profit predicted by Ricardian theory.

The foreign-trade sector of production differs from domestic branches in that its input/output coefficients are highly volatile. It may well be that the frequency of oscillation of international prices will be too high for the domestic economy to track effectively. Indeed this is almost inevitable since commodity price fluctuations are an expression of the differential time constants of supply and demand. For example, computer memory chip prices on the world market fluctuate in a two or three year cycle. At the peak of the price cycle the commonwealth might be faced with a price in terms of labour that was greater than that which would be incurred if a new factory were set up to produce memory chips at home. But to set up and commission that production line would take a year or two, by which point the world market price will have fallen to a trough level that would make imports cheaper than the domestic product. These world market price fluctuations depend on two time constants—the time it takes to commission new production facilities, and the time taken for new uses for computers to be found when chip prices are low. It is because both constants are of the same time order that fluctuations occur. If semiconductor wafers could be manufactured as easily as hamburgers then the production time constant would be a matter of weeks, and in that case prices would not fluctuate, they would just move steadily up with inflation or down with improvements in production technology.

To deal with such fluctuations the planning agency would have to apply weightings to prices that would dampen out short-term variations. Decisions to import or export would then be based upon long-run price trends rather than instantaneous prices.

Exchange rate policy, tourism and black markets

A phenomenon that could not but strike a visitor from the capitalist world to some socialist countries was the prevalence of a black market in foreign currencies. It may be that foreigners got an exaggerated impression of the significance of this from their very situation as foreigners, but it does seem to be a social evil that at the very least is politically damaging to the reputation of socialism. The black market in currency, as with all black markets, corrodes social values. It creates a subculture of semi-criminal petty capitalists whose outlook conflicts with the socialist ethic. Otherwise honest citizens are drawn into the black market and in the process break the law. When this happens frequently the prestige of socialist legality suffers. People become accustomed to fraud and hypocrisy and develop cynical attitudes. With the circulation of capitalist currencies for the black market in imports arises the chance for an internal black market. As socialism in the USSR decayed, managers of state enterprises took to disposing of goods onto the black market too.

So a socialist state would be wise to prevent the emergence of a black market in currency. There is no profit to be made by the black marketeer unless the domestic currency is officially overvalued: a black market implies that private citizens are willing to pay more for foreign currency than the state. Why do they want it? In many ex-socialist countries there were specialised shops which sold goods only for foreign currencies. In part these sold souvenirs and luxuries aimed at the tourist trade. The Russian *beriozka* shops might sell craft goods and fur coats. These goods may also have been available in the ordinary shops but they were cheaper in the *beriozka* shops. This encouraged tourists to spend more hard currency, with the proceeds going to the state treasury. In addition, however, these shops sold a motley collection of mediocre goods imported from capitalist countries, plus a variety of domestically produced consumer goods like washing machines, cars etc. These goods were unlikely to be bought by tourists and must have been destined for sale to Russian citizens with access to foreign currency. Given an officially overvalued exchange rate, they at once provided the motive for the black marketeer and allowed the state to soak up black-market holdings of dollars and marks. In order to fleece the tourist the state conspired with the black marketeer to undermine its own currency.

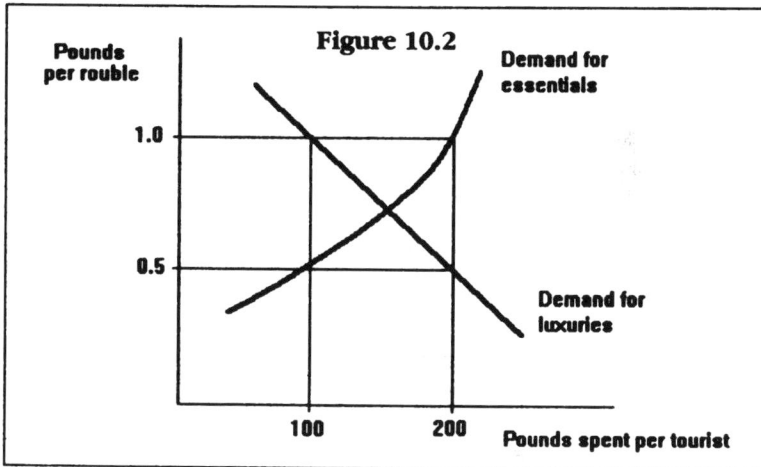

Figure 10.2

This policy is not entirely irrational. To understand it we must look at tourist demand curves for luxuries and for essentials like food and accommodation. There are shown in Figure 10.2. Demand for essentials is relatively inelastic: for instance, the number of meals that are eaten is insensitive to the exchange rate. So a high official exchange value of the rouble (say, £1 per rouble rather than 50p) will increase the total sterling revenue from the sale of accommodation and food to tourists. The demand for luxuries, on the other hand, is likely to be more elastic, so that a lower-priced rouble would bring in more foreign currency. At an exchange rate of 1 rouble to the pound a tourist might spend £100, while at an exchange rate of 50p per rouble she might spend £200. By offering what amounts to two exchange rates for different classes of product the state maximises its foreign exchange earnings. In the process it makes a black market profitable.

So long as foreign visitors are a rare phenomenon this may be an acceptable price to pay. Now that international travel is more common the corrupting effects of the black market become more serious and it is questionable whether the additional profits from tourism suffice to justify it. Suffice it to say that the scope for black marketeering would be greatly reduced if state shops only accepted domestic currency (or domestic labour tokens).

Another motivation for citizens acquiring foreign currency is to purchase privately imported goods. These may be commodities that the state chooses not to import—cocaine, pornographic videos, etc.—or may simply be goods on which substantial import duties are charged. Here we are dealing with the general problem of smuggling which affects both socialist and capitalist countries. When large profits are to be made from smuggling, the efforts of law enforcement agencies are notoriously ineffective, whatever the social system they are supposed to be upholding. The abject failure of Western customs agents to curtail the heroin and cocaine trade is testimony to this. The international drug cartels have not yet made great inroads into the erstwhile socialist states, but this may change as fully convertible currencies are established.

A socialist government coming to power in any of the present-day capitalist countries will have to deal with a situation where deprivation and despair have driven a significant fraction of the population into drug addiction. In the poor areas of great capitalist cities drug addiction is already an everyday fact of life and a subculture of drug black-marketeers is well established. The drug cartels demand payment in hard currency. At the street level payments are in cash. Front companies can always be found to launder illicit gains and introduce them into the banks. A system of convertible currencies in which private citizens or companies can transfer funds from country to country by bankers' draft is ideal for transferring the funds out to the countries where the drugs are processed.

The system of non-transferable labour accounts that we are proposing as a replacement for money would make this sort of black market very difficult. In the absence of cash how could street deals for drugs be paid for? We should not underestimate the ability of criminals and petty capitalists to devise new means of payment. The two immediate alternatives to cash are foreign banknotes and gold. A lot of the money for drugs already comes from theft, and jewelry has always been a prime target for theft, but were stolen gold the only means by which imported drugs could be obtained the volume of the drug trade would be sharply curtailed. There remains the problem of preventing the internal circulation of foreign banknotes. To deal with this, a socialist commonwealth should simply prohibit the import of currency. All domestic purchases will already be made using plastic cards. Arrangements could be made with capitalist banks to allow foreign tourists the use of their credit cards when visiting the commonwealth.

The remaining legitimate reason for citizens of the commonwealth to want capitalist currency is travel to capitalist states. This demand could be met by allowing citizens to use their labour credit cards when travelling in the capitalist world. A commonwealth citizen arriving in Tokyo could go to a Japanese bank and use her labour card to obtain yen. The procedure would be something like this:

1. Citizen transfers 20 hours labour credits to Japanese bank.
2. Bank gives her an equivalent in yen.
3. Electronic record transferred to commonwealth foreign trade computers, which credit account of Japanese bank with 20 hours labour.
4. These accounts then used by Japanese bank to finance purchase of commonwealth exports.

Note that although a citizen outside the country is free to use her labour card to purchase yen, she may not bring the yen back into the country or change yen back into labour credits. Correspondingly, although citizens can transfer labour credits to the account of a capitalist bank, the bank cannot transfer labour credits back to the accounts of citizens. This is necessary to prevent foreign currency circulating as an internal means of exchange.

Policy instruments

How can balanced trade be ensured using the exchange rate policy outlined above? A socialist commonwealth that carries out all payments associated with its international trade in domestic labour credits will not accumulate assets or liabilities denominated in foreign currency. In a way it would be like the United States, which after the second world war was able to use the special status of the dollar to carry out all its international payments in its domestic currency. This did not ensure that the US ran a balanced trade account—the US has frequently run trade deficits—but it did mean that these could be financed without negotiating explicit foreign loans. A trade deficit in dollars led to an increase in dollar holdings by overseas governments and companies, which in a sense represent liabilities of the US treasury. In accounting terms these are equivalent to loans from the rest of the world to the US, but in political terms far less onerous than explicit borrowing from the IMF.

Excessive issue of dollars has resulted in the long term depreciation of the dollar against the mark and the yen. This would tend to price German and Japanese imports out of US markets and bring trade back into balance were the process not interfered with by capital movements. High interest rates in the US induce overseas holders of dollars to convert some of their holdings into US government bonds and other dollar securities. This capital inflow prevents the dollar exchange rate moving far enough to bring trade into balance.

If a socialist country issues non-interest-bearing labour credits to finance foreign trade, the capitalist currency markets will establish an effective exchange rate for its labour against the leading currencies. This exchange rate, in the absence of complications due to capital flows, will tend to move very rapidly to bring trade into equilibrium. Let us examine how this would operate. We assume that the state sets 5 budgetary targets for foreign trade:

1. The planned quantity of producer goods imports
2. The planned quantity of consumer goods imports
3. The anticipated quantity of exports
4. The anticipated earnings from tourism
5. Anticipated tourist expenditure by its citizens when abroad

All of these are of course denominated in domestic labour units. Thus the budget for imports is denominated in domestic labour units. The actual collection of goods that foreign firms and states will offer for this, will depend on the valuation that they put in their own currency on the quantity of our exports that this could purchase. If the exchange rate remained constant, the planners could anticipate just what they would be able to buy in terms of raw materials and capital equipment with budget 1, and could draw up production plans accordingly. A similar argument applies to imports of consumer goods. Budgets 3 and 4, on the other hand, can only be anticipations: there is no way of knowing how much the country will succeed in exporting nor how many foreigners will chose to come as tourists. On the other hand the planners do have to make provision for producing the goods that are intended for export even if these are eventually unsold, and provide hotel rooms for visitors even if some of these go unfilled. Item 5 could in principle be regulated by setting controls on the amount that tourists could take out of the country.

Let us consider two ways in which the plans might be thrown out.

1. A portion of the goods intended for export remains unsold.
2. A change in international prices (*e.g.* an oil price increase) means that the terms of trade move in favour of the commonwealth.

Unsold Exports

The shortfall in exports leads to a decline in the exchange rate, and as a result the original import budget is too small to pay for the planned imports. The planners have to cut back on imports or try to deter people from taking foreign holidays. This implies some order of priority for import cuts, and some policy instrument to control what people spend on their foreign holidays.[5]

Improved terms of trade

If oil prices rose, an oil-exporting socialist country would find that its exchange rate improved. The import budget would be underspent. This means that the country is impoverishing itself by unnecessary exports. In the long term the plan could adjust for this by reducing planned exports and/or increasing planned imports. In the short term the surplus on the import budget account could be used to purchase extra consumer goods which could be sold on the domestic market at discount prices.

There is an alternative policy here. If the initially planned level of imports is maintained in the short run, so that the supply of labour credits to foreigners does not expand, then foreigners' purchases of the country's exports will be correspondingly restricted. One option open to the socialist economy is to accept payment for part of its exports in foreign currency, as a temporary measure. In that case the state would accumulate holdings of, say, dollars, and could then use these to buy additional imports in future. Under some circumstances, this could make more sense than encouraging extra current purchases of imported consumer goods. By delaying the expenditure of the 'windfall' due to the change in the terms of trade, the state may be able to select imports which fit better with the overall aims of the plan. (This would not mean that citizens acquire dollar balances—these would be held by the state bank.)

Notes to Chapter 10

1. It is beyond the scope of our current work to give an assessment of the theoretical validity of the labour theory of value when applied to market economies. An interesting and modern assessment is given by Farjoun and Machover.
2. This argument is due to Kalecki; see his *Theory of Economic Dynamics*, chapter 5.
3. Our reasons for calling them socialist are gone into in the next chapter.
4. The word commonwealth has taken on new overtones since the counter-revolution in the former USSR. Originating as an English translation of the latin Res-Publica, or republic, it was the tag attached to the revolutionary dictatorship established after the overthrow of the Scottish and English monarchies in the 17th century. It continued to have revolutionary associations well into this century with the term commonwealth being used by English socialists as a synonym for a socialist republic. It has the great virtue of directly expressing the idea of common ownership in its title. To give the 20th century monarchy some populist legitimacy in former colonies, this revolutionary title was incongruously adopted by the British state. It is in this conservative guise that it apparently appealed to Yeltsin.
5. In the long term, shifts in the exchange rate will tend to make individuals adjust

their holiday expenditure but there is no guarantee that this of itself will be fast enough. The obvious policy instrument here is a flexible tax on the export of labour credits by tourists. A citizen using her labour credit card outside the country might have to pay a specified surcharge on any purchases.

CHAPTER 11

Trade Between Socialist Countries

The last chapter examined trade between socialist and capitalist countries; in this chapter we extend the analysis by considering trade (and more generally, economic relations) between socialist countries.

In the long run trade as such should not exist between socialist countries. Trade presupposes the continued existence of distinct properties, albeit state properties, and in a socialist world economy these should not exist. Instead we can envisage a system in which productive resources and products belong to international organisations. This may sound a bit abstract but it was of course the situation in the USSR following the Stalin revolution of 1929–31. The 1936 Soviet constitution specified that

> land, mineral deposits, waters, forests, mills, factories, mines, railways, water and air transport systems, banks, means of communication, large state-organised agricultural enterprises . . . as well as municipal enterprises and the principal dwelling house properties in the cities and industrial localities, are state property, that is, the possession of the whole people.

The sections of the 1936 constitution dealing with political liberties and democratic process were honoured more in the breach than the observance, but the above assertion of state property corresponded to reality. The significant point here is that the state in question was an international one, and that effective disposition of resources was in the hands of an international planning organisation, Gosplan. The different nationalities of the USSR were not linked by international *trade* although they participated in an international *division of labour.*

Within this division of labour the Ricardian principles of comparative advantage still apply. By reason of natural resource endowments, the Republic of Azerbaijan had a comparative advantage in the production of oil, the Uzbek Republic in cotton, etc. Such advantages persist whatever the social system, and it was economically rational for the planners to make these republics centres of the oil and cotton industries respectively (although we shall return to some problems with the Uzbek cotton economy below).

This type of division of labour differs from that established by international trade in several respects. For a start, the products of the different national industries belong to an international organisation rather than a local company or nation state. There is thus no sale or purchase involved as the goods move across national frontiers. Instead they are allocated according to the needs foreseen in the plan, within a single system of property. Because there is no change in ownership, and because allocation is according to a plan rather than a market, exchange amongst the different republics need not be based on world-market prices for the goods involved. Individual republics are therefore cushioned against fluctuations in these prices. On the other hand, so long as the socialist state exists in the context of a capitalist world market, there are good grounds for not ignoring world-market prices altogether. If certain goods can be obtained more cheaply in the long run via trade with capitalist economies, rather than via the internal division of labour amongst the socialist republics, that should clearly be taken into account by the planners.

The general character of inter-socialist economic relations also makes possible a unified international system of payment for labour. Under a market system, wage levels differ between national economies. A newly industrialised economy with a large agricultural sector will tend to have wage levels held back by the standard of living of the agricultural sector. Any substantial rise in wages is prevented by a flow of workers off the land into the cities. In an international socialist state, wage rates are not determined by such market conditions but by state policy. The state can set standard international wage rates for the job. Thus the wage differentials between the different nations of the USSR were much less than would be the case between a collection of capitalist nation states with equally diverse starting points in terms of cultural and economic development.

In a system of international trade, a less developed country can catch up with more developed ones only if it (a) has a higher level of internally generated capital accumulation, or (b) finances its capital accumulation by borrowing from the more advanced countries. If the country cannot obtain inward investment its development is likely to be slower, but if it borrows it is likely to find itself heavily in debt with a large part of its labour going into the pockets of foreign capitalists. In an international system of socialist planning, on the other hand, resources can be allocated in the central plan to the development of more backward areas without the question of borrowing ever arising. Suppose the metallurgical industry of Siberia is developed using equipment produced in Russia. Under a trade system these transfers would have to be met by credits, and Siberia would become a debtor of Russia. With international planning no debts are incurred, as there is no transfer of ownership.

From the observation that national or regional differences in degree of economic development can in principle be eliminated more rapidly under socialism, without leaving a residue of debt, it does not, however, follow that this will actually happen. We must ask whether the more developed nations or regions will wish to help the less developed. This question bears some relation to the debate over the possibility of 'Socialism in one country' that took place in the Soviet Union in the 1920s. The position taken by Trotsky was that Russia was not capable, even along with the other nations of the USSR, of building socialism alone. The Soviet Union as a whole was simply too backward and isolated. Consequently, Trotsky and his supporters placed a high priority on encouraging revolutionary forces in Western Europe. Stalin, on the other hand, argued that the Soviet state had no choice but to go it alone following the defeat of the post-war revolutionary movements in Germany and elsewhere. The Soviets couldn't wait for the West. Further, one could not afford to sacrifice the interests of the world's only *actual* socialist state in favour of *potential* revolution elsewhere. If the survival of the USSR involved reaching some kind of accommodation with the capitalist powers, and if this in turn placed limits on the ability of the Soviets to support revolutionary forces in the West, then so be it.

Clearly, each side of this argument had some force. Trotsky's position could easily be represented as defeatist, given the non-appearance of the Western European Revolution; and Stalin's claims seemed to be borne out by the construction of the Soviet planned economy in the 1930s. Yet from the perspective of the 1990s, when the Soviet Union has collapsed in ruins, one may wonder whether the isolation and backwardness of the USSR, as diagnosed by Trotsky, contributed in an essential way to the ultimate weakness of Soviet socialism. Of course, whether any alternative action on the part of the Soviets could have been more effective in breaking out of that isolation is highly debatable.

At any rate, the point that is particularly relevant to our discussion here, is Trotsky's assumption that *if* the revolution had spread, the working classes of Western Europe would have willingly aided their

Eastern comrades in the construction of a more advanced socialism. That is, Trotsky was appealing to the same sort of international solidarity and idealism that we have alluded to above. The question arises again: How realistic is this conception?

For comparison, it may be worth briefly considering the reasons why an advanced *capitalist* country may wish to stimulate the 'development' (in some form or other) of less developed countries (LDCs). We can distinguish four sorts of reasons.

1. In order to exploit cheap labour available in the LDCs (which may also be used as a means of holding down wages in the metropolitan country). This may involve building factories and some infrastructure in the LDCs, but the labour farmed out to such countries is likely to be unskilled (assembly and the like).

2. In order to develop sources of raw materials and primary products. Again, this may involve building up the industries of the LDCs to some extent (*e.g.* mining and plantation economies). But such development carries the risk that the LDC enters into a relation of dependency, relying upon only one or a few products for its export earnings and hence becoming particularly vulnerable to adverse movement in its terms of trade. In addition, large-scale extraction of natural resources may of course be associated with environmental destruction.

3. In order to develop markets in the LDCs for the products of the metropolitan economy. This reason was stressed by Rosa Luxemburg, who argued that in the absence of the continuous development of new markets, the advanced capitalist economies would be inherently subject to crises of over-production.

4. Finally, we should recognise a motivation for 'developing' the LDCs that goes beyond direct economic self-interest, even in the case of capitalist economies. Ideology may play a role, either of the colonial variety (connected with the presumed superiority of the culture and social-political system of the metropolitan power, which zealous colonial adminstrators wish to impart to the natives), or in a social-democratic form which partakes to some degree of socialist internationalism. The practical impact of the latter is likely to remain marginal, however.

We may now ask how the above account relates to the possible motivations of an advanced *socialist* country, in its relations with LDCs. Reason number 1 above should be entirely absent in inter-socialist relations. Number 3 will also be irrelevant, as there should be no shortage of internal demand in a planned economy. That leaves 2 and 4. As regards point 2, a socialist economy will also have an interest in securing supplies of materials and primary products, and to that extent in developing the economies of LDCs as suppliers. From the standpoint of a socialist internationalism, however, one has to be careful with this sort of developmental path, because of the dangers mentioned above.

It used to be the proud boast of the Soviet state that the more advanced regions such as European Russia had contributed massively to the economic and cultural development of areas such as Central Asia, without the exploitative relationships inherent in capitalist development. While this claim was not without merit, there are nonetheless real grounds for concern over the developmental path of, for instance, Uzbekistan, with its virtual monoculture in cotton. Unlike an LDC in the capitalist world outside of the USSR, Uzbekistan was not at the mercy of fluctuations in the world-market price of cotton. On the other hand, the environmental destruction associated with the cotton economy has been particularly acute, with the Aral Sea being drained to service the massive irrigation projects required for growing cotton in the Central Asian desert. (Although it should be said that ecologically reckless development policies were not confined to the periphery of the USSR.)

Finally, then, we come back to the fourth motivation mentioned above: the ideological. One would hope that advanced nations or regions would be willing, in the context of socialism, to commit resources to aiding their less developed neighbours without relying upon any calculation of direct self-interest—or in other words, that the spirit of socialist egalitarianism would spill over regional and cultural boundaries. Is this too naive? Well, aside from the attempts at levelling up the relatively backward regions of the USSR, we can also cite as a precedent the case of 'regional policy' within capitalist nation-states under social-democratic governments. Such policies, which do seem to have involved real transfers of resources to less developed regions, have not been uncontentious, but nonetheless have been broadly accepted as legitimate. We would suggest that this case contains an important moral, particularly when the resource transfers involved in regional policy are compared with the relatively tiny amounts devoted to 'international aid'. That is, achieving popular legitimacy for an extended egalitiarianism across regions seems to be a more feasible undertaking when the regions involved are part of a unitary state, rather than separate nation-states. People seem more inclined to accept the project of levelling up as fair and reasonable when the levelling is to occur within 'their country', even when 'their country' is as large and diverse as the USSR.

In the absence of a developed sense of supranational community, having its counterpart in shared state institutions, a system of developmental transfers will be perceived as disadvantageous to the more developed nations. National resentments may develop in the more advanced countries against the less developed. Examples of this were the demands made by the economically sophisticated Baltic republics of the USSR for economic autonomy, in the face of the declining legitimacy of the Soviet state. Any concessions made to the developed nations in these instances are at the expense of the less developed nations.

In contrast to the situation of the nations within the USSR, the socialist states that were created in the postwar period—China, Cuba, the GDR, etc.—lacked unified international plans. Their economies related to each other as a series of distinct national properties. The division of labour between them was mediated by trade, which generally had to be balanced on a country by country basis. This represented a two-fold a disadvantage vis-à-vis the capitalist world. First, a system of bilateral trade balances provides less scope for the division of labour than is possible with multilateral trade and convertible currencies. Second, capitalist multinational companies organise an international technical division of labour, drawing up international plans for their production. Ford, for example, coordinates its car production on a world-wide basis, with particular national branches specialising in car bodies, engines, etc. Lacking this international organisation, the socialist countries suffer from wasteful duplication of basic industries and small scale production.

What we advocate
For the reasons spelled out above, it is in the interest of the socialist system as a whole for different socialist countries to subordinate their economies to an international planning system. This involves a surrender of national sovereignty which, at least at first, is likely to encounter strong political opposition.

In the capitalist world too, nation states find their sovereignty being encroached upon by the internationalisation of the world economy. This takes the form of trade liberalisation, the growing role of multinationals and the formation of international proto-states like the EC. Here too the process of internationalisation generates political resistance. Some national politicians, seeing their own institutional power undermined, try to impede the process. In doing this they have at their disposal the whole baggage of national chauvinist ideologies left over from an earlier stage of capitalist history. But politicians who oppose internationalisation are standing against the tide of history. It is notable that Mrs Thatcher failed to carry the Tory party with her in her hostility to European Monetary Union.

In general, since the 1970s capitalist politicians have been less prone to succumb to reactionary economic nationalism than socialists. Common action on the part of bourgeois governments prevented the recession of the late 1970s and early 80s leading to the sort of protectionism seen in the Great Depression of the 1930s. In contrast to this the leaders of the socialist states showed much less willingness to subordinate their national economies to a single planned system. Why?

One possibility is that the political class in the socialist countries has (or had) much more autonomy than in capitalist countries. The class with the strongest interest in the development of socialism is the working class, and the class of full-time politicians in socialist countries was supposed to represent the interests of the workers. The class with the strongest interest in the continued development of market economies is the capitalist class, and responsible politicians in capitalist countries take these interests into account. In capitalist countries top politicians are often also businessmen. They may be rich men who take up politics as a hobby, or they may be taken onto the boards of companies after they have risen to political prominence. In any case there is an interchange of personnel between commercial and political life.

Of the two, commercial life is the more financially rewarding. If a capitalist politician decides to give up politics and move into industry, his standard of living does not fall. This type of interchange was not seen between members of the political elite and the working class in socialist countries. A socialist politician who returned to the working class, as did Alexander Dubcek after the Soviet invasion of Czechoslovakia in 1968, suffered a fall in income and social status. Such transfers were rarely voluntary.

The status and income of socialist politicians rests entirely upon their position within their national state. They have a strong personal motivation to preserve national autonomy, whatever the longer-term economic arguments against it. These economic arguments go without any internal champion. While the capitalist classes in the West are vocal, and aware that they have a long-term interest in internationalisation, the same could not be said of the workers in socialist countries. Experience in trade and multinational companies schools the bourgeoisie in internationalism. Socialist workers, spending their whole life in one country, employed by their own nation state, are likely to be less concerned about it.

Working-class internationalism certainly existed in the socialist countries: witness the tens of thousands of Cubans who volunteered for service as soldiers, doctors or teachers in Angola. But as recent history has shown, it is also possible for local politicians to whip up nationalist sentiments to strengthen their local state machines.

Because of the important role of the state in socialist economies, it is not possible for them to internationalise at the economic level without political union. Had the Communist International not been disbanded during the second world war it might have provided the impetus required to achieve the political unification of the newly emergent workers' states. The existence of a single international political party would at the very least have acted as a brake on nationalist pressures.

Significance of national sovereignty

As economic relations become more internationalised the significance of national sovereignty become more and more a class question. The most significant right that remains to a nation is the right to decide whether to be capitalist or socialist. This was recognised by Mrs Thatcher when she railed that she had not eliminated the blight of socialism from British soil in order to have it reintroduced under the protection of the European Commission. Ironically, it is this same national right that the people of Nicaragua defended for years of bloody war against the *contras.*

It is possible even for small nations to break free of capitalism and establish an internal socialist economy provided that the political situation is favourable and provided the country can defend its borders. But if a small socialist country follows a go-it-alone policy on the Albanian model its economic development is retarded. Paradoxically, the best way for a newly emergent socialist country to secure its national decision in favour of socialism might be to apply for political union with other socialist countries.

CHAPTER 12

The Commune

There is a great deal of official cant going around about the 'community'. We hear talk about Community Care, Community Programmes and so on at the very time that economic development is destroying any organic basis for community. A community can only exist on the basis of shared cooperative activity. In present-day cities we see, for the most part, not communities but just residential areas. From these, people go forth to work across the city or even to other towns. In the area where they live they will scarcely know their neighbours; their friends will often live in quite different areas. Work and living areas become separated and people get to know workmates who may live miles away. Only for children who go to local school does the community live. Among mothers, the community of children finds an echo. But as children grow up the community of their peers slips away from them.

This inevitably leads to an intensification of individualistic values well suited to capitalism but a poor support for socialism. Amongst men this individualism is aggravated by long years of peace in which generations have grown up without knowing the discipline and cohesion of a military community. For socialism to thrive it needs community roots. It needs communities in which people get used to cooperating and working for the common good. But community can not be conjured out of thin air. It needs real economic support. There must be institutions that bring people together to meet real needs, and which meet them better than the institutions of capitalist society.

In the socialist countries the most ambitious attempt to develop community institutions was during the period of the People's Communes in China. This was the greatest cooperative experiment in history, involving some 800 million people. The communes were large, often having upwards of 30,000 members. They engaged in agriculture and light industry, and provided their members with education and health care. Through their militias they provided an element of military training and defense. They were also units of local self-government. In China the communes were created to replace the system of domestic economy in agriculture, and they made possible the development of land improvement programmes and social provision that were beyond the scope of the domestic economy. Within the context of the commune there was a marked advance in the social position of women.

If we try to apply the idea of a commune to advanced industrial societies then it must obviously be modified considerably. Since so few people now work in agriculture, we must think in terms of urban communes.

The activities of urban communes

The main function of communes is to replace the family. Chinese communes replaced the family as an agricultural unit; modern urban communes will have to replace the more vestigial economic roles of the bourgeois family. Since much of the economic activity undertaken by city people aims to satisfy needs in the wider economy, a city, or district of a city, does not have the degree of internal self-sufficiency that was typical of the Chinese communes.[1] It is for this reason that we concentrate on their potential role in the replacement of the domestic economy. We do not mean to exclude the possibility that similar principles of organisation might be applicable on a somewhat larger scale to small towns and large villages.

We should, however, preface the following discussion with the assurance that we do not envisage compulsory collectivisation. The point here is to explore the theoretical possibilities for forms of communal living; it will be up to the citizens of the future socialist commonwealth to explore those possibilities in practice. Communes will flourish only if they can demonstrate their desirability as an alternative to bourgeois family life.

Having said this, we can list the activities around which the commune might displace the family as follows:
1. Housing
2. Food preparation
3. Childcare
4. Some leisure activities
5. Helping senior citizens

Let us examine these areas of activity and the questions they raise.

The first question, and one that affects all of the others, is the number of people in a commune. We envisage it as being much smaller than the Chinese model—perhaps fifty to a couple of hundred adults. This choice of size may be justified on economic grounds, taking the different areas of communal activity in turn.

Housing

We assume that the communes will provide housing to their members. There already exist housing cooperatives that do this, but in this case there is no attempt to encroach upon the household economy. Hence in a housing co-op the physical form of the houses remains oriented towards the nuclear family. The co-op provides a series of individual houses for member households. A commune should provide accommodation for the individual members within a larger communal house.

Communal housing in the USSR was associated with overcrowding and inadequate facilities; the communal flats were comparatively small and not purpose-built. For communal housing to be an attractive proposition, it must offer individuals as much private space as they can obtain under familial housing, along with access to more collective space than they could obtain in the latter. We would assume that each adult member of a commune should have at least one room for his or her own exclusive use. It would probably be desirable to extend this principle to all post-pubertal members of the commune.

Communal life obviously has implications for the type of buildings that are suitable. The suburban 'semi' or the flat in a tower block are all in their way adapted to the nuclear family. Communes would have to develop a new type of architecture. An interesting and relevant recent discussion is offered by Durrett and McCamant (1989), based on their study of the Danish *bofoellesskaber* or 'living communities'. These architects do not envisage quite the degree of communality that we are suggesting, but their concept of 'co-housing' includes facilities for shared meals and child care, along with cooperative stores, laundry facilities, photographic darkrooms and so forth. It may also be possible to learn from the architecture of religious communities or colleges (although both of these types of buildings are basically for the celibate so that they lack space for children).

Food preparation

We assume that the members of the commune will be commensals, that is to say that they will eat together at least part of the time. This implies the existence of communal kitchens and a refectory, the ownership or at least disposition over large-scale cooking equipment, and an allocation of labour to the task of food preparation. We can envisage two basic principles on which the organisation of cooking could be carried out. Both are compatible with communist principles in the broad sense. In one case the commune would employ some of its members as full-time paid cooks, while in the other case there would be a roster system with duties rotating. We return to the relative merits of these systems below.

The size of the commune unit would be enough to justify a broader range of food preparation than is common in an isolated household. For instance, daily bread production is uneconomic in an individual household, but for 100 people it becomes quite feasible.

Childcare
The size of communes should chosen to be large enough to support at least a kindergarten and perhaps a primary school. The big economic advantages of adequate communal child care are obvious. It will free a significant percentage of the female population from individal child rearing, an activity with low labour productivity. These women can then participate in social labour of higher productivity. By doing so they contribute more to society and obtain an independent income.

Some leisure activities
We envisage that communes would have the wealth to provide certain sporting and leisure facilities that are currently available only to the upper classes. A commune of, say, 100 people should be able to afford a swimming pool, a small gym and one or two ponies for the children. The garden could be equipped with swings, climbing frames and so forth. It might be economic to provide commonrooms with space for playing music, or putting on dances. Pieces of equipment like sailing boats that are beyond the reach of most individuals might be affordable for a commune. An urban commune might own a house in the country that members could use in the holidays. They might own one or two minibuses and a car and cycle pool to provide transport.

Helping senior citizens
The basic infrastructure of communal life, such as collective cooking, and the presence of young fit adults in the building, would be of considerable assistance to the elderly. If cleaning and laundry services were also provided communally then senior members would benefit from this without the stigma and isolation associated with entering a separate old folks' home. For fitter senior members, the activities of the commune would provide opportunities to continue to play an active and productive role in society, rather than suffering the enforced idleness of retirement.

Basic rationale in terms of efficiency

The basic rationale for communes is that they reap economies of scale. It is this that makes them superior to individual households. It is because communal childcare saves labour that it is progressive and can be experienced as liberating. Obviously if the contrary were true, and communal life resulted in a greater number of person-hours spent looking after children, one would need other very compelling reasons to justify it. The economic efficiency of the commune has two aspects: economies in direct labour and economies in means of production. Economies in direct labour arise because the basic work of cooking or child-minding is not carried on the most efficient scale within the existing nuclear family. To cook supper for 50 people will take less labour than 50 people cooking their own supper. More realistically we can say that cooking for 50 people communally will take less labour than if these 50 people were spread across some 20 households as they would be today.

The economies in means of production are slightly more subtle. Consider the problem of going to the toilet. If you are in a typical British house there will be only one toilet, which is usually in the bathroom. If another member of the household is having a bath it can prove frustrating. If on the other hand 50 people lived in a large house with 20 toilets, the chances of them all being full would be minimal. Indeed, it should be possible to reduce the number of toilets per head and still ensure that there is always one free. The space and resources saved on toilets can then be made available for other activities.

The argument that applies to toilets can be extended to other fitments. A commune could justify the fitting of a small internal phone exchange and would use fewer outside lines than the equivalent population split into individual houses each with their own phone. The same argument applies to office equipment like computers and photocopiers, which one household could not put to adequate use, but which could be used efficiently by a commune. For a given percentage of their income spent on durable goods, the members of the commune will get access to a wider range of facilities than somebody in an individual household.

Our suggestion that the urban commune should be much smaller than the Chinese People's Commune rests on the assumption that the sort of economies discussed above are more or less exhausted at a size of a couple of hundred members. In the economics literature the concept of 'minimum economic size' (MES) refers to the smallest size of plant which reaps all significant economies of scale in a given industry. The MES can vary quite widely between industries; for instance it is much larger for oil-refining than it is for the injection-moulding of plastic toys. Our idea is that if we can identify the MES for urban communal living, then it does not make sense to urge the formation of communes bigger than this. 'Small is beautiful' may be a rather worn-out slogan, but it is clear that collective democratic decision-making and mutual concern are easier to achieve in smaller communities, and the point of the Commune is to seek these less tangible gains as well as economic efficiency.

Systems of payment and external trade

In China the members of the communes were paid for work that they did in work-units. These were internal units of account maintained by the commune. At harvest time people were entitled to a share of the harvest which depended on the amount of work they had done during the year. The work-units recorded in the commune accounts were distinct from the Yuan or national currency of China. The former units were a claim upon the resources of the commune, but did not directly entitle the member to national resources. This basic principle is generally applicable to economic systems based upon hierarchies of communally owned property. Let us see how it might work in a system of urban communes.

The work performed by commune members would be divided into two classes: work done within the commune, and work done for the national economy. This may or may not correspond to a division of the membership into those who work mainly for the national economy and those who work mainly for the commune. Work done in the national economy gives rise to values in the form of goods and services. These goods and services belong, in the first instance, to the people of the nation as a whole and the national community allocates labour tickets to those who have done the work. These labour tickets allow those who have performed the labour to get from the shops goods of equivalent value. The question arises: If a member of the commune works for the national economy is she personally credited with national labour tickets for the work done, or is her commune credited with these tickets?

In principle either system can be used. If individuals receive the national labour tickets, then the commune levies a membership fee on them. In the second case the labour performed by commune members is treated as the property of the commune. In a similar way, the work done by employees of a subcontractor in a capitalist economy is the property of the subcontractor. If J&M Consultants PLC supplies consultancy services to the government, the government pays J&M, not J&M's employees. The employees are then paid a share of the proceeds after J&M has creamed off a profit.

In the case of the commune there would be no exploitation involved, but a similar principle would apply: the proceeds of labour 'exported' to the national economy belong to the commune as a whole, not the individual who performed the work. The advantage of this procedure is that it puts internal and external labour on a par. If I perform a day's work in the commune kitchens or if I perform a day's work in the national economy, I as an individual will be paid by the commune in commune work-units. These units can be used to pay my commune dues, to pay for meals in the commune refectory, or converted into national labour tickets at the going exchange rate. We mention the exchange rate because it is not immediately apparent that communes will be able to redeem internal work-units at parity with national labour tickets. To understand this point we need to take a systematic look at the commune's accounts.

First consider the commune as a whole. Suppose the commune itself is credited with national labour tickets in the amount of the total hours of external work performed by commune members over the given accounting period. National taxes might be levied either individually or collectively. As we are working under the assumption that national labour-ticket incomes are paid directly to the commune, we shall also assume that the tax liability is treated collectively.

Under this system, the commune's *gross income*, in national labour tickets, is the total hours of external work performed by commune members. Its *net after-tax income* is equal to its gross income minus the total national tax obligation of the commune members over the same period. After making its collective purchases of national goods, the commune has a *distribution fund* left over. This is the total quantity of national labour tickets available for distribution to commune members, to enable individuals to buy national goods for themselves.

Now consider the individual commune member. If the commune treats all work at par for its internal accounting purposes, we can simply add up the hours she works inside and outside the commune to arrive at her total labour contribution. Call this 36 hours for communard Jane. Now we have to reckon the member's obligation to the commune's collective fund. This fund has to cover the external outlays referred to above (national tax and collective purchases of national goods), but in addition it must cover any collective *internal* labour needs, such as provision for the non-producing members and basic commune services such as cleaning and maintenance of the commune's assets. Our individual communard is assessed for a share of this fund, call it 12 hours. She will then be credited with disposable work-units to a value of 36 minus 12 = 24 hours. She can use these work-units to buy non-basic commune goods and services (*i.e.* those not provided by right of membership, but rather charged separately—such as, perhaps, meals or haircuts). Or she can convert them into national labour tickets to buy externally produced goods. Here is where the question of the exchange rate arises.

Suppose our communard Jane wishes to convert 16 hours' worth of commune work-units into national labour tickets. Other members will also want to convert some of their work-units. Faced with a certain total demand for such conversions, under what conditions will the commune be able to redeem its internal work-units at par with national labour tickets? This depends on the relationship between the total of demands, and the commune's distribution fund discussed above. If these magnitudes happen to be equal there is no problem—the demand for national tickets, at an exchange rate of 1 for 1, equals the supply available. Temporary random divergences between demands and the distribution fund need not be a problem either, provided the commune keeps a buffer stock of labour tickets on hand (perhaps in the form of a savings deposit—see chapter 7). But if there is a persistent discrepancy it will not be possible for the commune to offer free conversion of work-units at par. If the demand exceeds the distribution fund, then the commune will have to 'devalue' the work-unit. For example, if the distribution fund has a value of 1,000 national hours, while demand equals 1,200 work-units per period, the sustainable exchange rate is 1.2 internal work-units per national labour ticket.

To examine this issue further it may be useful to discuss an illustrative set of commune labour accounts, as shown in Table 12.1. As we can see from the table, the total disposable work-units will equal the sum of (a) the distribution fund (discussed above) and (b) the total non-basic internal work done. (For the definition of the latter term, see the note to the table.) In the example, their common value happens to be 2,200 hours, but the equality here is not a special feature of the illustrative numbers chosen—it follows from the accounting relationships posited, so long as the commune's collective fund is in balance, with total contributions equal to total expenditure.

Given a balanced collective fund, we can now see what is required for a sustainable one-to-one exchange rate between work-units and national labour tickets. Communards can do only two things with their disposable work-units: spend them on the

Table 12.1:
Illustrative set of commune accounts

1. *Determination of distribution fund:*

external labour credits	3000
less tax liability	1100
less collective purchases	900
equals distribution fund	1000

2. *Work-units credited by the commune:*

external work	3000
plus internal work, of which	
basic	1800
non-basic	1200
equals total	6000

3. *Collective fund obligations:*

tax liability	1100
plus collective purchases	900
plus basic internal work	1800
equals collective fund expenditure	3800

4. *Determination of disposable work-unit total:*

total work-unit credits (from 2 above)	6000
minus collective fund contributions (equal to collective fund expenditure, from 3 above)	3800
equals disposable work-units	2200

Note: 'Basic' internal work refers to work the product of which is available to commune members as of right, while the product of 'non-basic' internal work is in effect 'marketed' to the members through specific debits to their disposable work-unit accounts.

product of non-basic internal labour, or convert them into national labour tickets.[2] So if the members' expenditure of work-units on internal non-basic goods and services equals the amount of labour *credited* in this sphere, then the demand for conversions into national labour tickets will just equal the distribution fund available, and the one-to-one exchange rate is feasible. In Table 12.1, there are 2,200 disposable work-units, there is a distribution fund of 1,000, and 1,200 hours have been credited for non-basic internal work. If 1,200 of the disposable work-units are spent on the product of non-basic internal work, the demand and supply of national labour tickets will be equal at 1,000.

Here, then, are the three conditions required for a sustainable one-to-one exchange rate: the commune must do its accounts correctly; it must run a balanced collective fund (on average); and it must budget for just as much non-basic internal labour as commune members demand. A persistent shortage of distributable labour tickets, relative to the demand at a one-to-one exchange rate, must signal the violation of one or more of these conditions. For instance, suppose the commune gives more credit for non-basic work in the kitchens than it 'collects' as payment for meals—then there will be an excess demand for conversions into labour tickets, which will force the work-unit exchange rate below par. This could be a simple accounting problem. Perhaps meals are 'priced' too low in work-units; this could easily be rectified. On the other hand, there might be a substantive allocation problem. If too much labour is engaged in the commune's kitchens relative to the demand for commune meals, this calls for a real redistribution of the communards' labour time.

Assuming full employment in the external economy, this need not be a problem. The commune does not need to act as 'employer of last resort', mopping up excess labour in its internal activities, and indeed should not do so if it wants to maintain its work-unit at parity.

These arguments all presuppose that the commune is treating internal and external labour at par for accounting purposes. That is, the commune has decided to credit members with one work-unit per hour regardless of whether they are working inside the commune or in the national economy. In that case the exchange rate *ought to be* unity, and any sustained pressure away from parity indicates an error in accounting or in the allocation of labour. But in principle the commune could choose to value external labour more or less highly than internal. Say the members of a particular commune were to agree that external work is less attractive than internal, and therefore see it as fair to pay a premium for external work. Consistency requires that the work-unit exchange rate should be in line with the rate used for accounting purposes, so if the commune thought that a 10 per cent premium on external work was suitable, then a member working an hour in the national economy should be credited with 1.1 work-units, and the exchange rate for conversions should be 1.1 work-units per labour ticket. Since one of the objects of the commune is to break down the sexual division of labour and help establish a presumption of human equality, we would not recommend such a policy; we merely note it as a possibility.

Distribution of tasks

Two principles could be followed by communes in their distribution of tasks. In one case a member of the commune might be permanently allocated tasks. The commune might have full-time maintenance workers, full-time cooks, full-time child-minders and so on, and other members would work full time for the national economy. In the other extreme there would be a rotation of tasks, so that a person might be a child-minder one day, a gardener the next, and spend the following three days working in the national economy.[3]

There are advantages and disadvantages to both approaches. The rotation of tasks reduces the risk of people being typecast into sexually determined roles, but with permanently allocated tasks people may gain greater proficiency at their work. A radical form of task rotation would place a constraint upon the national economy. The efficiency of projects in the national economy might suffer if they could not count on their members turning up each working day.

The legal status of communes

Communes may own buildings and those means of production that are suitable for domestic production. This would include catering equipment, ovens, mixing machines, etc. In addition light transport equipment such as cars and vans might belong to the commune. It is assumed that they rent land from the public land agency. It may be expedient for communes to have the right to enter into contracts with public bodies. They obviously must be able to enter into contracts to supply labour to the national economy, but they might also contract to run whole projects[4] using communal labour. This would imply that the national economy lent them other means of production. For example, a commune might undertake the milk-delivery service to an area of the city and be lent milk floats for that purpose.

The means of production used by a commune are to meet the wants of its members rather than general social needs. In this sense they are analogous to such goods as pans, cookers and cars that are already used by households. These are means of production for the domestic economy within societies dominated by capital, but are generally thought of as 'consumer' goods. The popular categorisation of such goods derives from who buys them rather than their economic function. An electric drill marketed to the domestic economy is seen as a consumer good, a drill sold to a tradesman is categorised as a capital good. The good does not change, only the mode of production that employs it.

Socialist societies would continue to include a declining domestic economy in parallel with an expanding communal sector. Given the microsocial character of production within both of these sectors, their units of production can only relate to the socialised economy via the exchange of equivalents. Their purchases will comprise both consumer goods proper and small scale means of production. The instruments of production needed for a commune would be somewhat larger than for a single household—laundromat type washing machines rather than domestic models for instance—but this is a difference in scale rather than quality. In both cases it is assumed that they exchange against labour credits.

Public policy

As regards the formation of communes, at minimum there must be an agency set up to bring together people who wish to form communes—a kind of 'marriage bureau'. Beyond this, public funds could be made available specifically to encourage the formation of communes. They could be given stocks of publicly owned houses or provided with credit to build new purpose-designed communal dwellings. Taxation policy could be tailored to favour the communes over nuclear family arrangements. On the other hand, if communes really do yield substantial efficiency gains over family living, and are therefore able to offer their members a higher standard of living, it is not clear that they also need to enjoy officially favoured status in the long run. It may be, however, that a socialist government would wish to encourage experimentation and overcome social conservatism through a transitional policy of systematically favouring communes.

Notes to Chapter 12

1. The Chinese street and lane in the city had a similar economic-political function to that of the commune in the countryside.
2. People may not want to spend all of their income each period, but we assume that they cannot 'save' their commune work-units as such. If one wishes to save, one must first acquire national labour tickets. (On forms of saving, see chapter 7.)
3. Marx and Engels envisaged this kind of rotation, talking in *The German Ideology* (1947, p.22) of a community society in which one might "hunt in the morning, fish in the afternoon, rear cattle in the evening, criticise after dinner . . ."
4. For a further discussion of the notion of a 'project', and the distinction between a project and the traditional socialist 'enterprise', see chapter 14.

CHAPTER 13

On Democracy

Utopian social experiments are strongly associated in the public mind with brutal dictatorships and the suppression of civil liberties. Given our century's history this is to be expected. Although there is a growing realisation in Britain of a need for constitutional change, visions of what this might involve are modest. Devolution of power to regions and alternative parliamentary electoral systems may be open for discussion, but the supercession of parliamentary democracy itself is almost unthinkable. Our object in this chapter is to think the unthinkable—specifically, to advocate a radically democratic constitution. We outline a modernised version of ancient Greek democracy, and defend such a system as the best political counterpart to socialist economic planning.

Democracy and parliamentarism

It is one of the great ironies of history, that election by ballot, for millenia the mark of oligarchy, should now pass as the badge of democracy.

In his dystopian novel *1984* Orwell makes ironic reference to Newspeak, a dialect of English so corrupted that phrases like 'freedom is slavery' or 'war is peace' could pass unremarked. What he was alluding to is the power of language to control our thoughts. When those in authority can redefine the meanings of words they make subversion literally unthinkable. The phrase 'parliamentary democracy' is an example of Newspeak: a contradiction in disguise. Go back to the Greek origins of the word democracy. The second half of the word means 'power' or 'rule'. Hence we have autocracy—rule by one man—and aristocracy—rule by the *aristoi*, the best people, the elite. Democracy meant rule by the *demos*. Most comentators translate this as rule by the people, but the word *demos* had a more specific meaning. It meant rule by the common people or rule by the poor.

Aristotle, describing the democracies of his day, was quite explicit about the fact that democracy meant rule by the poor. Countering the argument that democracies simply meant rule by the majority he gave the following example:

> Suppose a total of 1,300; 1,000 of these are rich, and they give no share in office to the 300 poor, who are also free men and in other respects like them; no one would say that these 1,300 lived under a democracy (*Politics*, 1290).

But he says this is an artificial case, "due to the fact that the rich are everywhere few, and the poor numerous." As a specific definition he gives:

> A democracy exists whenever those who are free and are not well off, being in a majority, are in sovereign control of the government, an oligarchy when control lies in the hands of the rich and better born, these being few. (*ibid.*)

With regard to the filling of official positions, he further remarked that in Greece, "to do this by lot is regarded as democratic, by selection oligarchic." (*Politics*, 1294)

What the ideologists of capitalism call democratic procedures, would be accurately described as *psephonomic* procedures (Greek *psephos*: vote by ballot). By glossing over the nature of class relations, such ideologies confuse the right to vote with the exercise of power. In fact all capitalist states are plutocratic oligarchies. Plutocracy is rule by a moneyed class. Oligarchy is rule by the few.

These are the characteristic principles of the modern state. This state, the end or *telos* of history according to Fukuyama (1992), the most perfect form of class rule since the Roman republic, exercises such hegemony, spiritual and temporal, that it appears to have banished all competition.

Effective power resides in a series of concentric circles, concentrating as they contract through parliament and cabinet to prime minister or president: *oligarchy*. Now this power is openly exercised in the name of Capital, it being now accepted by all concerned that the job of government is to serve the ends of business, the highest objective of a state: *plutocracy*.

The plutocracy's power derives from its command over wage labour, a relationship of dominance and servitude whose dictatorial nature is not abolished by the right to vote. *Psephonomia* or election is merely a mechanism for the selection of individual oligarchs. It at once lends legitimacy to their rule, and enables these to be recruited from the 'best' and most energetic members of the lower classes (*aristoi*). At best, election transforms oligarchy into aristocracy.

Aristotle regarded oligarchy as a deviation from aristocracy:

> However the name aristocracy is used to mark a distinction from oligarchy . . . it describes a constitution in which election for office depends on merit and not only on wealth.
>
> But oligarchy readily passes for aristocratic since almost everywhere the rich and the well educated upper class are co-extensive. (*Politics*, 1293)

Substitute meritocratic for aristocratic and the verbal change well encapsulates the historical metamorphosis of British society since the early 19th century, as Parliament was opened to individuals of merit who were not necessarily well born. But the key question is not that some individuals of relatively humble origin are recruited to public office, it is who holds power. All else is illusory:

> What differentiates oligarchy and democracy is wealth or the lack of it. The essential point is that where the possession of political power is due to the possession of economic power or wealth . . . that is oligarchy, and when the unpropertied class have power, that is democracy. But as we have said, in actual fact the former are few and the latter many. (*Politics*, 1279)

Parliamentary government and democracy are polar opposites. Democracy is rule by the masses, by the poor and dispossessed; parliament, rule by professional politicians who, in numbers and class position, are part of the oligarchy. Marx and Engels quite explicitly followed the Aristotelean definition of democracy when they wrote, in the *Manifesto of the Communist Party* of 1848, that

> the first step in the revolution by the working class, is to raise the proletariat to the position of ruling class, to win the battle of democracy. (Marx and Engels, 1970, p.52)

The violent overthrow of the aristocratic state and the establishment of proletarian rule, were, for the founders of communism, synonymous with democracy. They spoke in 1852 of proletarian rule as the dictatorship of the proletariat.

Dictator is a word deriving from the Roman republic rather than Greece. It refers to one individual who was given temporary power to rule by decree in an emergency. There was a natural tendency for temporary dictatorship to degenerate into lifelong rule. Lenin and Stalin were dictators in this Roman sense.

Is this what Marx meant by the dictatorship of the proletariat? Certainly not. What he meant was a mass democracy unconstrained by existing laws. He meant a democracy that was unconstrained by entrenched constitutional rights defending private property. Two and a half thousand years earlier Aristotle had described such democracies:

> Another type of democracy is the same in other respects but the multitude is sovereign and not the law. This occurs when the decrees are sovereign over the provisions of the law.
>
> When states are democratically governed according to law, there are no demagogues, and the best citizens are securely in the saddle; but where the laws are not sovereign you will find demagogues. The people becomes a monarch, one person composed of many, for the many are sovereign not as individuals but in aggregate. (*Politics*, 1292)

And what did these demagogues propose? Communistic measures like the cancellation of debts and the redistribution of property.[1]

For a democracy to be of any use to the proletariat, the masses must be sovereign, unchained by the rule of law, able to issue decrees that violate well established legal rights to property in land or capital.

Direct democracy or soviet democracy?

On the left historically there have been two other candidates to replace parliamentarism: soviets and communist party dictatorship. The latter functioned as a viable political system for half a century in the USSR and Eastern Europe, but has now collapsed, and anyway few people in the West have ever openly advocated it. Instead there is a sentimental attachment to the idea of soviets. These are seen as the original unsullied form of proletarian power, before it was corrupted by Leninist dictatorship. We use the word sentimental advisedly, since many of those who say in their heart of hearts they would like to see a soviet system, are quite willing on grounds of 'realism' to accept parliamentary government. The idea of the soviet acts as a sort of moral insurance policy.

This is not to underestimate the importance of soviets as insurrectionary organs that might provide a focus for the overthrow of parliament. But certain generalisations can be made from historical experience:

1. Soviets tend to be formed only when a dictatorship or absolute monarchy is overthrown. They do not seem to arise in parliamentary states.
2. Soviets only provide a revolutionary challenge when they are armed (workers' and soldiers' soviets). Armed soviets are only formed under conditions of military defeat: France 1871, Russia 1905 and 1917, Hungary 1919, Portugal 1975.
3. They are able to overthrow the existing state only if they are led

by a cohesive group of determined revolutionists. Otherwise, like the Paris Commune, or workers' councils in the Portuguese revolution, they tend to leave the existing state power unchecked until they are themselves disbanded.

4. They provide the ideal medium for the establishment of a one-party state. This is because they are based upon a restricted franchise and indirect elections from lower to higher soviets. This tends to concentrate any initial preponderance of the communists. Such communist domination is probably a precondition for the overthrow of the bourgeois state in any case.

Soviets are transitory institutions, not lasting forms of state structure. Once they become regularised, it is necessary to write down and amend the *ad hoc* rules by which they were initially formed. There is a need to specify who is, and who is not, entitled to vote. The councils cannot be made up of only factory workers and soldiers indefinitely. There is then pressure to define territorial constituencies with universal suffrage: hence the Stalin constitution of 1936. In the absence of any clearly formulated alternative constitutional plans, a soviet system tends to evolve either in the direction of a one-party dictatorship, or towards bourgeois parliamentarism.

The harking back to the purity of pre-Stalinist (or pre-Leninist) soviet democracy, is no more than an unthinking nostalgia, derived from an uncritical acceptance of Lenin's *State and Revolution.*

Lenin, in this book, carried out a brilliant defence of the writings of Marx and Engels, in particular their reflections on the Paris Commune—the first workers' state. In the Russian context, he argued for the "complete destruction of the old state machine, in order that the armed proletariat itself may become the government" (Lenin, 1964, p.489). Sad to say, this genuinely democratic state, a state of soviets of workers' and soldiers' deputies, degenerated in short order into something rather different.

The historical process by which, to paraphrase Trotsky, the Bolshevik Party substituted itself for the proletariat, the Central Committee for the Party and then the supreme leader for the Central Committee, are too well known to require re-emphasis. This process, already well established under Lenin, was, with Stalin, carried to its conclusion.

Western socialist critics of the resulting system are united in applauding the theory outlined in *State and Revolution,* but highlight the conflict between Lenin's theory and subsequent practice. Some blame Lenin and his theory of the Party, some blame the difficult circumstances of Russia, some blame Stalin, some

Khrushchev, some Gorbachev. But few question the original model of a state of workers' councils described by Lenin.

A mere counterposing of theory versus practice, good intentions versus foul deeds is not a critique. Instead we must understand how the inner logic of the model described in *State and Revolution* led to the Soviet Union.

This model envisaged a system of councils of factory workers and soldiers electing deputies through a hierarchy of city regional and national councils to a Supreme Soviet. To ensure that the deputies responded to the workers' interests, the delegates would be subject to recall and receive only average workmen's wages. These latter provisions were drawn from the experience of the Paris Commune. Lenin defended these measures against the jibe of Bernstein that they were a reversion to primitive democracy with the rejoinder:

> the transition from capitalism to socialism is *impossible* without a certain "reversion" to "primitive" democracy (for how else can the majority, and then the whole population without exception, proceed to discharge state functions?) . . . (Lenin, 1964, p.420)

This is a crucial passage, and the rhetorical question is apt, but we must now, three quarters of a century later, ask if Lenin's understanding of 'primitive' was deep enough. It was characteristic of primitive democracy that all citizens without exception were called upon to discharge state functions, but the institutions by which this was done were far more radical than anything envisaged by Lenin.

Institutions of classical democracy

The first and most characteristic feature of *demokratia* was rule by the majority vote of all citizens.[2] This was generally by a show of hands at a sovereign assembly or *eklesia*. The sovereignty of the *demos* was not delegated to an elected chamber of professional politicians as in the bourgeois system. Instead the ordinary working people, in those days the peasantry and traders, gathered together en masse to discuss, debate and vote on the issues concerning them.[3] There was no 'government' as such, instead popular administration was carried out by a city council or *Boule*, with 500 members. Unlike the councils of our present plutocracy, the members were chosen by lot, not by election. There was rotation of offices and individuals only served on the council for one year before being replaced.[4]

This council had no legislative powers and was responsible merely for enacting the policies decided upon by the sovereign assembly. Every citizen had the right to speak and vote in the assembly and was paid for earnings lost through attendance.

The second important institutions were the people's law courts or *dikasteria*. These courts had no judges, instead the dicasts acted as both judge and jury. The dicasts were chosen by lot from the citizen body, using a sophisticated procedure of voters' tickets and allotment machines, and once in court decisions were taken by ballot and could not be appealed. It was held by Aristotle that control of the courts gave the *demos* control of the constitution.

Election was viewed with suspicion, and was not used except for military officials. Elections, Aristotle said, are aristocratic not democratic; they introduce the element of deliberate choice, of selection of the 'best people', the *aristoi*, in place of government by all the people (*Politics*, 1300). What he implies, as would be evident to any Marxist, is that the 'best' people in a class society will be the better off. The poor, the scum and the riff-raff are of course 'unsuitable' candidates for election. Wealth and respectability go together. Only where a specific skill was essential, as with military commanders, was election considered safe. The contrast with our political and military system could not be more striking.

With administration chosen by lot, anyone might be called to serve, producing a highly politicised population.

> The same men accept responsibility both for their own affairs and for the state's, and although different men are active in different fields they are not lacking in understanding of the state's concerns: we alone regard the man who refuses to take part in these not as non-interfering but as useless.[5]

For all his desire for a state run by pastry-cooks, Lenin was unable to conceive of the constitutional forms needed to achieve it. Referring to the workers' state he wrote

> Representative institutions remain, but there is no parliamentarism here as a special system, as the division of labour between the legislative and the executive, as a privileged position for the deputies. We cannot imagine democracy, even proletarian democracy, without representative institutions. (Lenin, 1964, p.424)

Lenin here completely misses the point. The reason why parliamentarism is a form of state suited to propertarian interests, is its basis in election, a principle that Aristotle had long ago shown to be anti-democratic. A proletarian dictatorship can be established by an elected assembly, as was the Paris Commune, where the electors and the candidates were exclusively drawn from the proletariat. But it cannot long be sustained by election.

'Democratic Centralism' a dead end

Lenin's notion of 'democratic centralism', whereby the outstanding class-conscious members of the working class, organised in a Communist Party, are elected through a system of workers' councils to form a workers' government, is fundamentally flawed. It seeks to build a democracy on an institution of class rule: elections. The fact that the vote is restricted to workers does not stop elections being an aristocratic system in the classical sense. Politics becomes a matter for the politicos. Like all aristocracies, it degenerates into a self-serving oligarchy, and is eventually replaced by an 'honest' bourgeois plutocracy.

The idea that a right of recall would be an effective constraint on this process is laughable. The right of recall is written into the state constitution of Arizona, and was in Stalin's Soviet Constitution without noticeable effect. It takes the collection of tens or hundreds of thousands of signatures to secure the recall of an official. It is bound to be a rare event compared to regular elections, but if elections do not keep officials in line why should recall?

As for average workmen's wages, who is to enforce this? What is to stop elected officials voting themselves other benefits?

Is democracy possible today?

In his recent book *Is Democracy Possible?* (1985) John Burnheim advocates a system that he calls *demarchy*, with striking resemblances to classical democracy. Instead of nation states he envisages a system in which power is decentralised and decision-making is carried out by representative bodies drawn by lot from among those with a legitimate material interest in the subject under consideration.[6]

The advocates of democracy present a radical critique of the 20th century bourgeois state, but the practices of classical democracy seem, paradoxically, so novel and alien that there is a danger that people will automatically reject them. Advocates of genuine democracy have to mount a persuasive case and fend off the standard objections.

Contemporary political science is overwhelmingly elitist in sentiment. It is held that the complexity of the modern state is such that only an elite of political professionals is capable of dealing with it. Ordinary Athenian citizens might have been able to run a simple city state, the argument runs, but they would be ill prepared to confront the full-time bureaucracy of the modern state. For this you need full-time politicians with paid research staffs.

In practice, we know that these full-time politicians are virtually powerless in face of a determined executive branch, and anyway are generally little inclined to question radically the system which furnishes their career opportunities. More fundamentally, the argument from expertise confuses two issues. On the one hand there is the question of technical expertise in specific matters such as public health, technology and military affairs, while on the other there is what Protagoras called *politike techne*, the art of political judgement. Protagoras held that all were equally endowed with this ability. When it comes to judging whether a decision is in her interest or not, a Drumchapel shop assistant is as well equipped as a Westminster MP to decide, given that neither has any relevant special technical knowledge.

Another common argument against classical democracy is that it was a democracy of the slave owners, and so has nothing to teach us. On the one hand this objection is just irrelevant—the modern advocates of direct democracy do not propose the reintroduction of slavery. It is also based upon a misconception about ancient Greek society. Athens was not a slave-owners' democracy, it was a democracy of the freeborn citizens. Slaves were excluded from citizenship, but the majority of the citizens were not slave-owners. The great bulk of the *demos* was made up of the working poor peasants and artisans. The *demokratia* was the instrument they used in their class struggle against the rich, the big landowners who were also the big slave-holders. The latter favoured an oligarchic constitution, and were eventually able to impose this with the help of Roman imperialism.

A more prosaic objection to direct democracy focuses on scale. You just cannot gather all the citizens of a modern nation in the *agora* or town square to debate affairs of state. But this is to overlook the power of modern technology. Television has created the global village.[7] There is no technical problem with fitting a voting console to each TV to allow us all to vote after seeing debates by a representative studio assembly. The TV current affairs programmes routinely invite randomly selected audiences to question politicians. On these programmes the public show themselves far harder on the politicians than the hacks who normally question them. It took an ordinary woman from the floor to put Thatcher on the defensive over the sinking of the Argentinian battleship, the *Belgrano*. We have every confidence in the people's ability to take important political decisions after such debate.

The modern state, as we have said, is based upon centralist, hierarchical principles. The institutions of democracy provide a quite different model. In a democracy there was no government, no prime minister, no president, no head of state. Sovereign power rested with the popular assembly. Particular branches of the state were run by juries or officials drawn by lot. Power flows neither up nor down, but is diffused. We can sketch out how these principles might be applied today. At one level, the sovereignty of the people would be exercised by electronic voting on televised debates. To ensure that this was universal, TVs and voting phones should be available free as a constitutional right. This would be analogous to the payment for jury service that the Athenians introduced to allow the poor to participate in the assembly.

Since only a minority of the decisions that have to be taken in a country can be put to a full popular vote, other public institutions would be supervised by a plurality of juries. The broadcasting authority, the water authority, the posts, the railways and so on would all be under councils chosen by lot from among their users and workers. Such councils would not be answerable to any government minister, instead the democracy relies upon the principle that a sufficiently large random sample will be representative of the public. A system of democratic control over all public bodies would mean that at some time in their lives citizens could expect to be called up to serve on some sort of council. Not everyone would serve on national councils, but one could expect to have to serve on some school council, local health council or workplace council. If people were to participate directly in the running of the state, we would not see the cynicism and apathy which characterise the typical modern voter.

Democracy and planning
For economic planning we envisage a system in which teams of professional economists draw up alternative plans to put before a planning jury which would then choose between them. Only the very major decisions (the level of taxes, the percentage of national income going towards investment, health, education, etc.) would have to be put to direct popular vote.

One of the great advantages of the system of labour-time prices advocated in earlier chapters is that it translates questions of national budgetary policy into terms that every citizen can understand. Today only a handful of professional economists and economic journalists are able to make an intelligent assessment of the budget. To make sense of it one has to know how big the national income is in terms of billions of pounds. That excludes the vast majority of the population for a start. Then one must know what proportion of the national income goes to the various categories of earners, in order to estimate the returns from different levels of income tax. One has to know how many billions of pounds of VAT-rated goods are sold, and the returns from excise duties. On the other side of the government accounts, one has to know about the cost estimates of different government spending programs, making allowance for inflation. A full understanding of the budget therefore rests on a vast body of data that is only really available to the Treasury.

Expressed in terms of labour hours the whole exercise could be made much more intelligible. People can understand what it means to work 3 hours a week to support the Health Service or 4 hours to support education. If people were presented with an annual ballot sheet, listing the main categories of public expenditure in terms of the hours per week that these cost them, they could form an opinion on whether they were willing to pay more or less for these services.

Suppose that for health service expenditure one could vote to increase expenditure by x per cent, leave it the same or reduce it by x per cent.[8] These votes could be tallied and averaged, with the resulting average being used as the proportionate increase or decrease that should be made in the NHS budget. Electronic 'ballot forms' could easily be set up in such a way that people are constrained to make consistent choices (for instance, they can't vote a 100 per cent increase in all kinds of spending!).

Over a period of years one would expect expenditure levels to stabilise then slowly change with shifts in public opinion. Under normal circumstances roughly the same number of people would want to increase expenditure as would want to cut it so any changes would be slight.

Although it is feasible to have democratic decisions on levels of public expenditure, this cannot be combined with independent democratic control over taxation. If both taxes and expenditure are subject to distinct votes, there is no assurance that the budget will balance (the US Congress can and does take inconsistent votes on expenditure and taxation, with notorious results). Rather, the level of the basic flat tax would have to be automatically adjusted to cover what people had voted to spend, allowance made for other forms of revenue such as rent. Voters would then have to take into account the tax implications when making up their minds on the expenditure side of the national budget. As a variant on this, a voter might first of all choose a level of overall spending (and therefore taxation). Then when she's making her choices on individual public spending categories, the 'ballot form' program would indicate the consequences for the rest of the budget of a vote to change spending in one area.

The acephalous state

A neo-classical democracy would still be a state in the marxian sense. It would be an organised public power, to which minorities are forced to submit. The *demos* would use it to defend their rights against any remaining or nascent exploiting class. But it would be acephalous: a state without a head of state, without the hierarchy that marks a state based on class exploitation.

The various organs of public authority would be controlled by citizens' committees chosen by lot. The media, the health service, the planning and marketing agencies, the various industries would have their juries. Each of these would have a defined area of competence. A committee for the energy industry, for instance, would decide certain details of energy policy but it could not disregard a popular vote, say, to phase out nuclear power. The membership of the committees need not be uniformly drawn from the public. The health service committees could be made up partly of a random sample of health service workers, and partly of members of the public. As Burnheim argues, the principle should be that all those who have a legitimate interest in the matter should have a chance to participate in its management.

This view is radically different from both Social Democracy and the practice of hitherto-existing socialism. Planning, for example, is not under government control but under a supervisory committee of ordinary citizens, who, since they are drawn by lot, will be predominantly working people. In the sense that they are autonomous of any government, these committees can be thought of as analogous to the autonomous bodies of bourgeois civil society: independent central banks, broadcasting authorities, arts councils, research councils, etc. It is not necessary for them to be under direct state control; their charters and the social backgrounds of their governors ensure their function. Provided that the socialist analogues of such authorities have founding charters open to popular amendment, that they have supervisory committees which are socially representative of the people, and that their deliberations are public, popular control would be assured.

The powers of demarchic councils would be either regulatory or economic or both. An advanced industrial society requires a complex body of regulations to function. In present society some of these regulations are what we recognise as laws, emanating from the decisions of politicians and enforced by state power, but a larger part already originate in autonomous bodies. Professional organisations define codes of practice binding on their members. Trade organisations define standards for industrial components, something absolutely essential for rapid technological progress. International bodies define standards for the exchange of electronic data by telephone, telegraph and fax.

In many cases these regulations affect only the internal operation of particular branches of production or social activity and the composition of their regulating councils should remain limited to people who participate in that area. In others, areas like broadcasting or processes which may impinge upon public health, general social ·interests are affected. In these cases the regulating council would have to be extended to include a majority of other citizens, selected by lot to represent the public interest.

The other power of demarchic councils would stem from their command over resources, human or inanimate. A council might be entrusted with the administration of certain immobile public property: buildings, historic monuments, transport routes, energy and water supply facilities. To the extent that these are immobile, the principal contradictions that may arise are over access. One thinks here of how the propertarian-dominated British commission responsible for ancient monuments denied the dispossessed access to Stonehenge. But to the extent that the property deteriorates and has to be maintained, even immobile properties presuppose an influx of labour and materials.

A council will also be entrusted with mobile public property in the form of machinery, vehicles and raw materials. This is more significant for demarchies administering manufacturing processes, but would affect them all to some extent. We assume that all such mobile property is ultimately allocated by the national plan. A council running a project has the use of the property unless and until a more urgent use arises.

Finally a council disposes of the labour of the members of its project. Since this labour is a fraction of society's total labour, and could potentially be devoted to other activities, it is, from the standpoint of the national accounts, abstract social labour. Similarly, the flow of mobile public property into the project presupposes a fraction of society's labour being devoted to the reproduction of these items. As a flow, therefore, it too is abstract social labour. The dynamic economic power of a council is, finally, command over social labour.

The magnitude of its power is measured in the hours of its labour budget. But by what right does it gain this power and who regulates its magnitude?

It is a power that is either devolved or in the last resort delegated by the people themselves. Consider a council administering a school. Its power might be devolved from some local or national educational council who vote it an annual labour budget. Let us assume that schooling is a local matter. In that case, the budget of the local education council would be set by the local electorate who would annually decide how many hours were to be deducted from their year's pay to fund education.

In the case of a manufacturing council, the delegation is more indirect. Its products, perhaps lead-acid storage batteries, meet an indirect social rather than concrete and local need. The number of batteries that society needs is a function of how many cars, telephone exchanges, portable radios, etc. are manufactured. Only the national, or in the long term federal, planning authority can calculate this. Thus only the planning authority can delegate a budget for battery production.

In all cases the people are the ultimate delegators of power. Either they vote to tax themselves and entrust a demarchic council with a budget to produce a free service, or they choose to purchase goods, in which case they are voting labour time to the production of those goods.

The great virtue of the rule of the *demos* was the elaborate constitutional mechanism they evolved to defend their power against usurpation by the upper classes. That rule flourished for some two centuries until crushed by the Macedonian and Roman empires. During that period it generated a beacon of art, architecture, philosophy, science and culture that illuminated the subsequent dark centuries. The enlightenment golden age of bourgeois culture was a self-conscious reflection of that light. The torch will not truly be reignited till the modern *demos* come to power.

Notes to Chapter 13
1. For a discussion of the role of demagogues (originally meaning just a leader of the people), see Ste Croix (1981, chapter v).
2. The requirement of citizenship excluded women, slaves and *metics*, or in modern terms resident aliens.
3. The similarity between the *eklesia* and those spontaneous organisations of modern workers' democracy, the mass strike meetings that are so hated by the bourgeois world, is immediately apparent.
4. Aristotle summarised the arguments of the classical democrats as follows:
    From these fundamentals are derived the following features of democracy:
    Elections to office by all from among all.
    Rule of all over each and each by turns over all.
    Offices filled by lot, either all or at any rate those not calling for experience or skill.

No tenure of office dependent upon a property qualification.

The same man not to hold office twice, or only rarely, or only a few apart from those connected with warfare.

Short terms for all offices or for as many as possible.

All to sit on juries, chosen from all and adjucating on all or most matters, i.e. the most important and supreme, such as those affecting the constitution, scrutinies and contracts between individuals.

The assembly as the sovereign authority in everything, or at least the most important matters, officials having no sovereign power over any but the most minor matters (the council is of all offices the most democratic as long as all its members do not receive lavish pay . . .).

Payment for services, in the assembly, in the law courts, and in the offices is regular for all.

As birth, wealth and education are the defining marks of oligarchy, so their opposites, low birth, low incomes and mechanical occupations are regarded as typical of democracy.

No official has perpetual tenure, and if any such office remains in being after a revolution, it is shorn of its power and its holders selected by lot instead of by election (*Politics*, 1317).

5. Pericles, as reported by Thucydides in Book II of the *History* (1988, p.85).
6. The potential relevance of the mechanisms of ancient democracy has also been discussed from the perspective of the historian by Moses Finley (1973). Further useful discussions of classical democracy are offered by G.E.M. de Ste Croix (1981) and David Held (1987).
7. Already in the 19th century, J.S. Mill was arguing that the development of the railways and newspapers made possible a modern, large-scale equivalent of the agora (see Finley, 1973, p.36).
8. We can specify how the votes should be counted more precisely as follows. Let x% be the maximal amount by which an item of the budget may be changed in one year. Suppose y% of the people vote for this increase. It follows, eliminating non-voters, that (100-y)% voted against the increase, giving a majority for the increase of y-(100-y) = (2y-100)%. The resulting change in expenditure should be (2y-100)x/100%. Where everyone votes for the increase, the budget will rise by x% where a majority vote against, it will fall by some fraction of x%.

CHAPTER 14

Property Relations

From the earliest written history of civilised society property—the ownership of people, animals, land, and human artifacts—has been the skeleton of social organisation. It has given to societies their shape and defined their degrees of freedom. Almost all revolutions have been driven by the desire to change property ownership in some way. The politics of Britain throughout the 20th century have revolved around the issue of public versus private ownership of property. The Labour governments in the mid-20th century were proponents of public property. The Conservative governments since 1979 have followed a policy of extending private property ownership at the expense of public property. These latter changes were considered sufficiently radical to be dubbed the 'Thatcher Revolution'.

The changes in property relations that we are proposing are more substantial than anything that recent governments have undertaken. They are as radical as the property revolutions that occurred in the Soviet Union in the first third of this century, or in China during the third quarter. Although what we are proposing is radically different from what has prevailed in Britain before it is also substantially different from the Soviet model.

Systems of property are familiar yet complex, and since people tend to take familiar things for granted it is worth examining property from first principles.

Who owns what?
That is the basic question which must be answered by any system of property law. The atoms of property relations are owners and the things they own; systems of property are like molecules built up of these atoms. We can represent them with diagrams like the ones chemists use for compounds. The simplest type of property relationship is shown in Figure 14.1.

In this relationship A is the owner and B is the property. The owner has the right to dispose of her property as she sees fit. At

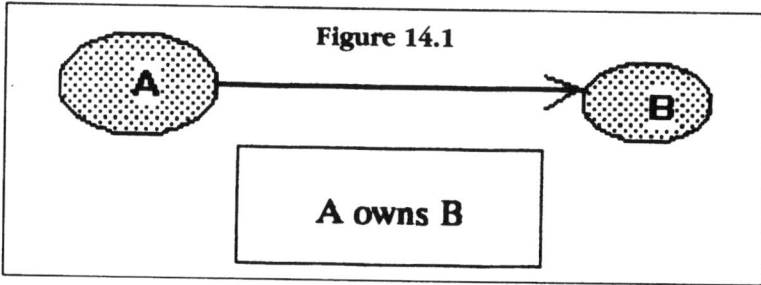

Figure 14.1

A owns B

different times and in different places this right of ownership amounts to different things. To a peasant farmer with property in land and a commodity dealer with property in wheat futures, ownership has a different practical significance. For our purposes we will consider ownership as being made up of three components: the right to use, the right to sell and the right to inherit. In the previous example the peasant is more interested in the right to use and to inherit; to the commodity dealer the right to sell is everything. By the right to inherit we include acquisitions by means of marriage.

Relations

We can order the component rights as follows: use, sale, purchase, inheritance. These rights can be treated as logical predicates. In logic a set of ordered pairs (A,B) for which some predicate holds is termed a relation. For instance, the relation of usufruct is the set of all pairs (A,B) such that A uses B.

We thus have four distinct relations that define property rights. These derive from four predicates: the relation Usufruct from the predicate (A uses B), the relation Sale from (A can sell B), Purchase from (A can buy B) and Inheritance from the predicate (A can inherit B).

A given pair of entities, for instance a trader on the wheat futures market (A) and a shipment of wheat (B) may be members of more than one of these sets. In this case the pair (wheat futures trader, wheat shipment) would be included in the relations Sale and Purchase. This is because the Sale relation includes all pairings of potential sellers with all that they can potentially sell and similarly for Purchase.

A property right between a class of owners **P** and a class of owned things **Q**, can therefore be characterised by the set of property relations that pairs (**p,q**) can be belong to, where **p** is an instance of **P** and **q** of **Q**. A property right between classes of entities is therefore a set of between 0 and 4 relations.

Encoding property rights

Since any form of property right is a small finite set of relations, the set of all possible property rights can be exhaustively enumerated. Our 4 defining relations can be combined to form 16 different sets of property relations, and thus 16 forms of property right. These can be assigned numbers from the sequence 0 to 15, ascending in proportion to the strength of the form of right.[1] This sequence is set out in Table 14.1. On this scale we can place the property rights of various different owners.

Table 14.1:
Exhaustive enumeration of possible property rights
(0 = weakest, 15 = strongest)

	A Uses B	A can sell B	A can buy B	A can inherit B	examples
0	no	no	no	no	(slave American law)
1	yes	no	no	no	(collective farm & land)
2	no	yes	no	no	(hired worker & labour)
3	yes	yes	no	no	
4	no	no	yes	no	
5	yes	no	yes	no	(consumer & electricity)
6	no	yes	yes	no	(commodity trader & commodity)
7	yes	yes	yes	no	(capitalist firm/factory)
8	no	no	no	yes	
9	yes	no	no	yes	(peasant & land)
10	no	yes	no	yes	
11	yes	yes	no	yes	
12	no	no	yes	yes	
13	yes	no	yes	yes	
14	no	yes	yes	yes	
15	yes	yes	yes	yes	(bourgeois right)

At the bottom of the scale are slaves. Slaves under American law had no ownership rights. They had no property to which they had a legally enforceable title. At the top of the scale is full bourgeois right, where an individual can use, buy, sell or inherit any property. In between are various combinations. A soviet collective farm prior to *perestroika* had the use of land but was not entitled to trade in land, and *a fortiori* could not inherit it. Note that some of the potential forms property rights may never have existed.

The socialist tradition holds that although wage workers in a capitalist economy have in theory full bourgeois rights over property, in practice their key right is the right to sell their labour. They are unable to use this labour effectively themselves since they do not own capital equipment. They are thus in position 2 on the scale. Of course hired labourers have the right to purchase and use or pawn consumer goods, but the most valuable property they own remains their labour.

Capitalist firms use, buy and sell all sorts of property, but do not have much use for rights of inheritance. In contrast a peasant farmer will typically inherit his land from his father and leave it to his son. The market in land is generally poorly developed, so inheritance and marriage remain the chief means of property transfer.

What can be owned?
For each of the capitalist, Soviet, and our proposed communalist societies we will consider what can be owned and who can own it. We rate the strength of that ownership on the 0 to 15 scale.

Property Relations Under Pure Capitalism and Mixed Capitalism
In capitalist societies there are four significant groups of property owners: individuals, the state, private corporate bodies,[2] and companies. The property system obtaining in Britain at the end of the postwar Labour government was as shown in Table 14.2.

The types of property can be grouped into four main classes. Things like money, information, buildings, etc., are thorough-going objects of property right. Any of the several classes of owner can

Table 14.2:
Property rights in postwar Britain

Owner Owned	Individuals	State	Private Corporations	Companies
Companies	15	15	15	15
Labour	7	7	7	7
Money	15	15	15	15
Information	15	15	15	15
Land	15	15	15	7
Buildings	15	15	15	7
Machinery	15	15	15	7
Mineral rights	5	3	5	5
Electromag spectrum	5	3	5	5
Transport infrastructure	1	3	1	1
Weapons	0	15	14	14

exercise full rights over them. They can be used, inherited, bought and sold by whomever or whatever owns them. Labour time is in the special position that it can be bought and sold by any of the categories of owner, but not inherited for obvious reasons. Companies form a special type of property as they can both be owners and property at the same time. Finally there is a group of objects over which the state holds relatively exclusive property rights. Certain natural resources like mineral rights and the electromagnetic spectrum belong to the state which can use them directly or hire them out (sell them for a period) to commercial companies. Then certain other objects can only be used by the state and not sold—military hardware like atom bombs and transport infrastructure like motorways.

The property system obtaining in 1988 was almost the same except that a few elements of the transport infrastructure had become ownable by companies. Surprising as it may seem, the Thatcher governments brought about a relatively small shift in the forms of property. This is not to deny that they achieved significant redistribution of property within the pre-existing legal categories. The amount of property held by the state has diminished, but with the exception of the legislation on local authority housing, the rights of different categories of owners have not been altered.

Property relations under the Soviet model
By the Soviet model we mean the system of property that obtained between the introduction of central planning in 1928–31 and the breakup of the Soviet Union in 1991. This system is shown in Table 14.3.

If we compare this to what exists in a capitalist country like Britain the most striking thing is how property relations are much 'weaker'.

Table 14.3:
Property rights matrix for Soviet system

Owners Owned	State	Individuals	Enterprises	Farms
Enterprises	1	0	0	0
Land	1	9	1	1
Machinery	5	0	1	3
Labour	5	3	5	1
Public goods[1]	1	0	1	1
Money	2	10	2	2
Buildings	7	15	1	7

1. Mineral rights, information, the electromagnetic spectrum, weapons.

There are few things over which bourgeois rights are exercised: money, personal possessions and houses are the only things that can be used, bought, sold and inherited. In contrast there are a great many weak links. Collective farms have use of land but may not buy or sell it since the notional owner of the land is the state. In terms of bourgeois rights the state ownership of the land is itself a very restricted relation since the state cannot buy or sell land—to whom could it sell?

Similarly, industrial machinery is used by the units of production but in the classic Soviet model they did not have full property rights over this machinery. In Stalin's day the machines used by farms were notionally owned by the state and kept in state-run Machine Tractor Stations; under Khruschev the farms got the right to buy equipment from the state. State enterprises are at the disposition of the state, but again the state can not buy or sell these enterprises, so in bourgeois terms its ownership rights are very restricted. The enterprises have the use of their means of production and have to account for it, that is to say they are charged by the state for means of production received. Despite this we cannot say that they had bourgeois right over industrial equipment since it was allocated to them by the state according to a national plan. If they produced means of production they could sell them, but again only to the state. There were sharp restrictions on the purchase of labour power. Only the state and state enterprises could do this, and they were not allowed to resell it, unlike a capitalist company which can hire out the labour time of its employees. The purchase of labour time by private individuals was strictly prohibited.

The enterprise as focus of contradictions

The property rights of Soviet industrial enterprises in the Stalin period differed in two important respects from those of capitalist firms. First, their rights to purchase commodities were restricted; they could purchase labour time from individual workers, but other goods had to be obtained from the state. The state charged the enterprises for goods received, and in this sense the supply of raw materials and other inputs to the enterprise looked like a purchase, but the ability to make this purchase was conditional upon goods being allocated in a plan. The second restriction was on the sale of goods produced in the enterprise. These could not really be said to be sold in the normal capitalist sense. They were produced to meet plan targets and although the state credited the enterprise with roubles for goods delivered, the enterprise had no choice but to sell them to the state.[3] Nonetheless all transfers between the state and the enterprises took the form of sales; they looked like sales in that goods moved one way and money moved the other.

The Soviet enterprise was thus a contradictory economic form. It appeared to carry out the same type of transactions as a capitalist firm, but in reality it was fully subordinated to the state which owned it. The relationship between the state and the enterprises it owned was quite different from that between a firm and its shareholders. The shareholders of a firm are usually neither its principal customers nor its principal suppliers, and they do not issue detailed directives to the firm about what to produce; they are interested in dividends. In accounting terms, however, the Soviet enterprise did provide the state with profits. The profits of state-owned firms made up a significant part of the national budget.

The Soviet industrial enterprise acted as an employer of the people who worked in it, that is to say it paid their wages out of its wage fund and also provided various bonus payments to workers out of profits. In this sense again it looked like a capitalist employer. But on the other hand socialist labour legislation made it very difficult for an enterprise to lay workers off, one of the principal objectives of the socialist state being the provision of full employment. Associated with this there was no mechanism for enterprises to go bankrupt; the enterprises were state property and the state could not go bankrupt. This led to inefficiencies in the allocation of labour between industries; enterprises and industries that were of diminishing importance to the national economy tended to hoard labour which could have been employed more effectively elsewhere.[4]

Here we see a major economic problem for the legal institutions of Soviet socialism. There are two contradictory imperatives—the provision of secure employment, and the need to ensure labour mobility between industries as the economy modernises. Labour could be released by allowing bankruptcies in sectors that were shrinking, but this would compromise a basic objective of socialism, and would be very unpopular. Allowing these older enterprises to continue would waste labour and involve the state in paying out subsidies to loss-making enterprises. These subsidies, generally provided in the form of credits from the state bank, would expand the money supply and lead to suppressed inflation. These are the circumstances that recently led to the introduction of bankruptcy laws in several erstwhile socialist countries.

We think that this was a retrograde step. Bankruptcy laws and the move towards cost accounting (*khozraschet*) involve emphasising the capitalist side of Soviet enterprises—their role as distinct economic subjects capable of buying and selling property—to the detriment of their role as social property. This capitalist form of solution to the problem of labour mobility is bound to be detrimental to the interests of workers, as is shown by the chaotic economic conditions in countries like Yugoslavia and Hungary where this course was followed longest.

We believe there is another alternative that involves emphasising the socialised aspects of the enterprise and eliminating its residual capitalist aspects. This approach, which we outline below, has to solve the same problems of economic efficiency that gave rise to the response of 'liberalisation'; it must allow the concentration of resources where they are most needed, but it must do so without undermining the social rights and liberties of workers.

Property relations under the proposed communalist model

We now describe the overall structure of property relations which we believe to be consistent with the economic and social system outlined in previous chapters. In the following, we discuss four aspects of this structure in detail: individual property rights; the rights of the central planning authority and of particular economic 'projects'; property in land; and ownership of natural resources.

Individual property rights

Property relations in a socialist commonwealth have to allow the smooth functioning of the economic system, to protect the legitimate interests of individuals and institutions, and to prevent the emergence of exploitation. In general, there are tensions between these requirements. Any system of property relations is at the same time a system of restraint and exclusion. When the law specifies that a resource is the property of one individual, that resource is thereby denied to others. If a man owns landed property his ownership denies others the free use of that land. Historically the right of some individuals to own property has allowed them to exploit others. The ownership of land allows landlords to exploit tenants; the ownership of capital allows entrepreneurs and bankers to exploit employees. Although this exploitation is unjust from a humanitarian standpoint it remains legitimate and necessary within the structure of Western society. Without secure property rights, capitalist industry could not thrive and the economy would decline into chaos and stagnation. So long as society provides no other mechanisms to organise production, capitalist firms have a legitimate interest in exploiting their employees. Property law has both a class character and an economic rationale; it protects the interests of those with property from those without, and provides the preconditions for economic development.

Socialist property law has to support analogous functions, but in this case the interests that have to be protected are those of the producers and those who must be constrained are the potential exploiters. It must give positive rights to workers and protect their legitimate interests in the new economy, while acting as a constraint upon any actions by individuals that would either disrupt the socialist economy or reintroduce exploitation. The key positive rights that a socialist commonwealth should grant individuals are as follows:

1. The right to earn a living;
2. The right to receive the full value of their labour; and
3. The right to dispose of the value of their labour as they wish.

These property rights constitute an essential aim of socialist society. They are components of the socialist 'good life'. The rights not to be exploited and to choose how to spend your income are ends in themselves. The right to earn a living has an additional social rationality: it is only by allowing all citizens to take an active part in the economy that the wealth of society as a whole is maximised.

None of these individual rights can be absolute. A citizen has the right to be provided with work, but only with such work as she is able to perform and for which there is a need. People have the right to the full proceeds of their labour, but this does not exempt them from the need to pay taxes; only part of the proceeds of labour can be made available for *individual* disposition, the disposition of the remainder being decided democratically in the light of common social objectives. Individuals may dispose of their income however they wish provided that they do not harm the environment or impinge upon the liberties of others.

For a commonwealth to give its citizens such rights it must have an appropriate institutional and economic framework. We will examine three aspects of this framework: the organisation of production, the nature of employment, and the protection of the environment.

Rights of Planning and economic projects

In earlier chapters the problem of planning was discussed from an economic standpoint; at that time little attention was paid to the legal framework that is needed to implement effective planning. Effective planning obviously cannot be carried out under the existing framework of company law, and we have criticised the legal framework of production in the erstwhile USSR. If socialist planning is to regain credibility it is necessary to explore alternatives.

We will refer to the body responsible for planning the economy simply as Planning. We are not concerned here with the constitutional mechanisms required to bring Planning under democratic control,[5] only with its property rights. Planning is assumed to own all collectively operated means of production except those held by local communes. By collectively operated means of production we mean instruments or collections of instruments that can only be put to effective use by several people. Planning owns everything that we would normally think of as industrial equipment: railways, roads, industrial buildings, communications equipment, computer networks, etc. It also owns stocks of intermediate goods and semi-finished products.

Planning is the institutional embodiment of common ownership of the conditions of production. This ownership is at once more absolute, and yet in a sense more limited, than capitalist property ownership. When the community is the sole owner of the means of production there will be nobody to whom it can sell them, nobody from whom it can buy (ignoring international trade for the moment), and nobody from whom it can inherit. Its powers of ownership shrink to those of disposition or allocation. On the basis of its production plans, Planning decides to what use each building, piece of equipment, etc. will be allocated.

We will refer to particular economic activities as 'projects'. By a project we mean a coordinated set of activities designed to produce a definite useful result. A project might be a large-scale activity such as constructing the third channel tunnel or an orbiting solar power station. It might be an ongoing production process like bottling milk for Peterburgh, or providing health care for Dumbarton. It might be a short-term production process like publishing a book or producing a film, or it might be a process taking several years like the development of a new range of computers. Whatever it is, the project uses resources—labour, buildings and machinery—that are allocated to it by Planning. Each project is registered, along with its intended output and its resource usage, on the network of Planning computers.

These production projects are units of work organisation, not legal personalities. In this respect the relationship between Planning and projects is the same as that between a capitalist company and the individual activities that it may be carrying out. A car company will have underway several projects to produce new models; each of these will be subdivided into projects to develop the car body, electronics, engine, suspension, and so on. These projects are allocated employees, workspace and equipment by the company, and are expected to produce results to a schedule agreed by the company management. The projects do not own the office or factory space they use, nor do they employ the people who work on them—the company does. The projects are managerial or administrative rather than legal entities.

It may be argued by the advocates of market socialism that the marxist idea of planning the economy like one vast enterprise is a threat to democracy. On the contrary, our case is that effective control by the citizens over the economy requires that the means of production be the collective public property of the citizens. We do not believe that state-owned enterprises as such, still less independent workers' cooperatives, provide an adequate form for public ownership of the means of production.

In the case of a state-owned enterprise the means of production are directly owned by the enterprise itself, and the enterprise is owned by the state. This ownership of the enterprise by the state may be of varying strengths. In some cases the state is just a shareholder in a Public Limited Company, with a right to a share of the enterprise's profits. This was exemplified by the British state's ownership of BP, whose operations were indistinguishable from that of any other capitalist company.

A stage up from this is the nationalised corporation like the former Coal, Gas and Electricity boards. In this case the state enterprises existed by special statute which placed obligations on them and provided for their governing boards to be appointed by the state. These are a step in advance of simple state shareholdings, as the statutory obligations of the corporations could go beyond the profit maximisation which governed BP's behaviour. They remained subject to many criticisms, however, some of the most important of which from a socialist standpoint were:

1. The class character of the state remained capitalist, and thus the management of the corporations could, when the government so chose, be used to carry out attacks on the interests of the workers in the industry. This was illustrated in the miners' strikes of the 1970s and 1980s.
2. Within the corporation there was no provision for workers' control of the industries.
3. The different corporations acted as relatively private bodies which prevented overall energy planning. Each campaigned to maximise sales of its own product and thus its revenues. This was directly contrary to the social goal which would have been to try and minimise overall energy consumption, and the pollution associated with it.

The first objection could only be met by a change in the character of the state. The second and third are related in a possibly contradictory fashion. The interests of the working class as a whole might well not directly coincide at all points with those of the workers in particular industries. There would be no problem with issues of a general class character that might be raised by workers' control: safety at work, better working conditions, opportunities for trying out workers' ideas for improving production, elimination of class hierarchy at the workplace. Where problems might arise is if other issues like overall equity, economy in use of labour or control of CO_2 emissions arise. It could be that the general public interest would be better served by, for instance, running down the coal industry in favour of more use of gas and energy conservation.

At this point it becomes important that the Coal Board, Gas Board and Electricity Boards are not treated as three separate enterprises with distinct corporate interests (including those of the workers they employ) but are treated as a single, co-ordinated process of energy production. This implies that there has to be a public body with both the authority and the capacity to regulate these industries in a co-ordinated way in the public interest.

An illustration of the inherent superiority of this centralised form of ownership can be made by reference to the NHS. There the hospitals are the property of the health boards, which, prior to the Tory reorganisation, had the obligation to organise their resources so as to best serve the health of the community. In our view the health service was the only really communist institution introduced by the Labour Party. As such it represents a higher form of socialisation than we are advocating for industry as a whole, but this higher form can be used as a benchmark for the socialist form that we are proposing for industry.

The NHS follows the communist principle of 'from each according to their ability, to each according to their need'. Treatment is free and based upon a disinterested professional assessment of what the patient needs. The parts are subordinated to the interests of the whole: a hospital was not an enterprise; it did not exist to make profits but to serve the community under the direction of the health board.

Recent Tory reforms move the system in the direction of a collection of distinct enterprises—opted-out hospitals, that would negotiate as private bodies to supply services. The general opinion of those working in the NHS is that the changes will result in a deterioration of service, a decline in morale and an increasing social stratification in health care, and a lack of local accountability.

These examples from British experience show that centralised ownership and planning are preconditions for democratic working-class control: without that, the working class is split into contending corporate groups pursuing sectional interests. In the case of both the capitalist firm and the NHS, if the superior body decides that a particular project or activity is no longer cost-effective it may close it down and reallocate its resources for other purposes. Consider the contrast with the situation in the USSR where three types of agency were involved: Gosplan, the industrial Ministries, and the individual enterprises. Gosplan set production targets which were directed to particular state officials in the industrial Ministries. The Ministries then passed these on to the enterprises under their control. In this arrangement the effective power to dispose of property was divided between the three levels. Parallel to this division of state property, there were various different forms of calculation—calculation in terms of material balances, in terms of labour balances, and, at the level of the enterprise, cost accounting in roubles. Although the enterprise has in the past been effectively controlled by norms set by the plan in material terms, it is also supposed to cover its costs in monetary terms. It is the enterprise that employs people and pays their wages. But given that prices have been centrally fixed, it is possible for the criterion of cost accounting to come into conflict with meeting the physical plan; it may be that under the given price structure it is actually 'unprofitable' for the enterprise to meet the plan.

A loss-making enterprise in a Soviet-type system may or may not be of net benefit to the economy, and whether it is or not cannot be determined from its monetary accounts. But since enterprises are, within limits, legal personalities (able to purchase labour, sell their products, enter into contracts, etc.) there is a problem deciding what to do with those that, on whatever grounds, are taken to be 'uneconomic'. The decisions in recent years in the ex-socialist economies to allow bankruptcy proceedings to be instituted against loss-making enterprises indicates that in these countries cost accounting at the level of the enterprise has become the dominant mechanism of calculation, and that the enterprise is no longer considered primarily as an object of state property. Instead it is operating as an owned/owner along the lines of a joint stock company with a state shareholding. This particular development of property relations is at the opposite pole from what we are proposing.

In our model projects have labour budgets set by Planning; these control the amount of resources that they can use. Although a project will not be allocated resources in excess of its budget, this type of allocation is functionally different from a monetary budget. It is not used to purchase resources. This can be illustrated by considering labour inputs.

Consider a project to run a local leisure centre. It is allocated an annual budget of 20 person-years, along with the use of a suitable building. The centre's budget acts as a control on its use of resources. The project registers with the planning authorities that half of this will go on staff and the rest on power, equipment and maintenance. The leisure centre itself does not pay the people who work on the project. The work these people do is deducted from the centre's budget, but unlike money it is not transferred into any other account, it is just cancelled out. Similarly any use of material resources like sports equipment will result in deductions from the budget, but nobody is 'paid' for the equipment, since the resources and the project are all equally community property. Staff in the centre are credited by the planning authority, not the leisure centre itself, for the work they have done. Since the project is in no sense an economic subject (*i.e.* a subject of property right), the issue of bankruptcy cannot arise. Planning must, however, be at liberty to terminate particular projects if they are deemed not to be cost-effective, just as a local education authority can close down a school if the school rolls no longer justify keeping it open.

Decisions to close projects—if they are to be better than arbitrary—presuppose the existence of a rational system of economic calculation. We have shown in previous chapters that there are no fundamental problems in carrying out such calculation without recourse to the market. At the same time such closures must not cause unemployment. At the gross level unemployment is prevented by balancing the national budget in terms of labour. As explained in chapter 7, any shortfall in aggregate demand is compensated for by the marketing authority marking down all consumer goods prices. This means that there is no possibility of a fall in demand sparking off a recessionary spiral, which is a major cause of unemployment in capitalist economies. But if generalised demand-deficient unemployment is ruled out, this still leaves the problem of redeployment. If your project is cancelled, the activity you were involved in has become redundant. That does not mean that *you* have become redundant; you have the right to expect society to protect your income and provide you with other work—but how exactly should this right be secured?

We envisage a system in which people are directly employed by the community rather than by companies or independent 'enterprises'. It is always in the interest of society that workers should be redeployed as quickly and efficiently as possible when their previous work is no longer useful; by making 'society' the actual employer this interest is borne home.

If Mary, say, were seeking a new project to work with, she would go along to an employment agency and register her skills, how hard she wanted to work, for how many hours a week, etc. The employment agency would then tap into the Planning data-net to find the best match between Mary's offer to work and the requirements of projects in the area. This means the planning authorities would have up-to-date records on the amount and types of labour available, making it possible to draw up gross labour budgets for the economy as a whole. Unlike present-day employment agencies, the positions available would match the workers seeking projects in overall numbers and approximate types. Once Mary has decided which project she wants to work on, and has convinced those currently working on it of her suitability, she signs a contract with the employment agency stating that she will work for so many hours a week on a particular project. This is then registered with the planning system, which starts crediting her account with the hours worked.

The social functions of labour credits overlap with those of money in the capitalist system but they are not identical. A worker receives from the community just as much as she or he gives to it in terms of work. After taxes have been paid these labour credits entitle the worker to withdraw from the community goods containing the same amount of labour. The similarity with money is obvious: the credits can be 'spent' on consumer goods. They differ in that they do not circulate; when something is bought the ticket is cancelled. In this respect they are like train tickets, which can be exchanged against a journey and are then cancelled by the ticket collector. The purpose of this restriction is to prevent the re-emergence of capitalist exploitation, money being the precondition of all capitalist activity.

Under such a system individuals would have the right to own personal possessions, consumer goods and houses. They could not own stocks and shares (indeed, these would not exist) or any other form of capital, nor could they own land or such productive equipment as can only be worked collectively. Individuals could not hire other individuals to work for them because of the non-transferability of labour credits.[6]

Self-employment
It may well be a good idea for the commonwealth to allow self-employment. Some sorts of activity are best carried out on an individual level. Examples are trades like plumbing and repair work. The propensity of these to give rise to a 'black economy' in the erstwhile socialist countries is notorious. According to classical

economics, self-employment does not give rise to economic inequalities. When individuals exchange the products of their labour, relative prices will tend to be set by labour values. Provided that entry into a self-employed trade is not artificially restricted, the tradesperson will earn the same sort of hourly rate as those employed in the socialist sector.

If people are to become self-employed they have to be able to open a company or trading account with the state bank, into which labour credits could be paid. This gives rise to the danger of disguised exploitation. A supposedly self-employed person might in practice be subcontracting his labour to another self-employed person. Perhaps the best way to prevent the emergence of hidden exploitation of labour is to harness the self-interest of the exploited. If the right of the workers to the full proceeds of their labour were assured by the constitution, and enforceable by recourse to a people's court,[7] and if the law provided for the award of punitive damages to the victims of exploitation, it would be impossible to hire people at exploitative wage rates.

Property in land

In contemporary Britain land is an object of private property like any other. It may be used, bought, sold, inherited or rented. In all socialist revolutions the land has been taken out of private ownership and nationalised. In all cases this nationalisation has resulted in a weak form of public property right over land. In the USSR, for instance, the state had disposition over the land. The planning bodies could decide to build a factory on a plot of ground, or sink a mine through it, without obtaining the permission of any landlord. But when it comes to agricultural land, or land used for housing, this right becomes tenuous in practice since the use of the land can be delegated to private individuals (private plots or privately built houses) or to corporate bodies (collective farms). These bodies have effective disposition over the land. In a capitalist country it is standard practice for landowners to grant use over land to other individuals, but the landlords demand rent in return for this. For some reason—probably the association of rent with gross exploitation by landlords in the past—socialist governments have been unwilling to introduce rent payments for the use of publicly owned land. But in the absence of rent, there is a tendency for public property in land to degenerate into private proprietorship by those with disposition over it.

The situation of the state owning land but charging no rent for it is both unjust and economically inefficient. To understand this it is necessary to have some grasp of the classical theory of rent.

Digression on the Ricardian theory of rent

We owe the theory of ground rent to the early 19th century English economist David Ricardo. He argued that rent arises due to a combination of two factors: scarcity of land, and differences between the productivity of different plots of land.

To establish that a shortage of land was the first requirement of rent he pointed out that in new colonies where land was to be had for the taking, no rent could be charged. He then observed that people settled first upon the most fertile soil. As population grew, settlement and agriculture would spread to less productive soils that were more difficult to work. Suppose that there were three grades of soil as shown in Table 14.4.

Table 14.4:
Soils of different productivities

Grade	Labour required per bushel	Production cost
1	10 hrs	£10
2	15 hrs	£15
3	20 hrs	£20

If in the first stages of population growth the people's needs could be met from the best soil alone, the price of corn would be £10. But as population expands, successively worse soils will have to be brought into cultivation and the price of corn will have to rise to meet the cost of production on these soils of declining fertility. Eventually the price would rise to £20 as soil of grade 3 was brought into use. At this point the cost of production of corn on the best land would still only be £10 leaving a profit of £10 on each bushel. In consequence, the landowners would be able to charge a rent equivalent to half the produce of the best land without driving their tenants out of production. The tenant farmer on the best land, who now pays half his produce over to the landowner, is no better or worse off than the farmer cultivating the marginal land of grade 3 who pays no rent. The situation is as shown in Table 14.5.

If the farmer happens to own his own land, he appropriates an income equivalent to the rent (an 'imputed rent') himself. In this example, an owner-farmer using grade 1 land would earn an excess of £10 per bushel over his cost of production simply due to the fact that grade 3 land is in use, and that the price of corn is set 'at the margin', where cost is highest. We can label this surplus 'rent', even if it is not paid over to a distinct person.

It is important to recognise that in the Ricardian theory land contributes nothing to the value of a product (Ricardo operated

Table 14.5:
Rents with grade 3 land in cultivation

Grade	Rent paid per bushel	Production cost
1	£10	£10
2	£5	£15
3	£0	£20

Price of corn = £20 = cost of production + rent on all land = cost of production alone on marginal land.

with a labour theory of value). Corn is not dear because land yields rent, rather, land yields rent because corn is dear.

The classical theory indicates that the existence of rent is an inevitable result of the differential productivity of land. This is true whether we are considering productivity in its narrowly agricultural context, or in the broader sense whereby land close to centres of population is more productive. In the latter case, the productivity springs from a saving in transport costs: "distance is equivalent to sterility" (Jean-Baptiste Say). Where a socialist society nationalises the land, but devolves the use of the land upon private bodies or individuals (family farms, communes), the public ownership of land has been effectively negated by allowing rent to be appropriated by the user of the land. In China, the marked differentiation in wealth between different communes, associated with differing local agricultural productivities, was due to the appropriation of rent by the communes on the more fertile land. On grounds of equity, private individuals or associations should be charged rent for the use of land. This rent can then be used to offset public expenditure, reducing the general level of taxation, and in effect transferring income to those burdened with less productive land.

One of the notable features of socialist countries that have allowed a resurgence of peasant cultivation has been the relative prosperity of peasants as compared to public employees. This is in large part due to the effective appropriation of rent incomes by the peasantry. Given the varying fertility of land, the majority of peasants will be cultivating non-marginal land and will therefore be in receipt of non-labour incomes.

In an advanced industrial society, a major form of rent income is that on building land. Although a socialist commonwealth may allow private ownership of houses, it should not allow the private ownership of the land on which they stand. Home owners should be liable for a ground rent based upon the current rentable value of the land used for their house. In this case somebody who buys a house is just buying the fabric of the building, but in addition to the purchase price home-owners pay a rent or land tax to the community, reflecting the differential convenience or amenity of the land on which their houses stand.

Ownership of natural resources

From the standpoint of a higher economic form of society, private ownership of the globe by single individuals will appear as absurd as private ownership of one man by another. Even a whole society, a nation, or even all the simultaneously existing societies taken together are not the owners of the globe. They are only its possessors, its usufructuaries, and, like *boni patres familias*, they must hand it down to succeeding generations in an improved condition (Marx, *Capital*, Vol III, p.776).

In the past the question of land ownership seemed primarily to concern conflicts of human interest. The interest of the landowner was opposed to that of the tenant, and political proposals concerning land ownership were the expression of the conflicting class interests of these groups. Now it is no longer good enough to look at things this way. We have to see the question of land ownership and use in the more general context of use of the earth's natural resources by humanity. The extent and scale of environmental destruction brought about by human activities has only recently sunk in on us.

It is now clear that human activity has been transforming the environment at an accelerating pace for several thousand years. Indeed it is possible that past transformations of our modes of production may have been forced upon our ancestors by ecological changes they themselves brought about. For instance the impetus to the development of agriculture in the Americas was probably provided by the hunting to extinction of the American megafauna (see Harner, 1977). One factor contributing to the collapse of the slaveholding civilisations of the ancient Mediterranean was the loss of a large part of their agricultural land due to deforestation and desertification. Genovese (1965) argues that part of the reason for the fatal clash between the slaveocracy of the Old South and Yankee industrial capitalism was the deterioration of the soil brought about by intensive cotton cultivation. This led to a pressure for westward expansion that brought the slave system into conflict with the free states.

The age-old phenomena of species extermination, deforestation and desertification remain with us still, and indeed occur at an accelerating pace. To this must now be added pollution of the sea and the atmosphere. The effects of environmental modification are no longer local to one society or one nation, but produce global effects through their influence upon the air and the oceans. It is likely that changes in the content of the atmosphere produced by a variety of economic activities are going to produce significant rises in average global temperatures. The possible consequences of this are now well known: flooding of coastal areas, polar shifts in the climatic belts, the loss of the world's main agricultural areas, the transformation of much of Africa and areas of South America into deserts, famine on an unprecedented scale.

These catastrophes are the indirect result of an inadequate system of property relations. Decisions on the use of natural resources are made by private individuals, companies, or even nations on the basis of their immediate interests. The long-term global consequences of these decisions do not enter into their calculations. It seems that the ultimate solution must be not the *nationalisation* of land and natural resources, but their *internationalisation*. In the long term, industrial society will be able to survive only if ownership of these resources is vested in some global authority. This would be responsible for licensing the use of resources in a way that is calculated to ensure environmental conservation and improvement. The powers of such an agency would run far beyond those of a conventional landowner, whose powers extend only to the use of the land itself. The global proprietor would have to regulate not just the use of land for agriculture, forestry and mineral extraction, but also the emission into the air and sea of all pollutants.

We can see some tentative steps being taken in this direction at the present with the UN Treaty on the Law of the Seabed, which introduced the notion of the resources of the seabed being the common patrimony of humanity. The Montreal Convention on the regulation of the emission of chlorofluorocarbons (CFCs) was a further step in this direction, but it is difficult to envisage the internationalisation of natural resources taking place while the major world powers remain capitalist. The USA and the UK refused to ratify the law on the seabed, as it was seen as undermining the rights of private property—which it certainly did. The establishment of global trusteeship over natural resources will probably have to await the victory of socialism in several of the world's major industrial centres.

Prior to that, the same general argument of principle holds—that natural resources should be under the control of the broadest possible public body. At the very least the ownership should be vested in a national body, better still a continental body.

Separation of control from benefit
Natural resources get abused because it is in somebody's interest to do so. Public ownership of resources in not itself a protection against this. In the USSR there was public ownership of land and

natural resources; there is also widespread environmental damage. The Caspian sea is heavily polluted and the Aral sea is in the process of drying out. This may be for lack of any strong institutions set up to regulate the activity of state bodies. The objectives of the industrial Ministries whose factories are causing the pollution of rivers is to maximise production, not to protect the environment. The objective of the Republican governments around the Aral sea has been to maximise the output of their cotton farmers, who demanded water, and not to preserve the fisheries of the Aral. To protect against these sorts of pressure it is essential that the country's, or later the world's, natural resources be owned and controlled by a body that is independent of those who stand to benefit from their exploitation.

Let us for the sake of argument call this body the Environment Trust. It owns all natural resources. It may grant licences to the Planning Agency to allow resources to be used. It may stipulate the conditions in terms of emissions and other parameters that are to be met by the industrial projects that use these resources. It may set rents for the use of land by individuals or communes. It may stipulate that surcharges are to be put on the prices of products whose production or use causes environmental deterioration. The revenues in the form of rents or surcharges should not accrue to the Environment Trust itself, but should be used to offset the cost of other public services. This is an important principle, since it ensures that the regulatory body does not acquire an interest in allowing the exploitation of natural resources for the sake of the revenue that might accrue to it. One wants the levying of rents and surcharges by the Environment Trust to be as disinterested as the levying of fines by a law court.

Notes to Chapter 14

1. Note that the numbering is the same as would be arrived at by expressing the original Boolean predicates as a binary expansion.
2. By private corporations we mean bodies like churches, educational institutions and political parties.
3. In various reforms of the post-Stalin period, enterprises were granted some nominal rights to choose their own customers, but the great bulk of output remained subject to state orders.
4. David Granick (1987) argues that the inefficiencies commonly ascribed to central planning in the Soviet Union are actually the result of immobility of labour, stemming from the effective right of Soviet workers to keep their existing jobs.
5. On this point, see chapter 13.
6. In a similar way, capitalist systems prohibit the purchase of people as slaves in order both to protect human rights and to protect themselves from unfair competition. A more civilised society is entitled to prohibit practices that were tolerated in more primitive societies.
7. On the pattern of the Greek dikasteria—see chapter 13.

CHAPTER 15

Some Contrary Views Considered

We have now completed the presentation of our views on the organising principles of a new socialist economy and society. In this final chapter we offer some responses to various contrary arguments that have been put forward by socialist writers over recent years. These responses are organised under two themes: distribution, values and prices; and the possibility of market socialism. Both of the themes connect in one way or another with the issue of markets and socialism. Under the first head, we defend our proposal for a market in consumer goods (spelled out in chapter 8). A market of this type, we argue, is essential for ensuring that the plan targets are continually adjusted in the light of consumers' preferences. In the second section of this chapter, however, we sharply distinguish our own 'market' proposal from 'market socialism' as such. We examine two examples of market socialist proposals from recent years, and find them wanting in relation to the basic aims of socialism.

Distribution, Values and Prices

When we first presented the arguments developed in this book, in an article in *Economy and Society*,[1] Gavan Duffy (1989) produced a response in the same journal. While we agree with some of Duffy's points, we think he has not fully understood our position, and perhaps we can sharpen the presentation of our ideas by considering some of his criticisms here. Two main points stand out.

First, Duffy suggests that there is something ironic about our argument in this sense: while we make much of the potential of modern computing technology, we stop short of advocating a purely quantitative planning system, *i.e.*, one which proceeds without using the intermediary of prices or values. Duffy seems to regard this as a kind of retreat from the positions of earlier socialist economists such as Lange, who saw computation as an alternative to markets of any kind.[2] Just as the technology required for the Lange-type model comes into view, Cockshott and Cottrell recommend a solution which relies on a market mechanism! Secondly, Duffy suggests that if one does think in terms of a socialist market in consumer goods, there is no good reason to use labour values as the benchmark of social cost: he argues that 'simple costs of production' would be preferable.

On the first point, we should stress that we are not proposing that all goods and services be distributed via a market. We recognise the existence of a 'social provision' sector (health, education, child care, etc.) where goods or services are provided as a basic right of citizenship (see chapter 5). Here the level and form of provision are not decided using market prices, but through democratic debate and politics. Nonetheless, we make no apology for advocating a market in many items of personal consumption.

The essential features of our consumer goods market are as follows.

1. Consumers receive incomes designated in labour tokens, either for work performed or as transfers.
2. Commodities have 'prices,' also designated in labour tokens, which may diverge somewhat from their actual labour content (also marked on the commodity) due to fluctuations in supply or demand.
3. When consumers acquire goods through the market their balances of labour tokens are 'cancelled' correspondingly, so that their acquisitions are limited by their incomes (plus some allowance for consumer credit).

In effect, each consumer is presented with this proposition: you are entitled to such-and-such a definite allowance of social labour time commanded, which you are free to enjoy in any form you wish.

What would an alternative 'purely quantitative' system, with no prices or values, look like? The state must place an initial 'order' for consumer goods to be produced in such-and-such proportions, and then presumably consumers are free to acquire whatever they like from the stores ('to each according to his need', as Marx put it in his *Critique of the Gotha Programme*). If there are no prices, then 'incomes' have no meaning either, and there is no pre-set limit to the quantity of goods the individual may acquire. As the stocks of some goods fall, the state simply orders the production of more, while the production rate is slowed down for goods of which stocks are increasing.

All very well, but what is to stop the stocks of popular goods going straight to zero, and how can there be any guarantee that production can be sustained at a level sufficient to meet consumers' wishes, within the constraint posed by the available amount of social labour? Or in other words, if consumers can acquire anything they like at zero cost to themselves, will the total of such 'demands' not likely exceed the total feasible production of the society? And will the practical result, therefore, not simply be 'first come, first served'?

Two points might be urged against this critical view: communist 'abundance', and the responsible, public-spirited attitude of the socialist consumer. But 'abundance', in the sense of a sufficiency of all goods when they are priced at zero, does not seem at all credible to us. Even as technology continues to improve, the need to cope with environmental problems and resource depletion, coupled with the need greatly to improve the material condition of the majority of the world's population now living in poverty, would seem to rule out the abolition of economic scarcity. And even if socialist consumers are thoroughly public-spirited, the right attitude is simply not enough. Without some guidance from objectively calculated social costs, people cannot know what is a 'reasonable' or 'responsible' amount for them to consume.

If one accepts the need for some kind of socially determined limitation on individual consumers, to keep people's total consumption demands within the feasible production set, what is the alternative to the payment of definite incomes and the (non-zero) pricing of consumer goods? The state could decide on an allocation or 'ration' of consumer goods per head, order the production of these, and then distribute them directly to the people. But it is hard to see how such a system could be adequately responsive to changes in consumers' preferences over time, or to the varied preferences and priorities of different individuals, households or communes. If people are to exercise (constrained) individual choice over their consumption pattern, there is no alternative to some form of market. Free substitution within a constraint requires that the consumer's allocation of goods takes the form of a scalar (any goods you like up to such a total value)[3] rather than a vector (a list of quantities of goods, or ration). And the payment of incomes and non-zero pricing of goods is simply a means of imposing such a scalar constraint.

Accepting the need for a market in consumer goods does not, of course, mean one has to accept our particular version of how such a market should operate. This brings us to Duffy's second point, concerning the use of labour values as a representation of social cost.

We accept that straightforward labour values are open to criticism as a measure of social cost. We have already addressed two relevant points in chapter 5. First, the use of labour values as the sole means of calculation arguably leads to an under-valuation of finite natural resources which cannot simply be 'produced' by the application of labour time. Second, strict labour-value calculation neglects the issue of the time-profile of the application of social labour. Two products might require the same total labour hours for their production, but the phasing of this labour over calendar time might be different. If such differences are relevant, then again labour-value calculation must be seen as incomplete. Also in chapter 5, we sketched means of solving these problems.

We are puzzled, however, by Duffy's suggestion that 'simple costs of production' might be preferable to labour values as a means of economic calculation under socialism. As discussed in chapter 8, 'cost of production' in the normal capitalist sense is far from simple. It presupposes that enterprises exist as subjects of right—in effect, presupposes private property in the means of production. In a socialist economy there is no 'simple', given cost of production; any candidate for a measure of social cost has to be socially defined and calculated. We have argued that labour time provides a rational basis for such calculation, even though it has to be supplemented in the ways indicated in chapter 5.

Market Socialism?
As we have already said, we are well aware that our arguments run against the recent tide of right-wing pro-market opinion. We make no apology for this; we believe that the fashion is mistaken and will ultimately be seen as such. Of more concern to us, however, is the fact that many avowedly socialist writers have, over the 1980s, expressed serious doubts over the 'classic' socialist project of a planned economy, and have advocated instead various forms of 'market socialism'.[4] The voices raised against this trend have been rather few.[5]

In this section we consider some of the market socialist views; we shall argue that market socialism is seriously inadequate as a goal of socialist politics. We agree with Devine (1988) that market socialism reflects not a bold new conception on the part of socialist theorists, but a damaging accommodation to the dominance of the right. Whereas Gramsci called for 'pessimism of the intellect, optimism of the will' (i.e. hard-headed realism combined with a passionate commitment to socialist objectives) the market socialism of the 1980s betrays a 'pessimism of the will', a debilitating loss of confidence in the ability of socialism to offer any really distinctive long-term political project.

We obviously cannot offer detailed comments on all the market socialist arguments that have been put forward lately. For our purposes here, we focus on one recent contribution in the West, that of Diane Elson, and one from the East, that of Abel Aganbegyan.

Diane Elson: the socialised market?

Diane Elson (1988) has argued that a 'socialised market' provides a third alternative between planning and the free market. We believe that her proposal for a socialised market concedes far too much to bourgeois economics. It appears to involve an uncritical acceptance of Alec Nove's claim that efficient central planning is impossible— a claim we have been at pains to rebut in previous chapters. Specifically we argue:

1. that by shifting her attention from the production to the exchange process Elson effaces the main point of the Marxist critique of capitalism;

2. that her socialised market system would retain most of the social and production relations of capitalism, and would be more accurately described as state capitalism rather than socialism; and

3. that it would be susceptible to all the characteristic instabilities of capitalism.

A large part of Elson's article is devoted to showing that real capitalist markets are far removed from the ideal markets assumed by most advocates of market socialism. She argues that they involve real costs in terms of resources to function, that they are rarely freely competitive, that consumer sovereignty is not really effective, that Say's law does not operate, etc. She makes reference to an extensive recent literature to reinforce her point. This sort of criticism, though it is of value in pointing out the lack of realism in the formulations of the outright pro-marketeers, seems to fill in for an absent concept. The concept of exploitation is missing from the critiques of capitalist markets to which she refers. Socialism as a political movement did not arise because consumers were dissatisfied with the way the market was organised. It arose because capitalism is an exploitative system whose victims sought redress. Capitalism allows the wealthy to exploit the labour of the poor. Socialism was the response to exploitation of wage labourers by capitalists.

We have made reference to the classical marxist conception of exploitation thoughout this book. In the present context, the important point is that one of Marx's central concerns was to refute the idea that exploitation arises from imperfections in the operation of the market. Instead, he argued, it arose from the very logic of commodity production. In order to demonstrate this theoretically, he made the 'generous' assumption that commodities exchange in proportion to their labour values. This was the ideal put forward by the most advanced bourgeois economist, David Ricardo. Marx was well aware that a whole series of complicating factors— different capital intensities, partial monopolies and so on—would prevent prices in a real capitalist economy being proportional to labour values. He nonetheless assumes this proportionality in Volume 1 of *Capital*. He assumes that in every sale or purchase of a commodity, equivalents are exchanged. The currency is based on gold, and in each sale or purchase the amount of labour embodied in the gold is equal to that in the commodity being purchased. In other words, he assumes no cheating in the exchange process. He knew that all this was counterfactual—that workers were routinely sold adulterated products, cheated through the truck system or extra deductions from their wages. But for the sake of argument he says: Let us grant the market to be completely fair, I will show that it still leads to the exploitation of the working class.

The key to exploitation, Marx argued, was the special character of labour power. Labour power is unique in that its utility to a capitalist is its ability to create value. Labour power is assumed, like every other commodity, to sell for its cost of reproduction. In many cases, of course, labour power will sell for less than its cost of reproduction, for instance where workers are part-time farmers and don't buy all their food on the market. But even if it does sell for its full cost of reproduction, exploitation still takes place. The working day is prolonged to produce absolute surplus value. Technology cheapens the means of subsistence and produces relative surplus value.

The political point of this argument was to rebut those who argued that fair trading, the abolition of monopoly, and a just level of wages would bring the salvation of the proletariat. Marx argued to the contrary that only the abolition of the wages system itself would end exploitation. No reform of the market could possibly remove the antagonisms at the heart of capitalism. But a reform of the market is just what Elson proposes.

Elson proposes a variety of publicly funded institutions that would set price norms. These institutions would have available to them detailed information about the cost of production of different products. On the basis of cost, plus some markup, they would set price norms for each commodity. (It is not made clear what the basis of the markup would be: Would it be proportional to the capital employed or to the recurrent costs?) The setting of these price norms, which are apparently not intended to be binding, together with the publication of the data on which they are based, is termed the socialisation of the market.

The term 'socialised market' is rather misleading since markets have always been social institutions. They are the typical way in which private individuals enter into social relations in the capitalist epoch. When the word social is combined with the word market —the social market economy, socialised market, market socialism

—we should be on our guard. Given that exploitation would exist even under the very generous assumptions made by Marx, the socialised market would also allow it. The socialised price norms are to be merely indicative, not binding on buyers and sellers: "Price and Wage Commissions can generate price and wage norms, and can supply the information to enable buyers and sellers to 'police' prices and wages in a decentralised way" (Elson, 1988, p.33). If the norms are not accepted by the market, then it is the norms, not the market prices, that are altered. The main difference between the socialised market and a normal one seems to be that in the former the taxpayer subsidises some costs of marketing that would normally be borne by the buyers and sellers. We can conclude that although this market might adjust more smoothly than an unsubsidised one, its effects would not be very different.

If we look at the crucial issue of the buying and selling of labour power, Elson's proposal looks suspiciously like the sorts of prices and incomes policies that were used to regularise exploitation in the 1960s and 1970s. The Price and Wage Commission is to produce norms for all wage rates. This clearly is not abolishing the wages system; it is a means of regularising it. The hierarchy of wage rates previously enforced by private economic contracts, now becomes a matter of public policy, to be legitimised by a state organ. At the same time the Price and Wage Commission will doubtless be mindful of the need to ensure industrial profitability. Here we come onto contentious ground, since the setting of wage rates affects the rate of exploitation. Any attempt to set higher wage norms will be resisted by employers, any attempt to set lower ones by the unions. If the wage norms are binding, actual wage rates will be determined by the relative strengths of employers and unions in the traditional way: strikes, lockouts, etc.

There is one measure that Elson proposes which could significantly alter the rate of exploitation. This is the idea that all citizens should be assured a basic minimum income whether they are employed or not. This policy is advocated by the Greens, and under capitalist conditions it is undoubtedly in the working-class interest. If workers on strike know that their families will always be able to eat, their position is strengthened, and strikes will be more solid and successful. But we should not overestimate the impact of this sort of unconditional social security benefit. Diane Elson indicates that she views it as very much a bare subsistence minimum, enough to provide a diet of lentils, a few pairs of cheap jeans and some coconut matting on the floor. It does not sound much better than living on contemporary social security benefits. It would be driven by the same contradictory factors as all social security schemes: it must keep people alive but not undermine their incentive to work, nor impose a heavy tax burden. People often have other commitments that they have entered into whilst working: mortgages, hire purchase, etc. Social security benefits can quickly be eaten up by these when people go on strike or become unemployed.

Unconditional social security benefits are a worthwhile reform in a capitalist country. They would help reduce poverty and would aid the class struggle. What they will not do is 'remove the basic cause of antagonism between buyers and sellers of labour power' (*ibid.*, p.30). The buying and selling of labour power is the prelude to exploitation and is inherently antagonistic. For the enterprises that purchase the labour power will still be juridical subjects whose objective is to use the labour power to make a profit. They will be legal personalities with the right to buy, sell and enter into contracts. In short they will be what Marx termed 'personifications of capital'. They might be owned by the state and have to pay interest to the state on capital advanced, but that would no more remove their capitalist character than did state ownership of British Leyland. Indeed, Elson proposes a auditor called the Regulator of Public Enterprises whose function is to ensure that the state obtains an adequate rate of return on its capital.

Where labour power continues to be bought and sold on the market there is bound to be a struggle over its price. In a capitalist economy unemployment is the ultimate regulator of wages. Under conditions of full employment the economic class struggle leads to wage inflation. It may be possible to regulate this to some extent by binding prices and incomes policies, but the purely voluntary mechanism which she describes is likely to be unstable. Either it will lead to inflation, with consequent pressure for a return to unemployment to discipline the workforce, or there will be demands for mandatory price controls. Society will be faced with the alternative of capitalist or socialist paths of development.

This is exactly the alternative that is posed with absolute clarity in countries like Poland or Hungary or Russia at the time of writing (1992). Either the economy reverts to the whip of unemployment, without which there can be no true labour market, or moves in a communist direction and establishes direct social regulation of production and income. This is not to deny that the sort of total state capitalism proposed by Elson would be progressive in a British context. One can see it as the asymptote towards which British social democracy tended in the pre-Thatcher period: almost total nationalisation, voluntary prices and incomes policies, comprehensive rights to social security benefits. As such it would be far more in the working-class interest than the present dispensation.

But we know from experience that the state capitalist type of social order is unstable. It retains the money, markets, and bourgeois income differentials of capitalism whilst removing the unemployment needed to make these effective, and at the same time weakening the state as an element of bourgeois class discipline. It is a transitional form of society which must either revert to private capitalism, as in Britain, or go in a socialist direction. The same holds good in the converse direction. But the move away from a planned socialist economy towards a state capitalist or market socialist one is unequivocally reactionary. The resulting form can only be an unstable one that will gravitate through class struggle into capitalism or else back towards communism.[6]

The irony is that Elson's socialised price-fixing agencies would have the computer networks and the information about production needed to make an effective transition towards planning. If she were advocating such agencies as a transitional measure leading up to a planned economy they might be justifiable. But in the current world situation, where capitalism is on the offensive, transitions towards capitalism seem more likely. Proposals for a third way between capitalism and communism will be just transient staging posts on the journey to full capitalist restoration.

All market economies are subject to macroeconomic instabilities. The two main forms that they take are recessions in which products cannot be sold, creating unemployment, or excess demand creating inflation. In those socialist countries that are reverting to the market, we see both of these: roaring inflation combined with millions being thrown out of work. Elson, like any intelligent left-wing economist, is clearly aware of these propensities of market economies; but she offers no real solution. Whatever one might say against the economic system that used to operate in the USSR before Gorbachev, prices were stable and there were no recessions. The Soviet system was not without problems, only the wilfully blind could think that. But any changes to the socialist system as it has been known this century should be a step forward for the working people. What Elson and similar thinkers in Russia are advocating is a retreat from Marx towards the doctrines of Adam Smith.

Aganbegyan: administrative and economic methods
The arguments developed here and in previous chapters also give us a basis for criticising the conception of Soviet economic reform put forward by Abel Aganbegyan, one of Gorbachev's key economic advisors in the mid- to late-1980s. In his book on

perestroika, Aganbegyan (1988) made repeated reference to the distinction between 'administrative' and 'economic' methods, and emphasised the need to curtail the former and develop the latter. He stated that "a chief characteristic of the existing system of management is the predominance of administrative methods, with economic methods having only secondary significance" (1988, p.20), and went on to claim that the essence of *perestroika* "lies in the transition from administrative to economic methods of management" (p.23).

If this simply meant that he is opposed to arbitrary bureaucratic directives ('admininstrative'), and in favour of the careful calculation of costs and benefits ('economic'), the point would be uncontroversial. But in fact there appears to be a slide between this conception and a much more contentious interpretation. First, Aganbegyan appears to identify 'administrative' methods with central planning as such. Commenting on the central planning of the Stalin period, he stated that "from the beginning of the 1930s economic methods of management were curtailed. Trade between production units was replaced by centralised allocation of resources and the market contracted" (*ibid.,* pp.21-22). Here 'economic methods' are counterposed against 'centralised allocation' as such. Matters become clearer when he spells out the content of the economic methods: these involve the transfer of associations and enterprises to full economic accountability, self-financing and self-management, as well as a greatly increased role for prices, finance and credit (p.23). Elsewhere he associates economic methods with the stimulation of market relations and an increased role for profit (p.58). Finally he proposes that the state plan be 'scrapped' in favour of a system in which ". . . enterprises and associations will work out and approve their own plans. They will not be subject to the approval of any higher authority and there will be absolutely no allocation of planned work" (1988, p.112).

Despite his positive comments on the role of the first 5-year plans in promoting Soviet industrialisation, Aganbegyan effectively identifies central planning with 'administrative methods' (out-of-date, arbitrary, bureaucratic, inefficient), while associating 'economic methods' (modern, efficient, progressive) with reliance on market prices, profitability, financial independence for enterprises and the complete abolition of central directives. It may well be that in the Soviet experience central planning has been associated with bureaucratic arbitrariness, but it is a serious mistake to identify the two. We have shown that central planning decisions need not be arbitrary, but can be made on the basis of a well-defined calculus of social cost. Indeed, we have been at pains to show that the social rationality of labour-time accounting is superior to that of the market. And there is no necessary association between the use of market-clearing prices for consumer goods (which we advocate as one component of the overall planning system) and the dissolution of socialist property via the granting of unbounded autonomy to enterprises. It is one thing to say that enterprises should be free to appoint their own managers, organise their own work democratically, and propose initiatives for new products— but quite another to argue that they should act as independent agents, drawing up their own plans in response to market signals. Indeed, if they are granted the latter role, then democratic control within the enterprise is likely to be one of the first things to go. A discussion such as Aganbegyan's, which loads the question by implicitly identifying economic rationality and market processes, must provide a misleading guide to the economic reform of socialism.

Over the last few years we have seen where this logic leads: the collapse of all effective economic planning, run-away inflation, general economic dislocation, mass unemployment and the eventual triumph of capitalist restoration. 'Reform' of socialism towards the market has been an unprecedented economic disaster for the working class in the countries affected. On a global scale, it has re-established the domination of the same few capitalist powers that ruled the world prior to 1917. At the political level it has led to a situation in which the socialist movement and the organised working class have effectively been excluded from the stage.

With socialism gone, what hope is there left for the dispossessed but fascism and nationalism? Nothing, unless it is a socialism that is more radical, more democratic and more egalitarian than any which went before, that is founded on clear economic and moral principles and that does not surrender its integrity to the demoralising myths of the market.

Notes to Chapter 15
1. Cockshott and Cottrell (1989).
2. In his earlier writings, Lange proposed a variant of market socialism, but by the 1960s he came to the view that modern computers had made it possible to dispense with the market altogether. See Lange (1938) and Lange (1967) in the bibliography for details. We have discussed Lange's arguments at some length in Cottrell and Cockshott (1993a).
3. More generally a scalar means a single number, in contrast to a vector which is a list of numbers. Thus 4.57 is a scalar quantity whereas [3.9, 1.2, 6.7] is a three element vector.
4. See, for instance, Alec Nove (1983), Geoff Hodgson (1984), Diane Elson (1988), Abel Aganbegyan (1988), David Miller (1989).

5. Defences of planning have been offered by Ernest Mandel (1986), and Nicholas Costello *et. al.* (1989), although the kind of planning advocated by the latter— in the tradition of the Benn/Holland current on the Labour left—falls short of our own proposals.
6. N. Scott Arnold (1987) presents an interesting argument along these lines, showing that market socialism is an inherently unstable socio-economic form.

Bibliography

Aganbegyan, Abel *The Challenge: Economics of Perestroika*, London: Hutchinson, 1988.

Arnold, N. Scott 'Marx and disequilibrium in market socialist relations of production', *Economics and Philosophy*, Vol.3, No.1, April 1987, 23-48.

Aristotle *The Politics*, Harmondsworth: Penguin, 1986.

Bacon, Robert and Walter Eltis *Britain's Economic Problem: Too Few Producers* (2nd edition), London: Macmillan, 1978.

Beer, Stafford *Platform for Change*, London: Wiley, 1975.

Beer, Stafford *Brain of the Firm*, London: Wiley, 1981.

Braverman, Harry *Labor and Monopoly Capital*, New York: Monthly Review press, 1974.

Burnheim, John *Is Democracy Possible?* Oxford: Polity Press, 1985.

Cave, Martin *Computers and Economic Planning: The Soviet Experience*, Cambridge: Cambridge University Press, 1980.

Cockshott, W. Paul 'Application of artificial intelligence techniques to economic planning', *Future Computing Systems*, Vol.2, 1990, 429-443.

Cockshott, W. Paul and Allin Cottrell 'Labour value and socialist economic calculation', *Economy and Society*, Vol.18, No.1, February 1989, 71-99.

Costello, Nicholas, Jonathan Michie and Seumas Milne *Beyond The Casino Economy: Planning for the 1990s*, London: Verso, 1989.

Cottrell, Allin *Social Classes in Marxist Theory*, London: Routledge & Kegan Paul, 1984.

Cottrell, Allin and Cockshott, W. Paul 'Calculation, complexity and planning: the socialist calculation debate once again', *Review of Political Economy*, Vol.5, No.1, 1993a, 73-112.

Cottrell, Allin and Cockshott, W. Paul 'Socialist planning after the collapse of the Soviet Union', *Revue Européene des Sciences Sociales*, Vol.XXXI, 1993b, 167-185.

Dasgupta, Partha 'Positive freedom, markets and the welfare state', *Oxford Review of Economic Policy*, Vol.2, No.2, Summer 1986, 25-36.

Devine, Pat *Democracy and Economic Planning*, Cambridge: Polity Press, 1988.

Duffy, Gavan 'A note on 'Labour value and socialist economic calculation' ', *Economy and Society*, Vol.18, No.1, February 1989, 100-109.

Durrett, Charles and Kathryn McCamant, *Cohousing: A Contemporary Approach to Housing Ourselves*, Berkeley, Ca.: Habitat Press, 1989.

Elson, Diane 'Market socialism or socialization of the market?' *New Left Review*, No.172, Nov/Dec 1988, 3-44.

Engels, Frederick *Anti-Duhring: Herr Eugen Duhring's Revolution in Science*, Moscow: Foreign Languages Publishing House, 1954.

Farjoun, Emmanuel and Moshe Machover, *Laws of Chaos*, London: Verso, 1983.

Finley, Moses *Democracy Ancient and Modern*, New Brunswick, NJ: Rutgers University Press, 1973.

Fukuyama, Francis *The End of History and the Last Man*, New York: Free Press, 1992.

Genovese, Eugene D. *The Political Economy of Slavery*, New York: Pantheon Books, 1965.

Granick, David *Job Rights in the Soviet Union: Their Consequences*, Cambridge: Cambridge University Press, 1987.

Gregory, Paul *Socialist and Nonsocialist Industrialisation Patterns: A Comparative Appraisal*, New York: Praeger, 1970.

Hahn, Frank *Equilibrium and Macroeconomics*, Oxford: Basil Blackwell, 1984.

Harner, M. 'The ecological basis for Aztec sacrifice', *American Ethnologist*, Vol.4, No.1, 1977, 117-135.

Held, David *Models of Democracy*, Stanford: Stanford University Press, 1987.

Hodgson, Geoff *The Democratic Economy*, Harmondsworth: Penguin, 1984.

Kalecki, M. *Theory of Economic Dynamics*, New York: Monthly Review Press, 1965.

Keynes, J.M. *The General Theory of Employment, Interest and Money*, London: Macmillan, 1936.

Lane, David *Soviet Economy and Society*, New York: New York University Press, 1985.

Lange, Oskar *On the Economic Theory of Socialism*, Minneapolis, Minn.: University of Minnesota Press, 1938.

Lange, Oskar 'The Computer and the Market', in Charles Feinstein (ed.) *Socialism, Capitalism and Economic Growth: Essays Presented to Maurice Dobb*, Cambridge: Cambridge University Press, 1967.

Lavoie, Don *Rivalry and Central Planning*, Cambridge: Cambridge University Press, 1985.

Leijonhufvud, Axel *Information and Coordination*, Oxford: Oxford University Press, 1981.

Lenin, V.I. *Collected Works*, Vol.25, Moscow: Foreign Languages Publishing House, 1964.

Lubeck, O., J. Moore and R. Mendez 'A benchmark comparison of three supercomputers', *Computer*, Vol.18, No.12, December 1985.

Mandel, Ernest 'In defence of socialist planning', *New Left Review*, No.159, Sept/Oct 1986, 5-38.

Marx, Karl *The Poverty of Philosophy*, London: Lawrence and Wishart, 1936.

Marx, Karl *The First International and After* (Political Writings, Volume 3, ed. D. Fernbach), Harmondsworth: Penguin, 1974.

Marx, Karl *Capital*, Vol. I, Harmondsworth: Penguin, 1976.

Marx, Karl *Capital*, Vol.III, Moscow: Progress Publishers, 1971.

Marx, Karl and Frederick Engels *The German Ideology*, New York: International Publishers, 1947.

Marx, Karl and Frederick Engels *Selected Works*, London: Lawrence and Wishart, 1970.

Miller, David *Market, State and Community: Theoretical Foundations of Market Socialism*, Oxford: Clarendon Press, 1989.

Nove, Alec *The Soviet Economic System*, London: George Allen and Unwin, 1977.

Nove, Alec *The Economics of Feasible Socialism*, London: George Allen and Unwin, 1983.

Nove, Alec 'Markets and socialism', *New Left Review*, No.161, Jan/Feb 1987, 98-104.

Pugh, W., *et al. IBM's 360 and Early 370 Systems*, Cambridge,

Mass.: MIT Press, 1991.

Ricardo, David *Principles of Political Economy and Taxation*, Cambridge: Cambridge University Press, 1951.

Sedgewick, Robert *Algorithms*, London: Addison-Wesley, 1983.

Smith, Adam *The Wealth of Nations*, Harmondsworth: Penguin, 1970.

Smith, Keith *The British Economic Crisis*, Harmondsworth: Penguin, 1984.

Ste. Croix, G.E.M. de *The Class Struggle in the Ancient Greek World*, Ithaca, NY: Cornell University Press, 1981.

Stalin, Joseph *Economic Problems of Socialism in the USSR*, New York: International Publishers, 1952.

Thucydides *History II* (ed. P.J. Rhodes), Warminster: Aris & Phillips, 1988.

Tribe, Keith *Land, Labour and Economic Discourse*, London: Routledge & Kegan Paul, 1978.

Varga, Richard S. *Matrix Iterative Analysis*, Englewood Cliffs, NJ: Prentice-Hall, 1962.

White, Lynn *Medieval Technology and Social Change*, Oxford: Clarendon Press, 1962.

Wolcott, Peter and Seymour Goodman 'High speed computers of the Soviet Union', *Computer*, Vol.21, No.9, September 1988, 32-41.

New Spokesman Titles

The Problem of China
Bertrand Russell

Marxism and Reform in China
Su Shaozhi

The European Imperative
Economic and Social Cohesion in the 1990s
Stuart Holland

A European Recovery Programme
Restoring Full Employment
Ken Coates MEP & Michael Barratt Brown (eds.)

Europe Can Afford to Work
Francis Cripps & Terry Ward

Forthcoming

The Practice and Theory of Bolshevism
Bertrand Russell

Community Work in the 1990s
Sid Jacobs & Keith Popple (eds.)

Complete list available from:
SPOKESMAN, Bertrand Russell House,
Gamble Street, Nottingham NG7 4ET.
Phone 0602 708318, fax 0602 420433

Printed in Great Britain
by Amazon